KNACK™
MAKE IT EASY

CANOEING
FOR EVERYONE

FUELED BY FALCON GUIDES®

KNACK™
CANOEING
FOR EVERYONE

A Step-by-Step Guide to Selecting the Gear, Learning the Strokes, and Planning Your Trip

DANIEL A. GRAY

Photographs by Stephen Gorman and Eli Burakian

Guilford, Connecticut
An imprint of The Globe Pequot Press

To buy books in quantity for corporate use
or incentives, call **(800) 962–0973**
or e-mail **premiums@GlobePequot.com**.

Editor-in-Chief: Maureen Graney
Editor: Katie Benoit
Cover Design: Paul Beatrice, Bret Kerr
Text Design: Paul Beatrice
Layout: Maggie Peterson
Cover photos (front and back) by Stephen Gorman
All interior photos by Stephen Gorman with the exception of
p. 3 (right): Kris Holland/shutterstock; p. 6: www.canoeing.com;
p. 7: www.canoeing.com; p. 22 (right): Stas Volik/shutterstock;
p. 100 (left): © David Coleman | Dreamstime.com; p. 100 (right): Joanne Stemberger/shutterstock; p. 101 (left): © Jennifer Lind | Dreamstime.com; p. 103 (left): © Yegor Piaskovsky | Dreamstime.com; p. 104 (left): © Frhojdysz | Dreamstime.com; p. 123 (left): © Sorin Alb | Dreamstime.com; p. 123 (right): George Peters/istockphoto; p.124 (right): © Vincent Dale | Dreamstime.com; p.125 (left): Crystal Kirk/shutterstock; p.127 (left): Courtesy of Ben Morookian; p.134 (right): © Beisea | Dreamstime.com: p. 135 (left): © Kushnirov Avraham | Dreamstime.com; p. 137 (right): Chris Hill/shutterstock; p. 138 (left): istockphoto; p. 146 (right): Arthur Kwiatkowski/istockphoto; p. 166 (right): shutterstock; p. 181 (right): Jaimie Duplass/shutterstock; p. 183 (left): shutterstock; p. 183 (right): shutterstock; p. 184 (left): shutterstock; p. 184 (right): shutterstock; p. 185 (left): shutterstock; p. 185 (right): Jason van der Valk/istockphoto; p. 186 (left): shutterstock; p. 186 (right): shutterstock; p. 187 (left): shutterstock; p. 187 (right): shutterstock; p. 188: Courtesy of Cindy Dillenschneider; p. 221 (right): Rick Olson/istockphoto

Library of Congress Cataloging-in-Publication Data is available on file.

ISBN 978-1-59921-524-2

The following manufacturers/names appearing in Knack Canoeing for Everyone are trademarks:
Armor-All®, Band-Aid®, Benadryl®, Bisquick®, Camp Suds®, Chota, Coleman™, Crazy Creek Products®, Duluth Pack, EpiPen®, GORE-TEX®, JetBLADE, Jet Boil®, Kevlar®, Luna®, Mad River Canoe®, MSR®, Nalgene®, NRS®, Old Town®, Poland Spring®, Potable Aqua®, REI®, Royalex®, Sky Blazer®, Styrofoam®, Teflon®, Therm-A-Rest®, Thermos®, Under Armour®, Velcro®, Whisper Lite™

The information in this book is true and complete to the best of our knowledge. All recommendations are made without guarantee on the part of the author or The Globe Pequot Press. The author and The Globe Pequot Press disclaim any liability in connection with the use of this information.

Printed in China

10 9 8 7 6 5 4 3 2 1

Dedication

To Sara, my paddling partner and life companion

Author Acknowledgments

My thanks to my parents for exposing me to the great outdoors, to the Urban Ecology Center in Milwaukee where I did the bulk of my canoeing instruction, and to the Milwaukee Riverkeeper for involving me in protecting our rivers.

Photographer Acknowledgments

We would like to thank the following people for their support: Kate Fisher, Josie Fisher, Alexandra Zagaria, Todd Uva, Mary Gorman, Steve Brownlee, the staff of Umiak Outfitters (Stowe, Vermont), the staff of Canoe Imports (Burlington, Vermont) Cheers, Steve Gorman & Eli Burakian.

CONTENTS

INTRODUCTION

The world of canoeing is a broad and varied one that has a lot to offer the casual weekend paddler and the hardcore enthusiast.

Canoeing can be done by a solo paddler and by groups of nearly any size. Canoes can be used in many ways; for fishing, nature watching, exercise, transportation into the deep wilderness, a way to see an urban landscape from a new perspective.

Canoeing can be a weeklong adventure with friends, a family outing, and engaged in by people with a variety of disabilities.

My first canoeing experience was a weekend trip on Sugar Creek in Indiana with the Boy Scouts when I was eleven years old. I immediately fell in love with the simplicity and excitement of that form of travel; a canoe, a paddle, a body of water. Canoeing soon became my favorite outdoor activity, an instant and reliable doorway to the woods and wilds. Throughout my teens, I went on weeklong trips to Michigan and Ontario, as well as numerous day trips on the creeks and rivers near my hometown.

At the end of high school, "senior skip day" was spent paddling Wildcat Creek. Much of that day was also spent prying loose our swamped canoe that was trapped under a downed tree, implanting in my psyche the power and strength of moving water.

Years later, as a high school teacher, I led some trips to the Boundary Waters in northern Minnesota, reliving the joy of canoeing while watching my students learn to canoe.

After a shift in career, I taught paddling and other outdoor activities for an urban nature center. I led canoe and kayak trips in and around Milwaukee, Wisconsin, for over five years.

Knack Canoeing for Everyone is a compilation of those years of paddling, teaching, reading, and taking classes. I have attempted to convey the many components of a suc-

noeist sits more upright, as in a chair, with legs bent at the knee. The canoeist is a little higher above the water and can see much further. A canoe is easier to step into and get out of than many kayaks.

A canoe can carry more gear and passengers than a kayak. While there are tandem kayaks, the kayak is primarily a one-person vehicle. It is virtually impossible to bring a couple of children and the dog along in a typical kayak, while this is quite routine in a canoe. Canoes are typically easier to portage longer distances than kayaks. Canoes are roomier and easier to fish or hunt from than a kayak.

cessful paddling experience as clearly and simply as possible. This book is geared for the beginning paddler.

Why canoe instead of kayak? Canoeing and kayaking are similar in many ways. Both canoes and kayaks are small, human powered watercraft. Both are relatively light weight and easily carried and transported on top of nearly any vehicle. Both canoes and kayaks allow access to shallow and remote waterways that are impossible for large motor powered boats.

While in a kayak, the paddler is basically sitting on the floor of the boat, with her legs straight out in front. The ca-

The choice between a canoe and kayak is similar to the choice between a motorcycle and a car. They have differing attributes in regard to comfort, load capacity, and number of passengers. The choice depends on your preferences. If you haven't paddled much, be sure to paddle both kayaks and canoes, before purchasing one. Also, consider how you will be using the boat and what types of outings you plan to take.

In this book, you will become acquainted with the basic design features of canoes and how they impact canoe performance. Also included is information on life jackets, paddles, and other gear needed for safe canoe outings. You will learn how to launch and land your canoe, and how to paddle a solo and tandem canoe. All of the basic strokes for maneuvering and propelling your canoe are included in great detail.

Knack Canoeing for Everyone also addresses common hazards encountered while canoeing and how to deal with a swamped or capsized canoe. It also compares and contrasts canoeing on small lakes, river canoeing, and coastal paddling.

And you certainly can't take a paddling trip without first learning about ropes, knots, maps, compasses, first aid kits, and other tools you will need.

Flip to the resource directory to find information on additional Web sites, manufacturers, and other information.

Throughout the text, I emphasize safety. Canoeing is an active sport that takes place on water. Accidents, injuries, and a variety of other mishaps are always possible. It is incumbent on the paddler to maintain awareness of the risks involved and to take all possible steps to minimize the inherent dangers. It truly is important to wear a PFD (lifejacket) while canoeing. It is equally important to gauge the potential risk of any paddling situation, and to maintain a healthy respect for water.

Canoeing is great fun and an ongoing adventure. I encourage people to challenge themselves in order to build their skills and overcome any apprehensions related to being on the water. However, the fun can end abruptly if someone gets hurt. Be careful out there, keep learning, and stay safe.

Paddling is an experiential learning activity; you have to actually do it to learn it. There is much you can teach yourself using this, or a similar book. However, a qualified instructor can enhance your experience quite dramatically by focusing on your individual needs and abilities.

The vast number of canoes on the market, and the gear available to go with them, is mind boggling. However, *Knack Canoeing for Everyone* hopes to give you a heads up on the basic information you will need to get started. When you are ready to buy your own canoe, do a lot of online research, but be sure to locate a reputable paddle sports shop. The staff at most shops are eager to help you find the right boat and gear for you, and they will be able to answer more questions than any book.

Canoeing can be as expensive as or as cheap as you want to make it. You can rent or borrow canoes, adapt camping gear you already have, and stay close to home to minimize cost. My only request for the frugal paddler is to not skimp when it comes to your lifejacket. Buy a quality PFD that fits well and is comfortable to wear.

For those who have the money to spend, there are some really beautiful canoes out there. They handle well, slice through the water, and are as light as a feather. But be sure to shop carefully to find a canoe that suits you and feels right. The best canoe for you may not be the most expensive. There is also something to be said for a high quality, lightweight paddle. In general, paddling is a very affordable sport that the whole family can engage in.

I hope that you find the information presented in *Knack Canoeing for Everyone* to be useful in getting you out on the water. Remember, have fun and be safe! And happy paddling!

SOLO VERSUS TANDEM

What to consider when picking a canoe that will satisfy your paddling needs

A solo canoe is designed for one paddler. A tandem canoe is designed for two. Solo boats are excellent for fishing, photography, and bird-watching or for someone who paddles simply for solitude. A tandem boat can be paddled solo by adding a center seat or kneeling behind the middle thwart. A tandem canoe is well suited for hauling gear and bringing along children and for paddlers who like paddling with a partner. Solo canoes are usually a little shorter and narrower (and lighter) than tandems.

When buying a canoe consider your main interests and expected activities. A tandem boat can be paddled solo, but a solo canoe can be very uncomfortable if not nearly impos-

Solo Canoe

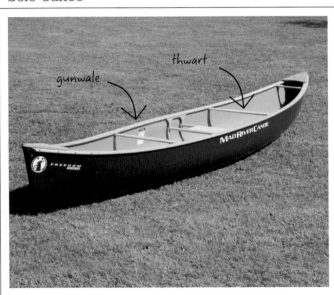

gunwale
thwart

- A solo canoe is perfect for the independent minded. It is lightweight and easily manageable by one person.

- The solo boat works well for fishing, photography, birding, and other solitary paddling pursuits.

- It is big enough for overnight trips on calm water but generally isn't suited for long wilderness trips.

- Solo canoes vary in length from about 12 feet to 17 feet. They range in weight from 30 to 60 pounds, depending on the material used in their construction.

Tandem Canoe

stern
yoke
seat
bow

- Designed for two paddlers, this is the typical canoe style. Tandems range in length from about 12 to 19 feet and can weigh between 30 and 82 pounds.

- Tandems come in various styles. Recreational canoes are for all-around use by the occasional paddler.

- Expedition/tripping canoes are designed for lengthy wilderness trips.

- Sporting canoes work well for fishing, hunting, and nature viewing.

- Whitewater canoes are for running fast-moving rivers and playing in rapids.

sible for two adults to paddle. People who can afford, and have storage space for, two canoes often acquire both a solo and a tandem.

After deciding between solo and tandem there are numerous other considerations regarding the design and construction of your canoe. A longer boat will tend to track better than a shorter boat. *Tracking* is the ability to maintain a straight line with minimal effort. A shorter canoe is much easier to turn and maneuver. Touring and tripping canoes tend to be longer to allow for paddling greater distances in a straight line. Whitewater river canoes are short for dipping around rocks and playing in rapids.

The width (also called *beam*) is another consideration. A wider canoe will feel more stable than a narrower canoe. A wider canoe will also hold more gear, although a narrower canoe will turn more readily.

Depth is the distance from the top of the gunwale to the bottom of the canoe. The greater the depth, the more gear a canoe can hold and the less likely water is to come over the side.

Solo versus Tandem

- Choose your canoe based on the kind of paddling you expect to do the most.

- If you plan to paddle alone—for exercise, solitude, or nature study—you will probably want a solo canoe.

- If you always paddle with a partner, purchase a tandem.

- Tandems are usually larger and will carry more gear for overnight trips.

Tandem for Three

- If you will frequently be canoeing with two partners, buy a longer tandem with a third seat in the middle.

- If you already have a canoe, the middle thwart can be replaced with a third seat.

- For three paddlers, choose from canoes designed to carry more weight.

- Temporary "drop-in" seats can be clamped into the canoe to provide a third seat or to allow one person to paddle a tandem boat solo.

CANOE MATERIALS

The materials a canoe is made of impact its weight, durability, quietness, and handling

The original North American canoes were wood frames covered with birch bark or large hollowed-out logs. Birch bark was replicated with wood-ribbed canoes covered with canvas. This was the canoe of choice until sheet aluminum developed for airplanes during the 1940s was adapted to canoes. Aluminum canoes were affordable and durable and soon became the workhorse of summer camps and canoe liveries. Aluminum is reasonably light and easy to maintain but is noisy and has been mostly displaced by fiberglass, plastic, and Kevlar.

Plastic (polyethylene, Royalex) canoes are made from large sheets of plastic that are heated and fitted into molds. These boats are durable and can slip quietly over rocks, although

Plastic

- Canoes made from polyethylene, Royalex, or other types of plastic are durable and can withstand a lot of use and a fair bit of abuse.

- Plastic boats tend to be heavier than fiberglass or composite canoes, although they are usually also less expensive.

- Plastic canoes require very little maintenance but can be damaged and discolored by extended exposure to direct sunlight.

- Treat your plastic canoe with Protectant 303 or Armor-All to prevent sun damage.

Fiberglass

- The durability, weight, quality, and price of fiberglass canoes vary immensely.

- Inexpensive fiberglass boats tend to be heavy, clunky, and unresponsive in the water. Well-made fiberglass canoes are relatively light and seem to skim through the water.

- Fiberglass is very strong but can be damaged by excessive scraping and direct collision with rocks.

- Fiberglass is fairly easy to repair, and the fiberglass cloth and epoxy resin needed to do so are readily available.

2

they will abrade with excessive scraping. Plastic boats used to be quite heavy but have become much lighter while remaining durable. They are less efficient in the water due to blunt entry lines (rounded ends).

Fiberglass boats vary considerably in weight, strength, quality of construction, and price. Kevlar is about 40 percent stronger than fiberglass and almost half as light. A Kevlar tandem can weigh about 38 pounds. However, Kevlar is very susceptible to abrasion and, although it is very strong, can be fragile if it is dropped or receives uneven pressure. Car-

bon fiber is very light, very strong, and very expensive. Many canoes are now made from composites of fiberglass, Kevlar, and carbon fiber. To protect them from abrasion and ultraviolet light most composite canoes have an outer layer of gel-coat. Gel-coat is an abrasion-resistant, waterproof resin. It adds weight to the canoe, but for most purposes the added protection and durability are worth it.

The staff at established paddle shops will be happy to guide you through the maze of available boats and help you select a model that meets your needs and budget.

Kevlar

- Extremely lightweight and durable, Kevlar is a woven cloth soaked in resin and then shaped to create the canoe hull.

- Kevlar frizzes up when it is abraded and requires a protective gel-coat to maintain its integrity.

- Although very strong, Kevlar can be cracked by a severe shock. It is difficult to repair, and the repairs can be unsightly.

- Kevlar is very expensive and is often combined with fiberglass to create composite canoes.

Aluminum

- After dominating the canoe market from the 1950s to the 1970s, aluminum was replaced by plastic and fiberglass/Kevlar composites.

- Aluminum canoes are moderately heavy and tend to be noisy on the water. They "grab" onto rocks rather than slide over them.

- Aluminum is durable and virtually maintenance free. It can take a lot of rough use, although it is not indestructible.

- Although most dents can be pounded out, a broken spine or caved-in bottom may be irreparable.

CANOE PARTS
Know the names of the basic components of your canoes

Regardless of design innovations, all canoes share the same basic components. Being familiar with the names of the parts of a canoe is crucial for clearly communicating with your paddling partners and for making sense of instructions on how to paddle.

As with all watercraft, the front of the canoe is called the *bow*. The back of the canoe is the *stern*. The rim, or upper rail, of the canoe is the *gunwale* (pronounced *gunnel*).

Most canoes will move through the water the same forward or backward. The bow and stern are usually determined by where the seats are installed. The bow seat will have leg and knee room for the bow paddler in front of the bow *deck plate*. The stern seat will be placed closer to the stern deck plate.

Thwarts are cross-braces that are attached to both gunwales. Thwarts strengthen the canoe and provide excellent tie-down points for gear. The center thwart often

Deck Plate

- This is the flat spot at the bow and stern of some canoes. Some Kevlar canoes forgo deck plating for a simple handle made of aluminum tubing.

- The deck plate serves as a handle and a place to secure painters (ropes on bow and stern) when not in use.

- Deck plates are made from wood, fiberglass, aluminum, or plastic, depending on the canoe.

- The deck plate is also a spot to mount a bracket for a night light.

Thwarts and Gunwales

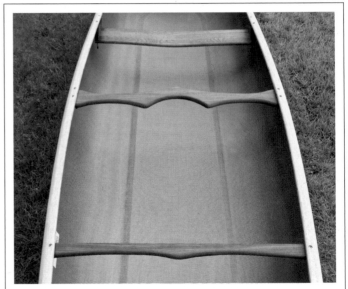

- Gunwales are the rail that runs around the edge of the canoe.

- Thwarts are support braces placed between the gunwales. Thwarts maintain the shape and rigidity of the canoe.

- Thwarts are made from wood or aluminum tubing. Thwarts are used for securing gear in the canoe.

- The center thwart is often a portage yoke for carrying the canoe on one's shoulders.

takes the form of a *yoke*. The yoke allows one person to carry the canoe over his or her head. A yoke may merely be a curved piece of wood or have attached shoulder pads to make it more comfortable.

The *hull* is the body of the canoe. *Ribs* are internal supports that run from side to side. Ribs provide support and structure for the hull. Ribs are common in aluminum canoes but are not used in some plastic and composite boats.

The *keel line* runs along the center of the bottom of the canoe. Most canoes are smooth bottomed, and others have a strip of wood or metal, called a *keel*, that runs along the keel line. The purpose of the keel is to help keep a straight line in wind or waves. The keel also helps the hull maintain its shape.

Seats

- Traditional canoes didn't have seats. Paddlers knelt on the floor of the canoe.

- Seats are now universal in contemporary canoes. Seats vary from flat bench seats to molded tractor-type seats. Some seats have wooden frames woven with cane or nylon webbing.

- Some seats are adjustable, sliding forward and backward on a metal track. Many seats are immobile, bolted in place.

- Canoe seats can vary remarkably in how comfortable they are. Try out several kinds to see which you prefer.

Keel

- The keel line runs along the bottom of the canoe from the bow to the stern.

- Most canoes have flat or rounded bottoms. Some canoes have a keel, a metal or wooden strip that follows the keel line.

- The purpose of the keel is to help the canoe travel in a straight line on a windy lake.

- Keels can be hazardous during river travel. The keel can get hung up on rocks and in strong currents cause the canoe to capsize.

5

SPECIALTY CANOES
Canoes come in designs for many purposes and classifications

Canoes are classified by their primary intended purpose. *Recreational* canoes are general-purpose boats. They are wide, flat bottomed, stable, and relatively slow. *Touring* boats are designed to carry people and gear over a distance. Touring canoes have a shallow-arch hull shape, are longer, and quicker and have large capacity. *Whitewater* canoes are short, round-bottom boats with lots of rocker (rocker is the upward sweep of the keel line toward the bow and stern). They are highly maneuverable for skirting around rocks and rapids but track very poorly. *Racing* canoes are long, narrow, lightweight boats with a shallow-arch or shallow-V hull.

When describing the stability of a canoe people differentiate *initial* from *secondary* stability. *Initial stability* describes the feeling when you first enter the canoe or are sitting in a nonmoving craft. High initial stability feels solid and predictable. High initial stability is not tippy while sitting flat in the water.

Rocker

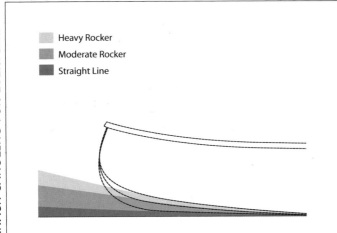

Heavy Rocker
Moderate Rocker
Straight Line

Tumblehome

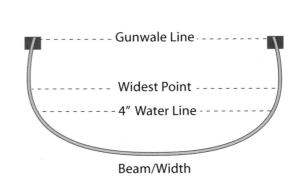

Gunwale Line

Widest Point

4" Water Line

Beam/Width

- Rocker is the upward curve of the keel line at the bow and stern of the canoe.

- The more rocker a canoe has, the easier it will turn and the less well it will track (keep a straight line).

- For general paddling, ½ to 1 inch of rocker is probably about right. A longer touring canoe can use 1½ inches of rocker.

- Whitewater canoes, which are built for rapid turning, can have 3 to 5 inches of rocker.

- Tumblehome is the inward curve of the sides of the canoe above the waterline.

- Curved sides are more rigid than flat sides and require less support.

- A canoe with tumblehome is wider at the waterline for stability and narrower at the gunwales. Narrow gunwales make paddling easier.

- Some paddlers prefer as little tumblehome as possible. In rough water, tumblehome tends to allow more water into the canoe.

Secondary stability refers to how the canoe performs when leaned over on its side when it is moving. A canoe with high secondary stability can lean pretty far without tipping over. Boats with high initial stability may be more likely to capsize in waves or when leaned far.

When purchasing a boat consider its primary use. For an occasional jaunt, fishing, or just hanging out at the lake house, a recreational canoe will probably be just great. If you lean more toward lengthy expeditions, consider a touring canoe. Is paddling rapids your main interest? Look into a whitewater boat. Many paddle shops rent all sorts of canoes. Why not rent a few different styles to see what "floats your boat"?

Research any paddling clubs in your area and attend a few meetings. Most members are more than happy to answer questions and encourage interest in their beloved sport.

Flair

- Flair is the opposite of tumblehome. The sides of a canoe with flair are wider at the gunwales than at the waterline.

- Flaired hulls shed waves away from the canoe in rough water and tend to ride up over waves rather than cut through them.

- Flair-sided canoes are wider than straight-sided or those with tumblehome.

- Wider canoes are harder to paddle because you have to reach out farther.

Bottom Shapes

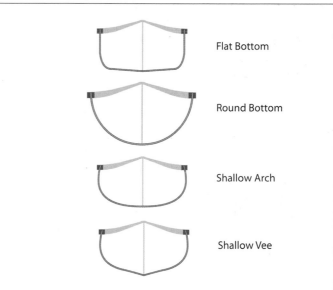

Flat Bottom

Round Bottom

Shallow Arch

Shallow Vee

- The bottom shapes of canoes include flat, round, shallow V, and shallow arch (sort of halfway between flat and round).

- A flat bottom has lots of initial stability and is comfortable for novice paddlers and stable for activities like fishing or photography.

- Flat-bottom hulls have little *draft*. They don't sit very deep in the water. Other hull shapes have much more draft.

- Round-bottom, shallow "V," and shallow-arch hulls have less initial stability but are faster than flat-bottomed boats.

CANOE GEAR

Although canoes tend to be a one-piece affair, there are some accessories to consider

In many canoes the seats are permanently attached. Some canoes have adjustable seats that can be moved at the discretion of the paddler. Some tandem canoes are large enough for a third seat to be added in the middle.

For canoes without seats, or for the paddler who prefers the increased stability of kneeling, a variety of knee pads is avail-able. Foam knee pads can be glued to the floor of the canoe. Paddlers can also opt for the wearable knee pads worn by athletes or carpet installers.

A portage yoke is shaped to fit the curves of the neck and shoulders. A yoke is invaluable for solo carrying a canoe any distance. Many canoes have a built-in wooden yoke for the

Movable Seat

Knee Pads

- Many canoes have fixed seats.

- Some canoe seats can be slid horizontally on rails or aluminum tubes. Sliding the seat forward or back-ward allows to you to adjust the trim of the canoe: how flat the boat lies in the water.

- Other seats can be adjusted vertically to account for how close to the water the paddler wants to be.

- This somewhat "perma-nent" adjustment is made by placing or removing wooden spacers between the gunwale and the seat bracket.

- Kneeling increases stability, decreases the chance of capsize, improves control over steering, and allows for efficient paddling. Kneeling can also make your knees hurt.

- Enhance comfort while kneeling by gluing foam knee pads to the floor of

the canoe. Contoured knee pads will help brace your knees in place.

- Removable nonslip kneel-ing pads are also available.

- Another option is to wear athletic knee pads or the more rugged versions used by floor installers.

middle thwart. There are yoke pads available to cushion the load as well as padded yokes with which to replace the wooden thwart yoke. Removable portage yokes are available that can be attached as needed. These are especially useful for the solo canoeist who finds resting the central solo seat on her shoulders uncomfortable. There are yokes that can be inverted to serve as a seat for the third person in a tandem boat.

Foot braces allow you to apply more body weight and strength to your paddling. Braces let you push solidly with your feet, increasing your leverage and stability. There are canoe brace kits available to modify your canoe with, or you can create your own braces.

Nylon thigh straps can be added to a boat to brace the kneeling canoeist between the straps and the thwart behind. Properly adjusted thigh straps "lock" you into the boat, making the canoe and paddler a single entity. To release yourself from the straps, just relax the pressure on your legs.

Yoke

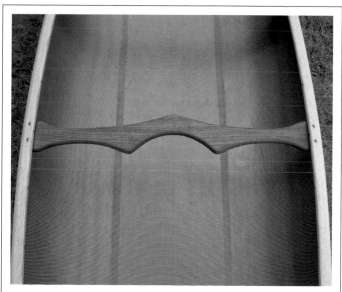

- If you will to portage your canoe, a yoke will permit you to carry the canoe comfortably on your shoulders.

- If the center thwart is not already a yoke, it can be replaced with a number of yoke/thwart options. There are also clamp-on yoke pads available.

- If you will be paddling with three people you might choose a canoe yoke seat.

- There are removable yokes that are particularly useful on a solo canoe where a permanent yoke interferes with the centrally placed seat.

Foot Braces

- Foot braces make paddling more comfortable and efficient. They permit more leverage and power while battling wind and waves.

- Foot braces can be installed in the bow and stern. They are especially helpful if there is not a bulkhead or other feature to wedge your feet against.

- Some foot braces are fixed in place, and others have an adjustable crossbar to accommodate legs of all lengths.

PADDLES

Paddles allow you to propel and maneuver the canoe

Paddles are designed for all types of canoeing situations, are manufactured from a variety of materials, and range in price from quite economical to extremely expensive.

To start with, all you need is a paddle that is the right size for you and that feels comfortable in your hands.

Paddles may be constructed from a single piece of wood, multiple pieces of wood laminated together, plastic, plastic and aluminum, carbon fiber, or other synthetic materials. The

blade is the large end of the paddle that pushes and pulls the water. Blades come in three general shapes. The beavertail is long, narrow, and rounded and thought to be the easiest blade for beginners. Tulip-shaped blades are wider and move a little more water. Square-tip blades are often chosen by whitewater paddlers. The blade is a shorter but wider for powerful maneuvering in whitewater.

The shaft of the paddle connects the blade with the grip. The

Parts of the Paddle

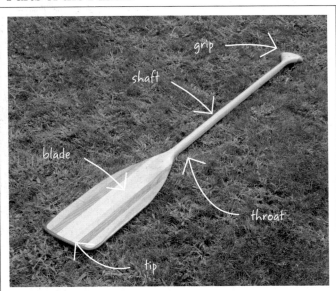

grip

shaft

blade

throat

tip

- The tip is the edge of the blade. It is the part of the paddle that enters the water first.

- The blade pushes against the water, providing power and steering.

- The shaft connects the blade to the grip. Shafts can

be round or oval shaped. The throat is the lower part of the shaft, where your lower hand grasps the paddle.

- The grip is the top of the paddle. The grip is where your upper hand holds the paddle.

Paddle Grip Options

- The main consideration is to pick a paddle grip that is comfortable for you.

- The T grip and the pear-shaped grip are the two main options.

- Pear-shaped grips can be contoured in a number of ways. Grips can be plain

wood or varnished. Plain wood is easier to hold on to when wet.

- The T grip can be firmly held by locking your thumb and fingers around the T. Whitewater paddlers prefer the T for this reason.

shaft can be round or oval shaped. The lower part of the shaft is the throat. The grip is usually pear shaped or T shaped. The T shape is easier to hold on to firmly.

Depending on material and design, there is a range of how much paddles weigh. Lighter paddles can be handled more quickly and put less strain on arm muscles.

The most important consideration in selecting a paddle is that it is the right size for you. A paddle that is too long is cumbersome and harder to use. A paddle that is too short is inefficient and much more tiring. The scientific method

for sizing a paddle is to sit in your canoe and measure the distance from your nose to the waterline. This is the length of the shaft from the grip to the top of the blade. Add the length of the blade, and this is the size paddle for you.

Bent-shaft versus Straight Shaft

- The bent-shaft is more efficient for lake cruising than a straight-shaft.

- The angle of the bent-shaft paddle keeps the blade more perpendicular in the water, minimizing resistance. The paddle is held so that the blade angles *forward*.

- Bent-shaft paddles are awkward for steering and can be very difficult to manage in rapids.

- Some canoeists bring two paddles: a bent shaft for wide-open water and a straight paddle for faster currents.

Sizing a Paddle

- Quickly select a paddle by holding the paddle by the throat and grip.

- Lay the shaft of the paddle on top of your head. Your elbows should be bent about 90 degrees.

- For more precision, sit in a canoe and measure from your nose to the waterline. This is the length of the shaft. Add 20 to 22 inches for the blade.

- Approximate the second method by sitting in a chair and finding a paddle that reaches from the floor to your eyebrows.

PFDs
The most important piece of safety equipment when you are on the water

PFD stands for *personal floatation device,* commonly known as a *life jacket.* The United States Coast Guard approves five types of PFDs. Type I PFDs are offshore life jackets for use in rough, open water. Type I PFDs are heavy and bulky. Type II are near-shore buoyant vests for calm, inland water. The orange horsecollar PFD is that type. Type III PFDs are floatation aids. These are vest-type PFDs that are most comfortable for paddling. Type IV PFDs are throwable seat cushions and ring buoys. Type V PFDs are special use. This type includes floatation belts for water skiers, work vests, and other hybrid vests.

Paddlers wear Type III PFDs. They are comfortable and come in a huge variety of styles and designs. It is important to

PFD

- Select a Type III Coast Guard-approved personal floatation device. There are many styles and designs to choose from.

- Some PFDs are adjustable, and others are sized very specifically.

- PFDs can zip up the front

like a jacket or pull over like a sweater. Some PFDs fasten with buckles.

- The size and placement of floatation greatly affect comfort. Try on lots of models at the store. Grab a paddle and see how each PFD feels when swinging a paddle.

PFD, continued

- Proper fit is very important. If your PFD is too loose it will shift up and float around your head instead of buoying your chest.

- A PFD that is too tight will constrict your movement.

- Be sure your PFD will fit over your cool weather clothes and your rain jacket.

- The PFD should always be your top layer. A fleece or rain jacket worn over a PFD can float up and entangle head and arms during a capsize.

choose a comfortable PFD that fits well because you should be wearing it whenever you paddle.

Some PFDs are adjustable, others come in specific sizes. Be sure to try on a number of models before buying one. There are PFDs designed especially for women. Children should always wear a PFD in or around the water. Purchase them a high-quality, comfortable PFD. If you bring your dog canoeing, consider a canine PFD. Dogs can drown as easily as a person, especially in moving water. Never tie your dog into the boat. This is a serious threat to the dog if you capsize.

Throughout this book I emphasize the necessity of wearing your PFD. Most canoeing fatalities happen to paddlers who are not wearing their life jacket. Canoes capsize under chaotic conditions. You do not have time to grab your PFD as your canoe hits a rock, spins around, tips over, and fills with water. If your PFD is on and fastened, you know you will float and can focus on maneuvering the canoe and keeping track of your paddle.

PFDs for Women

- Women's PFDs are designed to fit a woman's body. Try on numerous models to find the right size and fit for you.

- Some women find that men's or unisex PFDs fit more comfortably. Everybody's body is different. Base your selection on fit and comfort first, style and color second.

- Many paddlers select bright colors for improved visibility by other watercraft.

- Brightly colored gear is less likely to get left at a portage, launch, or landing site.

Children's PFDs

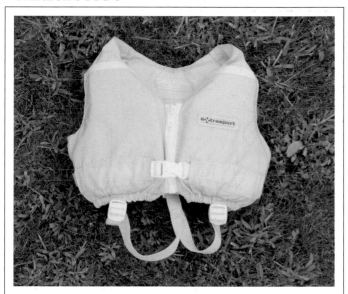

- Let the kids help shop for their PFDs. Be sure to buy those that fit well and are comfortable.

- If the PFD is uncomfortable, keeping it on can become an ongoing struggle.

- For adults, PFDs are selected by chest size; for children, PFDs are selected by weight.

- For smaller children, some PFDs have crotch straps to keep them from floating up around the child's head.

FOOTWEAR

Protect your feet with shoes that will stay on in the water

It is important to wear some kind of shoes while paddling. Your feet will likely go in the water, and there is no way of telling what is under the surface. Rocks, broken glass, rebar, torn beverage cans, fishing lures, sticks, and other objects can all inflict serious injury to bare feet. If you capsize you don't want to worry about cutting your feet.

There are a number of options available for paddling footwear. Many paddlers wear canvas sneakers. They are lightweight, have nonslip soles, don't absorb a lot of water, and dry fairly quickly. In cooler weather add warmth with wool socks.

There are a number of "water shoes" on the market. They are designed to stay on your feet in the water, drain easily, and dry fast. Some are thin and slipper-like, and others are very sturdy and suitable for rocky portage trails.

Traditionalist wilderness paddlers wear lightweight leather

Sandals

- Select sandals that will stay on your feet during capsize. They will protect your feet from sharp rocks and other objects.

- Flip-flops *will* come off your feet and float away. Also flip-flops provide no support while walking.

- Wear sandals with sturdy straps and good treads to assure solid footing during portages.

- In cooler weather you can add wool socks to keep your feet warm.

Water Shoes

- Water shoes are comfortable, durable, stay on your feet, and easily drain water.

- Some water shoes are like slippers, and others are closer to low-cut hiking boots. Some are simply designed, and some are high tech.

- Water shoes have holes or mesh to let the water escape. The soles can vary from smooth rubber to sturdy treads.

- They are a good option for a comfortable paddling shoe that will protect your feet.

hiking boots and wool socks. They just endure having damp feet for the duration of the trip. Neoprene booties will keep your feet warm in cold weather.

In warmer weather, sandals are a good option as long as the straps will keep them firmly on your feet.

For overnight trips, bring one pair of shoes for paddling and keep another pair of dry comfortable shoes in your pack for wearing in camp.

Remember that paddling is a water sport. Expect your feet to get wet. Sometimes launching or landing the canoe will require stepping into the water. Anticipate this likelihood and wear appropriate footwear.

Leather and canvas shoes can be treated with waterproofing compounds to reduce the amount of water they absorb. Don't dry shoes near a campfire. Leather will shrink and become brittle. Rubber soles will melt. Other materials can burn. Take care of your shoes, and they will take care of your feet.

Sneakers

- An old pair of sneakers makes great canoeing footwear. You probably already have a pair in the closet.

- Sneakers are comfortable, don't absorb tons of water, and dry fairly quickly. They have good tread for portaging and provide some ankle support.

- In cooler weather, wear wool or neoprene socks to keep your feet warm if they get damp.

- On overnight trips, bring a second pair for nice, dry comfort around the campsite.

Neoprene Booties

- These can be worn with or without a wetsuit. They will keep your feet warm even in cold water.

- There are several styles. Most have rubber soles. Some have straps and buckle fasteners.

- Neoprene socks offer insulation without the solid sole. They can be worn inside sandals or other shoes.

- Neoprene booties, like all neoprene products, can become quite odiferous after prolonged use.

WARM WEATHER CLOTHING

Dress in active clothing appropriate to the weather

Most canoeing takes place outdoors during the summer months. You must be prepared to deal with hot temperatures and the rays of the sun.

Canoeing is an active sport; wear clothes that fit well and allow you to move. Lightweight nylon is a popular material because it breathes, dries quickly, and is durable. Nylon and similar synthetic materials work well as a first layer when other clothes are added during cooler periods.

Cotton is comfortable and is acceptable in warm weather when hypothermia (see page 176–77) is unlikely. However, cotton provides virtually no insulation when it is wet and dries very slowly.

You can wear your swimsuit under shorts and T-shirt or bring it in your day pack. A lot of swimsuits aren't comfortable for all-day paddling.

Protect your head from the sun and shade your eyes with

Warm Weather

- Wear light, comfortable clothing that allows movement.

- Nylon or other synthetics will wick away perspiration and dry quickly if wet.

- Even on the warmest days, bring a long-sleeved shirt of some kind. It is often cooler on the water than on shore. The wind can pick up, and clouds cover the sun. A nylon rain jacket makes a good windbreaker.

- Broken glass can cut your feet in any temperature. Always wear sturdy water shoes or sandals when paddling.

Sun Protection

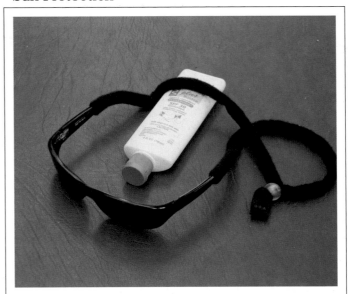

- Sunburn is preventable. You know you will be in the sun, so apply sunscreen to all exposed skin.

- Don't forget the ears, tops of your feet, or the part line in your hair. Remember that UV rays can still burn on cloudy days.

- Wear a hat to protect the top of your head and neck and to shade your eyes.

- Wear sunglasses to protect your eyes and to cut the glare off the water.

a broad-brimmed hat. A baseball hat works well, although a full-brimmed hat will keep the sun off of your neck. A brimmed hat will keep rain from getting in your eyes and from running down your neck when the weather turns.

Apply sunscreen to all exposed skin. The sun is more intense while paddling because it reflects off the water as well as striking you directly. Wear polarized sunglasses to protect your eyes. The glare of the sun can become quite uncomfortable and can damage your eyes.

Even if you anticipate high temperatures all day, be prepared for cooler and wetter weather. Pack a long-sleeved shirt or light fleece along with your rain jacket and pants. The wind can pull away a lot of warmth from your body, and with clouds blocking the sun, it can be rather cool, especially early and late in the day.

Rain Protection

- Nylon rain pants and jackets are lightweight, roll up quite small, and take up little room in your day pack. Bring them!

- You may choose not to put them on for a sudden cloudburst on a hot day, but hot days *can* cool off, and a steady rain will leave you soaked and chilled.

- Rain gear also blocks the wind and provides a protective layer from the elements.

- A broad-brimmed hat will keep rain out of your eyes.

Hot Weather Considerations

- Dehydration: Drink lots of water. Bring along more water than you think you will need.

- Sun exposure: Prevent sunburn. Wear sunscreen but also bring loose-fitting clothing to block the sun.

- Be alert for signs of heat exhaustion (see page 178).

- Dip your hat in the water or wear a wet bandanna around your neck to help stay cool.

17

COLD WEATHER CLOTHING

Dress in layers to stay comfortable as the weather and your activity level change

Use the three *W*s—wicking, warmth, and weather—to guide your clothing strategy.

Wicking is the layer next to the skin, often called the *base layer*. This layer uses highly breathable fabrics to remove moisture from the skin. Wear a wicking T-shirt on warmer days and a long-sleeved shirt on cooler days. Many people also wear wicking underwear, and women might want a wicking bra.

Wicking materials are nylon, polypropylene, and other synthetics. One name brand is Under Armour. Some products have UV or bug protection woven into the fabric.

Warmth is the second layer and provides insulation. Fleece, wool, or pile works best. These fabrics are breathable, allow-

Fleece for Cold Weather

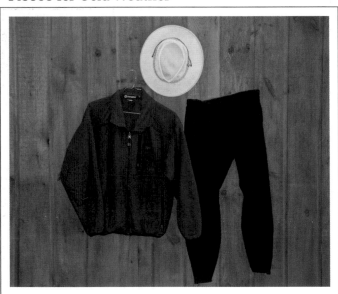

- Fleece, or pile, provides a lot of insulation and allows freedom of movement.

- Fleece is very breathable, allowing body moisture to be drawn away from the skin so that it can evaporate.

- However, fleece by itself lets the wind right through. Plan on an additional layer to block the wind.

- Although warm and comfortable, fleece can be bulky and take up room in your pack.

Wool for Cold Weather

- Wool, the hair that lets sheep exist comfortably in snow and rain, provides insulation and warmth.

- Wool wicks away moisture and can insulate when wet but becomes heavy and takes a long time to dry.

- Wool is a favorite of many paddlers. It is versatile, and there are various thicknesses and blends available.

- Some blends combine the natural warmth of wool with the elasticity of synthetics.

ing moisture to evaporate while providing insulation. Do not wear cotton! If the weather is too warm for your second layer, keep it packed in an accessible dry bag in case the temperature drops or you take a swim.

Weather refers to the third, or outer, layer. This layer protects you from wind, rain, and splash water. It includes windproof, waterproof, or water-resistant fabrics that still breathe, and is usually made of nylon treated to repel water and block wind. Avoid plastic rain gear or heavily coated nylon. These materials will keep out the rain but won't let perspiration out.

Wet Weather Gear

- Light nylon rain pants and jackets work well in moderate weather.

- For extreme conditions, select heavier-duty gear. GORE-TEX and other heavier-duty waterproof materials that are designed to breathe are available.

- You will need to paddle while protecting yourself from the elements.

- Layered clothing and a lightweight rain jacket will keep you warm enough while paddling. Then change into a heavier waterproof jacket and dry clothes while in camp.

Paddling Jacket

- Paddling, or spray, jackets shed water and block wind.

- Made of breathable materials like GORE-TEX or heavy nylon treated with water repellant, they keep spray out while allowing perspiration to evaporate.

- Spray jackets have neoprene cuffs at the wrists and neck or other fastenings to keep water out.

- Paddling jackets can be pullovers or closed with zippers.

- Paddling jackets, like all clothing, are worn beneath your PFD.

WETSUITS & DRY SUITS

Protection in more extreme conditions due to cold temperatures or prolonged exposure

Hypothermia is the condition when a person cannot generate more heat than he or she is losing. Immersion in very cold water brings with it a very real risk of hypothermia. Getting wet on a cool, windy day without wearing proper clothing can also lead to hypothermia.

Paddlers canoeing in cold weather or on cold water or who may be some distance from land or the means to get warm after immersion can get increased protection and insulation by wearing a wetsuit or dry suit. Wetsuits are made from neoprene, a spongy rubber. They keep a person warm by trapping a thin layer of water between the skin and the neoprene. The person's body warms the thin layer of water, and the

"Shorty" Wetsuit

- A partial wetsuit provides good insulation for the torso while allowing for maximum movement.

- This is a good option in cold weather if prolonged exposure after immersion is unlikely.

- While the body core is kept warm, take care to protect extremities. Wear gloves or poagies on your hands and booties on your feet.

- Think of wetsuits as part of your overall clothing strategy rather than as a single item that will meet all of your needs.

Full-Length Wetsuit

- A full-length wetsuit provides more insulation for your legs and will help retain heat in cold weather or during immersion.

- Wetsuits work by warming a layer of moisture between the neoprene and your skin. Wetsuits should be skin tight.

- A loose-fitting wetsuit allows in too much water to work well.

- Scuba divers often wear a full wetsuit with arms, whereas paddlers tend to prefer sleeveless wetsuits for the increased movement while paddling.

neoprene insulates the thin layer from the surrounding cold water. It is important that the wetsuit fit snugly, like a second skin. A baggy wetsuit will fill with more water than your body can easily warm. Also, a baggy wetsuit will not fit comfortably. Thicker neoprene is warmer than thinner neoprene but allows less mobility. Neoprene can be worn alone or under an insulating layer like fleece, rain gear, or spray jacket. Feet can be protected and kept warm with neoprene booties.

A dry suit keeps you warm by keeping you dry. Made of waterproof fabrics, with waterproof zippers and latex gaskets at the neck, wrists, and ankles, a dry suit keeps water away from your skin. Dry suits are one piece or a top and pants combination. The two-piece suit may leak at the waist but will keep you fairly dry in the event of a quick immersion. Dry suits go over other layers of clothing.

A drawback to dry suits is that they can be very hot. Neoprene wetsuits can develop a hefty aroma after a few hours or days of use.

Hand Protection

- In cold, wet weather, hands become numb and easily chapped.

- Neoprene gloves will protect your hands while absorbing minimal water.

- Poagies are mitten-like hand protectors designed for paddling. Some poagies attach to the paddle, protecting your hands but allowing you to hold on directly to the paddle.

- Some paddlers wear leather work gloves to prevent blisters and calluses. Leather gloves can double as hot pads while cooking.

Dry Suits

- Dry suits keep in warmth by keeping out water. They are preferred by people who don't like the "wet" part of wetsuits.

- Dry suits are made of waterproof materials with latex gaskets at the neck, wrists, and ankles.

- Dry suits, suitable in very cold weather or if immersion is likely, tend not to breathe well and to get hot.

- Great care must be taken with dry suits. A small hole or tear will allow wat⬛ enter.

HEAD GEAR

Pick the proper lid to protect your head from heat, cold, and concussion

A wide-brimmed, water-repelling hat will protect you from the sun and rain and will help keep bugs out of your hair. A long-brimmed, baseball-type hat with a cloth fringe will also keep the sun out of your eyes and UV rays off of your neck.

During hot weather, dunk your hat in the river to help keep your head cool. A wet bandanna can also be tied around your neck to provide moisture to evaporate, pulling the heat from your skin. If you forgot or lose your hat, tie a damp bandanna or T-shirt on your head.

For cooler days, wear a wool or pile stocking cap. You can lose a huge percentage of body heat through your head. If the cap fits snugly, it will more likely stay on your head during capsize.

Sun/Rain Hat

- Some hats work well as both sun and rain protection.

- A broad-brimmed nylon hat will keep the sun off your head and shed the water without directing it down your back.

- A hat with a chin strap will stay on your head in the wind and if you capsize.

- Some hats float, and others sink like a stone. Know which of these your hat is before you watch it disappear below the surface, never to be seen again.

Sun Hat

- A good hat keeps the glare of the sun out of your eyes and the burning UV rays off the top of your head and neck.

- Options include broad-brimmed nylon or straw hats and baseball-style hats with a cloth neck cover.

- Pick a comfortable, light-weight hat with plenty of ventilation.

- Pick a hat that will stay on in heavy wind, or secure the hat with a chin strap.

On Class III rapids many paddlers consider helmets a requirement to maximize safety. Some paddlers will always wear one on Class II whitewater as well.

A fairly rigid helmet lined with crushable foam and designed to provide good temple protection is safest. A similar helmet with resilient foam is next best. Helmets with sling suspension support are third. Many helmets have drain holes for water to run out, but this is not considered essential. A properly fitted helmet sits snugly on the head without sliding around. A helmet that is too small exposes the temples. A helmet that is too big can slide forward, exposing the base of the skull and blocking your vision.

If paddling in the north woods during insect season, consider bringing a mesh head net to keep mosquitoes and black flies out of your face and off your neck. Select a head net that is lightweight and folds up small.

Improvised Head Protection

- If you forget your hat, wear a bandanna, T-shirt, or other cloth on your head to prevent burning.

- Dip a bandanna in the water before tying it on. The evaporating moisture will keep your head and body cooler.

- If it's sunny, and you have no head gear whatsoever, apply extra sunscreen to the top of your head, ears, and neck.

- In cold weather, tie two wool socks into a loop to make ear muffs.

Whitewater Helmet

- If you intend to paddle whitewater or run lots of rapids, invest in a rigid helmet with crushable foam padding.

- Select a helmet that has adequate temple protection and that fits properly. Drain holes for water are optional and generally considered unnecessary.

- A helmet that is too large will slide forward and expose the base of the skull while also blocking your vision.

- A helmet that is too small will sit too far back and expose the temples.

DRY BAGS

Pack your gear to fit in the canoe, stay dry, and be easy to portage

Keeping your food, sleeping bags, and extra clothing dry is very important. Wet food doesn't stay usable for very long, and wet clothes do not protect as well from exposure and hypothermia.

The dry bag is a heavy duty plastic or rubberized cloth or waterproofed nylon bag that can be sealed to keep water out. Dry bags range in size from just big enough to hold a camera and wallet to large enough to carry all of your gear.

Some dry bags are made of clear plastic or have opaque strips so you can more easily see the contents.

Most dry bags are sealed by folding down the top and then buckling to keep it closed. It is important to not overfill the dry bag. If the top edge isn't able to fold over enough times, then it won't be watertight.

Although many dry bags are very durable, take care to not abrade or puncture them. While in camp try to keep dry bags

Dry Bags

- Dry bags are durable, reusable waterproof bags. They can be made from flexible plastic, rubberized cloth, and waterproofed nylon.

- Dry bags range in size from just big enough for a GPS unit or a wallet to large enough to carry whatever you'll need for several days.

- Dry bags will keep your stuff dry only if they are closed properly. Overfilling makes it hard to maintain a watertight seal.

- It's usually a good idea to double-bag food, clothes, and sleeping bags.

Dry Bag with Shoulder Straps

- Once limited in size, dry bags are now available in very large sizes.

- Pack-size dry bags with shoulder straps and hip belts can hold a lot of gear, keep it dry, and make it easy to portage.

- As with all dry bags, don't overfill and make sure that the bag is well sealed.

- Stow bags in the canoe so that the openings point up. This prevents any water in the bottom of the canoe from seeping in.

that hold food off the ground; mice can chew a hole through a dry bag in very little time.

As effective as a dry bag can be, it's a good idea to double-bag all items that should stay dry. Put sleeping bags, clothes, and food inside their own plastic bags before packing in the dry bag.

If you don't have dry bags, line cloth Duluth packs or duffel bags with heavy duty plastic bags. These can be sealed by tying in a knot or tying off with cord. Double- or triple-bagging is important; even thick plastic can easily get holes.

Select packs with comfortable shoulder straps for easier portaging. Shoulder straps can also be used to tie packs into the canoe. For large packs, you may also want a hip belt to assist with long portages.

Duluth Pack

- Duluth packs are designed for canoeing. They are durable, hold lots of gear, and sit upright in the canoe.

- Duluth packs have shoulder straps for carrying easily and for securing into the canoe.

- Line your Duluth pack with two large heavy duty plastic bags to keep gear and clothing dry.

- You can adapt whatever gear bags you already have. Canvas duffel bags will work for canoeing, although they may be more awkward to portage without shoulder straps.

Thwart Bag

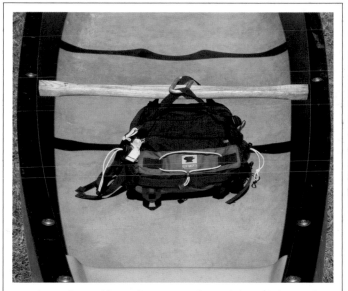

- A thwart bag is like a glove compartment for your canoe.

- This bag hangs on the canoe thwart or seat frame. It is a convenient way to keep track of your water bottle, binoculars, map, and compass.

- Thwart bags can be made of nylon, waxed canvas, or rubberized material like dry bags.

- They can be closed with buckles, snaps, zippers, or Velcro. Select a thwart bag that is easy for you to get into with one hand.

ACCESSORIES
You'll want to include other items with your paddling equipment

The essential items for canoeing are a canoe, a paddle, and a PFD. There are some items to add to the essentials in order to avoid potential mishaps, deal with the unforeseen, or just be more comfortable.

Because a paddle is essential, and it's possible to lose or break your paddle, it's a good idea to bring along a spare. The spare paddle need not be a top-of-the-line model. It just needs to be enough paddle for you to steer the canoe and propel yourself to the landing site. A shorter-than-usual paddle will suffice in a pinch and takes up less room. Some canoeists bring along half a kayak paddle for their backup. Some people keep the spare paddle lashed to the thwart so it is always handy, much like the spare tire in the trunk of the car.

Canoeing is a water sport. Water will get into your canoe. Be prepared for this by bringing a large sponge to mop up

Extra Paddle

- It's hard to steer or move the canoe without a paddle. Bring along a spare in case you lose or break your first paddle.

- The spare paddle just needs to be big enough to get you to your destination.

- Almost any undersized paddle, or half of a double-bladed paddle will suffice.

- Be sure to tie the spare paddle securely into the boat, or else the same capsize in which you lose your first paddle may carry away the spare.

Bailers

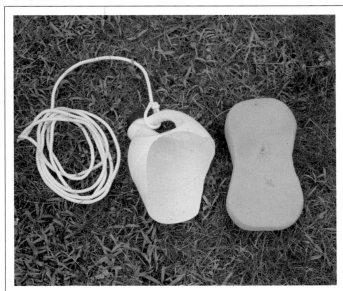

- Your paddle will drip water into the boat. Rain will collect at your feet. A surprising amount of mud can rapidly appear on the floor of your canoe.

- Bring a large sponge to remove water from the canoe and keep the inside clean.

- Keep the sponge secure under a bungee cord on the thwart or tied with a cord.

- Bring an old plastic bottle or a plastic cup to bail out larger volumes of water.

moderate amounts of water. Keep the sponge tucked under a bungee cord on the thwart or tied to a cord. For the gallons of water that can flow over the gunwales, have a bailer near at hand. Cut off the bottom of a plastic bottle with a handle to make a bailer. Run a cord through the handle to tether the bailer to your thwart.

To ease, or prevent, sore back muscles, purchase a canoe seat backrest or a Crazy Creek-type camp chair. Strap this to the canoe seat to keep it in the boat.

If you will be canoeing at night anywhere there might be other boats, always have a light to keep from getting run over. Check your state's laws regarding boat lights.

Seat with Backrest

- If your back gets sore easily, or if you want to paddle more comfortably, install a backrest on your canoe seat.

- Options include removable backrests that hook onto the seat. You can also replace the original seat with a seat that has a folding backrest.

- Another option is a folding camp chair that rests on the canoe seat.

- Secure any added backrests, seat cushions, and chairs to prevent loss during capsize.

Night Light

- If you will be paddling between dusk and dawn where there may be other boats, you need a light of some kind.

- Most states require a single white light on canoes and kayaks; be sure to check your state's regulations.

- In many cases, a headlamp for one or both paddlers will suffice.

- There are permanent marine lights that can be installed on the deck plate of the canoe or brackets that will hold a removable light.

ROPES & PAINTERS

Have plenty of quality nylon rope for use on and around the water

Rope is very useful while canoeing and in some situations is a real lifesaver. Rope is used to keep gear secured in the boat and to rescue struggling swimmers.

Rope has endless applications around the campsite, ranging from hanging food bags to serving as clothesline to keeping tents and tarps over your head.

Select quality nylon rope and cord. It is more durable and pliable than cheaper plastic rope and is stronger than clothes-

line. Plastic rope doesn't hold a knot well and becomes stiff and brittle over time. Clothesline frays and rots and doesn't retain its strength. Clothesline is also harder to untie.

A good knot is easy to tie, easy to untie, and does the job. Nylon rope helps meet all three of these criteria. Nylon rope is easy to keep from fraying. Melt the ends of nylon rope immediately after cutting.

A *painter* is rope tied to a boat. All canoes should have a

Throw Bag

- Paddlers can fall out of canoes or end up swimming due to capsize.

- Keep a throw bag near at hand to provide assistance to anyone in the water who needs help getting to shore.

- When throwing a rope to someone in the water, aim *past* the person to avoid hitting the person in the face.

- Occasionally practice tossing the throw bag. This will keep your aim sharp and keep the rope from being tangled and unusable.

Throw Rope

- If you don't have a throw bag, keep 30 to 40 feet of rope coiled to throw to a struggling swimmer.

- Coil rope carefully and then wrap a few turns around the top of the coil to keep the rope coiled neatly.

- Keep a throw rope tied to the thwart with a quick-release loop (see pages 160–61).

- You can place a knot at the end of the rope, but do not tie a loop there; it might get looped over the person's neck.

12- to 20-foot painter on the bow and stern. Painters are used to tie up the canoe at a dock or on the shore. A painter can be used when your canoe is being towed or when towing another canoe. Painters help secure the canoe to the roof of the car while being transported.

When it is not in use, coil the painter and secure it under a bungee cord or other rope. Don't let the painter drag in the water. It can get snagged and pull your canoe up short. If you capsize, a loose painter can get tangled around your arms or legs, creating a very dangerous situation. When portaging, a loose painter will get underfoot or caught on trailside brush.

Keep a couple of small coils of cord in the pocket or bottom of your day pack. It may come in surprisingly handy.

Painter Secured

- Painters are the ropes tied to the bow and stern of the canoe. They are used to tie up the boat at docks or other landings.

- Painters are used to help secure the canoe onto a vehicle for transportation.

- They can be useful for towing, or being towed by, another canoe.

- Your canoe should always have a bow and stern painter, and the painters should be secured so that they won't get snagged or entangle you during a mishap.

Many Uses for Rope

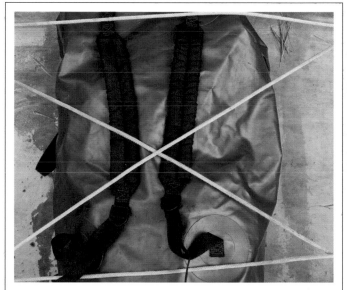

- Have a variety of lengths of cord on hand. It is useful for tying gear into the canoe.

- Cord is handy around camp for setting up tents, tarps, and clotheslines and for hanging food bags.

- Rope can serve as an emergency belt or a leash for the dog and have endless other creative adaptations.

- Whenever you cut nylon rope or cord, melt the ends with a flame to prevent fraying. Keep cords neatly coiled to avoid annoying tangles.

FLOATATION

Most canoes have enough built-in insulation to keep from sinking

Because canoes are small craft and easily filled with water, they are usually manufactured to have enough floatation to prevent them from sinking to the bottom.

Wooden canoes have enough natural floatation to keep them near the surface. Aluminum canoes have large blocks of Styrofoam built into the bow and the stern that make them virtually unsinkable. Royalex has an internal foam core sandwiched between the layers of vinyl to make that

material more buoyant. Because fiberglass will not float, buoyancy is achieved with the use of air chambers or foam compartments.

Although a canoe may not sink when it is full of water, it can be very difficult to move. The less water that will fit into a canoe, the lighter it will be and the more buoyant it will remain. Water is displaced by equipment and by additional floatation. Waterproof gear bags that are tied securely into the ca-

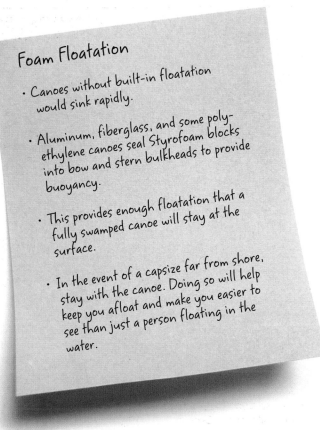

Foam Floatation

- Canoes without built-in floatation would sink rapidly.

- Aluminum, fiberglass, and some polyethylene canoes seal Styrofoam blocks into bow and stern bulkheads to provide buoyancy.

- This provides enough floatation that a fully swamped canoe will stay at the surface.

- In the event of a capsize far from shore, stay with the canoe. Doing so will help keep you afloat and make you easier to see than just a person floating in the water.

Air Pocket Floatation

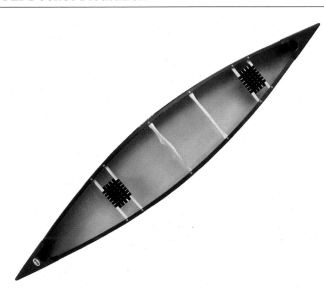

- Royalex canoes are double walled with an internal ABS foam core from end to end.

- The foam core provides buoyancy, eliminating the need for float chambers.

- Canoes that rely on air pockets within the main material (foam core) will

stay at the surface but not be as buoyant as those supported by foam blocks or sealed bulkheads.

- Swamped canoes can be difficult to move through the water, are unstable, and easily spin.

noe will keep that much water out. When sealing dry bags leave some air in them to assist with floatation. That extra air will help displace some water, and it will keep that particular gear afloat if it gets separated from the canoe.

For whitewater canoes there are special floatation bags that are installed in the canoe and then inflated. They can fit in the bow and stern, be placed under seats, or secured in the middle of the canoe. Placement of floatation has varying effects on how the canoe handles in heavy water.

Alternatives to factory-designed floatation bags include blocks of Styrofoam, inflated tire inner tubes, and even duffel bags filled with empty milk jugs. Be sure that any supplemental floatation is well secured in the boat. It won't be very helpful if it gets loose and floats away.

Floatation Bags

- Floatation bags displace water and add buoyancy to the boat.

- Floatation bags come in various sizes and shapes. They can be placed under seats, or lashed between thwarts.

- They can be inflated with a pump or by mouth and have a threaded valve to seal air in.

- Floatation bags are best kept in place by lacing them into the canoe with nylon cord. A bag "cage" is a more elaborate lacing system that keeps the extra floatation tightly in place.

Inner Tube Floatation

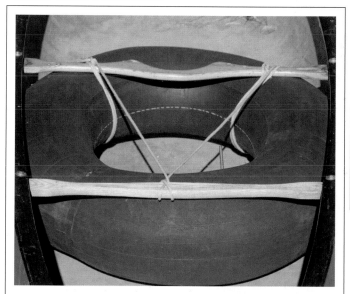

- Inner tubes or any other durable inflatable object that is secured in the boat will displace water and increase buoyancy.

- Place uninflated under a canoe seat and then inflate with a bike pump. Secure with cord.

- Wedge foam blocks or other floatation materials under seats or thwarts and tie in place. If using extra PFDs for this, be careful not to tear or cause other damage.

- Dry bags, with gear or empty, can be sealed to trap air and provide floatation.

WATER & FOOD

Bring plenty of water and nutritious snacks to maintain hydration and energy

Always bring water to drink, even on a short trip. Your body is more than 60 percent water, and even light exercise can decrease that percentage. Staying hydrated will allow you to have more energy and endurance, stay cooler, and feel better. After you begin to feel thirsty, dehydration has already begun. Other early signs of dehydration include a dry mouth and a decrease in energy. Further symptoms include cramps, nausea, and headaches.

Avoid this unpleasantness by drinking plenty of water. Start to drink water up to two hours before starting to paddle or engaging in other exercise. Take frequent sips rather than gulps during the course of your outing. Drink after paddling

Water Containers

- Bring water in unbreakable containers that are easy to pack and easily carried.

- Each person should have her own water bottle for frequent drinks. Durable plastic Nalgene-type bottles have been popular.

- Stainless steel and alumi-num bottles are widespread among people concerned about possible health risks related to using plastic.

- Refill bottles from water jugs or water bladders. Choose larger containers that are durable, are easily carried, and can be easily secured in the canoe.

Water Treatment

- On day trips it is easy to bring enough water with you or to refill containers at park spigots (when they exist and are working).

- On longer trips you will want to be sure of a clean water source. Bring at least two ways of treating water.

- Water filter pumps are lightweight, effective, and quick. But have a chemical backup: iodine tablets or liquid bleach in a small dropper bottle.

- See page 218 for details on treating water.

to replace fluids that were lost.

Drinking water helps counteract heat exhaustion, allows you to paddle longer, and feel better while doing it.

For a short paddle of two to four hours on a cool day, bring at least 1 liter of water per person. If it is warm, or if you will be out more than half the day, bring 2 liters per person. It is unlikely you will ever regret taking more water than you end up drinking. Get in the habit of taking enough water that you always have some at the end of the trip. You will regret not having enough.

Bring along trail mix, power bars, fruit, or other easy-to-eat snacks to keep up your energy while paddling. As blood sugar drops, so do energy, concentration, awareness, and enjoyment.

On a day-long trip, be sure to include a lunch stop. It is important to get out of the canoe, stretch, and just enjoy your meal and the company without having to steer, paddle, and watch for obstacles. Bring sandwiches and other easily packed foods. In cool weather, stay warm with a Thermos of soup.

Trail Food

- Bring easy-to-eat snack foods to keep your energy up. Trail mix, fruit, and power bars are old standbys.

- Include a plastic bag of carrot strips, broccoli, and other sliced veggies to balance out high-fat snacks like nuts and chocolate.

- Bring fig bars and other crumble-resistant cookies. Beef jerky and fruit leather pack lots of energy.

- Make sandwiches for lunch, slice cheese and sausage to eat on crackers, or stir up some tuna salad and spread on pita bread.

Hot Lunch

- On a cool day, a Thermos of hot soup tastes good and raises the spirits. Use a stainless steel Thermos bottle, not the glass-lined variety.

- A small stove will rapidly heat water for soup or a hot beverage of your choice: tea, coffee, cocoa.

- Be sure to pack spoons and cups. Bring plenty of matches, stored in at least two separate watertight places in your gear.

- Test light the stove at home to assure it is working.

FIRST AID KIT

A basic first aid kit will permit you to respond effectively to mishaps

First aid kits vary in size and purpose, depending on the length and locale of the trip and specific needs of group members. The first aid kit for a week-long wilderness trip will be more elaborate than that for a four-hour paddle, but the concepts are similar.

Your first aid kit should allow you to respond to *likely* injuries and discomforts. Your first aid kit and, more important, your first aid knowledge will allow you to provide emergency care

until medical help, if needed, can be obtained.

Likely injuries and discomforts include minor cuts, scrapes, burns, blisters, insect bites, headaches, and diarrhea. These are easily treated with a Band-Aid, antibacterial ointment, and a few over-the-counter medicines.

More serious injuries include deep cuts and puncture wounds with severe bleeding, deep burns or burns covering a large area, and fractures. These conditions require medical

Personal First Aid Kit

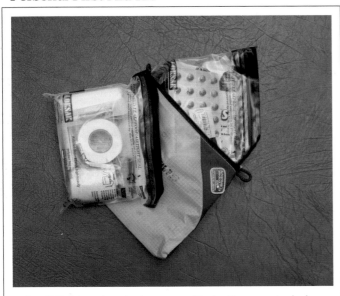

- Small, light, and packed with the basics, the personal first aid kit should go everywhere you go.

- Include adhesive bandages, gauze, tape, antibiotic ointment, tweezers, and nail clippers. Bring along alcohol pads or soapy tow-elettes to clean wounds.

- Medications can include aspirin or the equivalent, an anti-allergen like Benadryl, an anti-diarrheal, and perhaps a decongestant.

- Additional items might include throat lozenges, moleskin (for blisters), a needle (for slivers), and an elastic wrap.

Group First Aid Kit

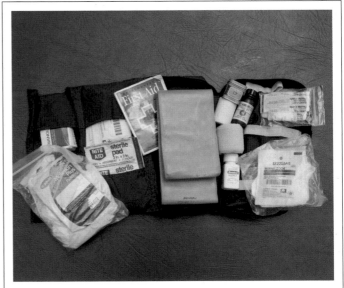

- A group first aid kit is larger because it addresses the needs of more people.

- Bring more bandages, gauze, and tape. Include a few sanitary napkins. They can absorb blood from in-juries and are also available for their intended purpose.

- Include latex gloves as a barrier to infection and a couple of plastic bags to put any bloody bandages in. For longer trips include a thermometer and some cloth triangular bandages.

- Bring a small first aid manual. It provides instruc-tion and reduces panic.

attention as quickly as possible. The role of the first aider is to stop or slow further injury, get the person into a safe situation, and arrange for medical care.

The everyday first aid kit should contain items for dealing with cuts and bleeding. Band-Aids, gauze pads, a roll of gauze, and tape will allow you to stop the bleeding of minor cuts and then cover the wound. For burns bring a tube of antibiotic ointment. Include tweezers for removing splinters. Bring aspirin, acetaminophen, or ibuprofen for headaches, cramps, and muscle soreness. Include some Benadryl to counteract

allergic reactions to bug bites. Bring a small bar of soap or liquid soap for disinfecting wounds and washing hands.

For longer trips, increase the standard contents of the everyday kit. Bring more gauze pads and roller gauze. Increase the amounts of pain relievers and include an anti-diarrheal. The goal is basic care for a longer period of time.

Waterproof Container

- The first aid kit needs to stay dry. Store in a plastic bag or box inside a dry bag.

- Keep your first aid kit inside of a Nalgene water bottle. It is waterproof and crush-proof, and you may already have an extra one at home.

- It's a good idea to have a pre-trip orientation to the first aid kit and a review of first aid procedures.

- Be sure that everyone knows the whereabouts of the group first aid kit.

Medical Considerations before Canoeing

- As with any vigorous activity, use common sense. Stay within your physical and medical abilities.

- If you have high blood pressure or any history of heart problems, consult with your physician before beginning to canoe.

- Be careful while lifting a canoe or other gear.

- Many medications make a person more sensitive to sunlight. Others can cause dizziness. Read all precautions carefully, and if you have any concerns check with your doctor's office.

CARRYING A CANOE

Moving the canoe safely and efficiently on land leads to an enjoyable trip on the water

Although many modern canoes are extremely light, they are still large and can be cumbersome to carry. Proper attention while moving your canoe can minimize frustration. It can also reduce dings, dents, or serious damage to your craft. Most important, proper carrying can prevent injury to bystanders and those moving the canoe.

Have a plan. First, scan the area where you will be moving the canoe. Be alert for uneven ground, rocks, logs, steps, or anything you or your partner might trip over. Be sure to look for obstacles that are not on the ground: tree branches, clotheslines, eaves of buildings. View the place where you will set the canoe down. Are there sharp rocks that might dent or

Hand Carry Canoe

- The suitcase carry: One person is on each side of the canoe near the bow and stern. Grab the canoe by the handles, deck plate, or bow and stern thwarts.

- Underarm carry: Reach over the deck plate and grab under the bow or the stern.

- With four people, space your selves two on a side and grab the canoe by the gunwales or thwarts.

- Lift with your legs, not your back!

Overhead Carry: Step 1

- Drain any water from the canoe to reduce the load and to prevent getting drenched when you flip it over your head.

- Secure any dangling painters. If you don't, you *will* trip over them.

- Face the same direction. This will be your direction of travel when the canoe is lifted.

- Put your "inside" hand on the near gunwale. Put the other hand on the far gunwale.

puncture? Will the canoe be flat and stable? Will the canoe be blocking a path or obstructing other canoeists or hikers?

Second, take a look at the canoe. How will you hold it while carrying? Some canoes have secure, comfortable, well-designed handles. Some canoe handles have uncomfortable edges or break easily. The decking on an aluminum canoe looks like a great place to grab but can easily tear, leaving a sharp metal flap. Other canoes have no handles at all. Carrying a canoe by the handles can suffice for short distances, although your legs will rub against the canoe. Many people find it more comfortable to hook their arm over the decking and grab the canoe under the keel.

Get in position. Coordinate with your partner. Lift with your legs, not your back! While walking with the canoe, be alert for things the canoe can bump into. Swing wide while rounding corners or trees. Watch for other people. Small children dart around, and dogs easily get underfoot. Do not *ever* drop your canoe. Gently place the canoe onto the water or flat ground.

Overhead Carry: Step 2

- Bend your knees. This will help you to lift with your legs.

- Lifting at the same time, raise the canoe in a sweeping motion over your heads. You can rest the gunwales on your shoulders.

- You may also be able to rest the front of the seat behind your neck.

- An alternative is to rest the deck plates on one shoulder. This improves visibility but can be harder to balance the boat.

Overhead Carry: Step 3

- Before walking, be sure both people are situated and ready to move. Proceed carefully; the view of the trail may be partly obscured by the canoe.

- Some gear may be tied into the canoe. Gear can also be carried in packs by the portages.

- Check the ground for a suitable place to set the canoe. Decide on which side you will put the canoe down.

- On signal, bend your knees and lift the canoe off to the side, setting it right side up, gently onto the ground.

CARRYING A CANOE SOLO

Your partner isn't available? Master the skills needed to enjoy paddling alone

Moving a canoe alone might seem like a daunting task, but with practice it can be done as easily as a two-person carry.

As in the two-person carry, check out the surroundings before you begin moving your canoe. Look for objects the boat might hit while you are walking or making turns. Inspect your path for obstacles, holes, or other trip-ups. Scan the area where you will put the canoe down.

For short distances, carry the canoe on your thighs. With the canoe on the ground, stand at the center point of the boat facing the middle thwart. Tilt the canoe away from you and, holding on to the middle thwart, hoist the canoe up onto your thighs. Walk with your back straight.

Shoulder Carry

- To raise the canoe, grab the center thwart with both hands, lift onto your thigh, then hoist canoe up onto your shoulder.

- Place a hand flat on the inside of the canoe hull. This can be tiresome on your wrist for long distances.

- Be alert to where the ends of the canoe are as you make turns and move.

- The boat may block your vision to the side, so set the canoe down gently.

Overhead Carry: Step 1

- Roll the canoe onto its side away from you. Hold the near gunwale with both hands placed on either side of the center thwart.

- Lift the canoe up on your thighs. Grab the thwart (yoke) with your near hand and the far gunwale with your other hand.

- Take a breath and prepare for the next step.

- You will toss and roll the canoe in a single, quick maneuver.

For moderate distances, use a shoulder carry. Stand at the center point of the canoe with one foot close to the canoe and the other leg back to provide support. Grabbing the thwart with both hands, lift the canoe onto your thigh, then hoist canoe up onto your shoulder.

For longer distances or along narrow portage trails, employ the one-person overhead carry. Getting the canoe up over your head is easier than it looks after a little practice. Be aware of nearby items while hoisting the canoe and making turns.

Overhead Carry: Step 2

- In a quick, fluid movement, thrust out with your thighs, pull the high side of the canoe over your head, and push up on the near side.

- Toss the canoe up over your head while rolling it over.

- Practice this move in a large area free of obstacles.

- This move must be done with vigor and commitment. It's very hard to do if broken into parts.

Overhead Carry: Step 3

- Settle the yoke over your shoulders. Hold onto the gunwales with your hands.

- Shift the canoe around until it is balanced on your shoulders.

- Every canoe rides a little differently. With some canoes you will need to push the bow up. With other canoes you will need to pull down on the gunwales to keep the stern from dragging.

- To unload, reverse the process: Make a quick push up with both hands, roll the canoe to your thighs, and then transfer it to the ground.

TO THE WATER

TRANSPORTING THE CANOE BY CAR
Getting your canoe to and from the water is part of paddling

There are numerous ways to attach a canoe to the top of your car. The most secure method includes a canoe rack designed to go on your particular vehicle, adjustable load brackets, and cinching tie-down straps. The load brackets prevent any side-to-side movement by the canoe, and the straps quickly secure the canoe to the rack. A high-quality canoe deserves a high-quality rack.

However, there are other approaches to securing a canoe that will work fine in a pinch. Foam blocks can be purchased that slip onto the gunwales and protect the car's roof from scratches. In the event of no foam blocks you can improvise with seat cushions, folded towels, and so forth. Straps or ropes can be passed over the canoe and through the passenger compartment of the car. Pass straps through open car doors, then close doors. If they go through an open window, you won't be able to open the door to get in and out of the car.

Car Rack: Two People

- Lift with your legs. Pick up the canoe from the ends. Flip the canoe so that it is upside down.

- Move the canoe so that it is parallel to the vehicle. Move your feet carefully. Be cautious of mirrors, radio antennas, or other accessories on the vehicle.

- From the ends, place the canoe so that it is centered on the rack in between load brackets.

- Watch out for things to trip over (curbs) or things to hit with your legs (trailer hitch, bumper).

Car Rack: One Person

- Pick up the canoe as in the solo overhead carry. Move the canoe parallel to the car. Slide the canoe off your shoulders onto the rack.

- Or load the canoe from the end of car. Place the front of the canoe on the rack and slide it forward.

- Or place the canoe on the ground parallel to the car. Lift up one end and place it on the car rack. Hold it in place while lifting the other end and placing it onto car.

- Use extra caution when loading a solo canoe. It can be easy to bang it into the car or hit a window.

Without a rack it is particularly important to tie off the ends of the canoe to car bumpers or tie-down loops. Be careful that ropes or straps do not contact the muffler or exhaust pipe; nylon ropes will melt, and cloth ropes will burn!

Canoe Straps

- Run a strap under a bar on the canoe rack. Lay both halves of the strap over the canoe. Run the strap under the bar and fasten the buckle.

- If your rack does not have load brackets, make sure the strap is right next to the side of the canoe. This prevents sideways slipping.

- Tighten securely, but don't overtighten.

- If using rope, see pages 159–63 for knots you can use: two half hitches and the trucker's hitch.

Secure the Ends

- Use the painters (ropes attached to bow and stern) or additional ropes to secure the ends of the canoe.

- Use two half hitches and a trucker's hitch. Run rope through the tie-down loops, bumper brackets, or a secure spot on the vehicle.

- Avoid sharp edges. Don't tie around a tailpipe or have the rope too close to that source of heat. It can melt the rope.

- Be sure that all ropes are tight but not too tight. The leverage can crack a Kevlar boat.

LAUNCHING THE CANOE: SOLO

Keep your weight low and in the middle of the canoe to avoid tipping

Getting in and out of a canoe is when most beginners get wet! Awareness of how canoes work, combined with paying attention to what your body is doing, will keep you dry. Canoes are lightweight, move easily on the water, and respond quickly to any change in weight or pressure. If you jump into a canoe like it is a yacht, it will instantly move from under you

and leave you in the drink. Keep your weight low. Step gently into the middle of the canoe and feel the effect of your weight on the boat. Squatting with your weight over your feet and your hands on the gunwales will keep the canoe steady and allow you to get situated.

A flat canoe is a stable canoe. A canoe that is partly on

Get Ready

- Lay the canoe *flat* on the water. Place the paddle on the bottom of the canoe where you will be able to reach it. (Lay paddle flat, not like in the photo, so you don't trip over it.)

- Stow day packs or other gear out of the way, but be

sure that the water bottle is within reach.

- Have your PFD on and fastened! Always do this first.

- Be sure that painters are on board, not dragging in the water.

Get In

- Place a hand on each gunwale. Step on the keel line (middle) with one foot, keeping your weight on the on-shore foot.

- Shift your weight smoothly but all at once to the first foot. Bring your second foot into the canoe.

- Don't divide the weight between your feet! The canoe will move away from the shore, and you will do a split.

- Carefully lower yourself into a seated or kneeling position. Pick up your paddle.

water and partly on shore is *extremely* unstable. This is called *bridging*. Place the canoe parallel to the shore or dock before getting in. A shallow beach may require that you walk the canoe out where the water is deep enough that the canoe will not touch bottom after you get in. Be aware of the durability of your craft. An aluminum or plastic hull can endure quite a bit of scraping and bumping around. Gentle treatment of a wooden or Kevlar canoe will keep it seaworthy for much longer.

ZOOM

Kneeling keeps the canoe more stable by lowering your weight and distributing it more widely. However, most canoes come with installed seats, and most paddlers are inclined to use them. Become comfortable both ways. Kneeling is very helpful when in windy conditions or when encountering rapids, providing more leverage and power.

Push Off

- Gently push off shore with your paddle.

- Or use a draw stroke (see pages 62–63) to move the canoe sideways to deeper water.

- Watch for obstacles in or under the water.

- First time in a canoe? Gently shift your weight from side to side. Notice how the canoe responds. Now carefully lean from side to side and note how much effort it takes to get the gunwale near the water line. Every canoe is different.

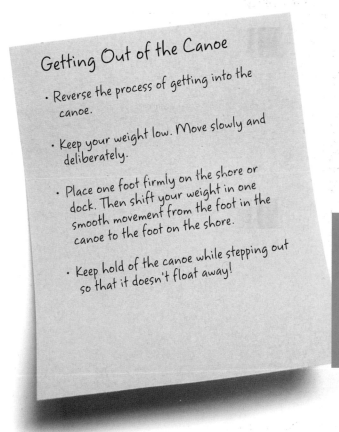

Getting Out of the Canoe

- Reverse the process of getting into the canoe.

- Keep your weight low. Move slowly and deliberately.

- Place one foot firmly on the shore or dock. Then shift your weight in one smooth movement from the foot in the canoe to the foot on the shore.

- Keep hold of the canoe while stepping out so that it doesn't float away!

LAUNCHING THE TANDEM: PART I
Keep your weight low and communicate with your partner for a smooth launch

Launching a canoe with a partner allows one person to steady the canoe while the other person is getting in and getting situated. However, launching a canoe with a partner also provides more opportunities to swamp if both people are not working together.

Successful launching follows a process. Get the canoe onto the water, floating flat and not *bridging*. Be sure that the canoe is in deep enough water that it won't be stuck after loading with gear and people. Sometimes this requires both paddlers to walk the canoe to deep enough water. As you take turns getting in, let excess water drain off your shoes to minimize water that collects in the bottom of the canoe.

Get Ready!

- Place the paddles on the bottom of the canoe, and stow gear out of the way. Have both hands free to grab the gunwales.

- Be sure that the canoe is flat on the water. Sometimes this means getting your feet wet by walking the canoe out far enough to be free of the shore and the bottom.

- Communicate! One person steadies the canoe while the other gets in and gets situated.

- Keep your weight low and evenly distributed. Step into the middle of the boat.

Getting In

- Take your time. Relax. Know that the boat will move a little bit as you enter and shift around.

- As you move to your position, stay low and keep your weight centered over the keel.

- When climbing over thwarts and seats, be sure to lift your feet high to avoid tripping.

- In a fully loaded canoe, the first person might need to crawl over the gear. Stay as low as possible. Stay centered.

Enter the canoe one person at a time. The second person waits until the first is seated, situated, and has his paddle. While the second paddler steps into the canoe, the first person stabilizes the canoe by leaning forward as far as possible to lower his weight. If possible, the first person can also hold onto the dock to increase stability.

When getting in or out of a canoe, always remember to keep your weight distributed over the keel line of the canoe. Keeping a hand on each gunwale spreads the weight and keeps your center of gravity low.

Steady the Canoe

- The first person should get into position. If seated, sit in the middle of the seat.

- Bend forward or squat down to lower your weight. This stabilizes the canoe for the second person to get in.

- Be prepared to lean a little to counterbalance as the second paddler enters and gets situated.

- The second paddler grabs the gunwales, steps onto the keel line, and stays low.

Push Off

- When both paddlers are settled in, pick up paddles and prepare to get under way.

- Push off from a dock using your hands if possible.

- Ideally, the canoe will be floating free of the bottom. Use the draw stroke (pages 62–63), forward stroke (pages 56–57), or back stroke (pages 58–59) to move into deeper water.

- When pushing off with the paddle, be gentle. Wood can crack, and plastic can break.

TO THE WATER

LAUNCHING THE TANDEM: PART II
Launching perpendicular to the shore involves a different approach

Sometimes when setting out from a river bank or beach it is not possible to place the canoe parallel to the shore. In this situation, the canoe is placed at a right angle to the shore as flat on the water as possible. One person stabilizes the canoe by squatting down and holding the deck plate. This person can squeeze the end of the canoe between his or her legs to provide more stability. The other paddler then steps into the canoe and, keeping his or her weight low and a hand on each gunwale, walks up the keel line to his or her seat.

After the first paddler is situated, the second paddler makes sure that the bottom of the canoe is free from the river bottom. He or she then steps into the canoe with one foot, puts a hand on each gunwale, and pushes off, bringing his second foot into the canoe. After being sure that the canoe is free floating, the second paddler then settles into his seat and grabs his paddle, and off they go!

Perpendicular Entry

- Point the canoe straight out from the bank, bow or stern first. Lay the canoe flat on the water. This might require getting wet feet.

- Have gear stowed and paddles flat on the bottom of the canoe.

- Stabilize the canoe by using your hands and by clamping the end of the canoe between your legs.

- When entering, stay low and evenly distribute your weight.

Get In

- Take your time. Rushing the canoe launch can lead to swamping the canoe or falling into the water.

- While entering and moving about the canoe, keep three points of contact at all times: hands on gunwales and feet planted near keel line.

- Keep the craft stabilized the entire time the other paddler is shifting about.

- Lift feet high enough to clear seats and thwarts.

Take your time. It's easy to tip when launching. Communicate with your partner, and pay attention to how you move and how this affects the canoe.

ZOOM

Landing the canoe means reversing the steps for launching the canoe. Approach the landing gently. Banging into the dock or hitting land at full speed can dent your canoe and remove the protective gel-coat. Get out of the boat one at a time. Step carefully, shifting your weight to the shore foot in one movement. Remember to hold on to the canoe so that it doesn't float away.

Push Off

- After the first paddler is seated and ready, the second paddler gets into the canoe.

- Keeping hands on gunwales, step onto the keel line with the first foot.

- Push off from the shore with the second foot, then bring the foot into the canoe. This is a fluid, continuous movement.

- Maintain your balance as the canoe begins to move.

Get Settled

- Keeping his or her weight low, the second paddler turns and lowers into the seat.

- Pick up your paddles and begin to move farther out onto the water.

- If pushing off in reverse, check to be sure that the space behind you is clear of obstacles, swimmers, and other boats.

- Near shore, be especially alert for submerged logs and rocks.

TO THE WATER

47

HOLDING THE PADDLE
Correct hand placement allows for efficient paddling

The paddle is the steering and power mechanism for your canoe. Proper grip and hand placement allow you to comfortably maneuver and propel your canoe for long periods while minimizing fatigue and chance of injury.

Place one hand over the grip on the paddle. This is the control hand. It allows you to turn the paddle blade in the water and affects how the canoe responds. Place your other hand on the shaft of the paddle 8 to 12 inches above the

blade. Hold the grip and throat with relaxed hands. There is no need to white-knuckle the paddle. The distance between your hands is a little more than shoulder width. Get comfortable with this placement of your hands. This is where your hands will be on the paddle for virtually every stroke. Switch hand placement when you change sides of the canoe you are paddling on. When paddling on the left side, your right hand will be the control hand on the grip and your left hand

Hand Placement

- To determine hand spacing on the paddle, hold the shaft resting on your head with elbows at a right angle.

- This shows you hand positions for almost every canoeing stroke. Grip the paddle firmly but not overly tight.

- Having hands too close together sacrifices control. Having hands farther apart requires you to lean out farther than necessary.

- This spacing allows maximum torso rotation.

In the Canoe

- Whether sitting or kneeling in the canoe, the purpose is to be able to power and steer the canoe as efficiently and comfortably as possible.

- You will need to be able to reach as far out as possible without whacking the paddle on the gunwales or

- mashing your thumbs.

- Unless the canoe is fitted with a middle seat, kneeling is often the best position for solo paddling.

- Spread your weight so that the canoe stays level and flat.

will be on the throat. When paddling on the right side of the canoe, your left hand will be the control hand.

Placing your hands a little more than shoulder width apart permits the most efficient use of energy by allowing for torso rotation. Torso rotation is *the key* to maximizing muscle use and preventing sore arms. Practice this by sitting in a wooden chair and holding your paddle. Your arms should be parallel to each other. The shaft of the paddle and your chest should also be roughly parallel to each other. Now move the paddle as if you were pulling it through the water. Your torso and shoulders should be turning to cause the paddle to move, and your arms should remain parallel to each other. Switch hands and practice on the other side.

Paddling Position

- While forward paddling, maintain the "paddler's box": arms parallel to each other and paddle shaft parallel to your chest.

- This allows for *torso rotation*, which maximizes back and trunk muscle use and preserves arm muscles.

- Arms, paddle, and chest move as a unit. Shoulders pivot forward at the start of a stroke.

- Look down at your PFD zipper or buckle. It should move back and forth with every stroke as you rotate your shoulders.

End of Stroke

- At the end of a stroke, your arms, paddle, and chest should still be in the paddler's box position.

- Your shoulders and torso will have turned 60 to 70 degrees.

- Feet and knees remain in the same position during the stroke.

- Torso rotation may feel awkward at first, but it's worth the effort to master it.

THE PADDLE STROKE

All paddle strokes contain the same four components

Although the form and purpose of canoe strokes vary immensely, the different parts of each stroke share the same names and functions within that stroke. Although each stroke is a fluid and unified movement, using the names of each part of a stroke isolates that component of the process so you can focus on each of the different aspects of a paddle stroke.

The *catch* (also called the *plant*) is the beginning of the stroke. This is where the paddle enters the water. The *power*

phase of the stroke pushes against the water, causing the canoe to move. The paddle is removed during the *exit* phase of the stroke. The *recovery* phase of the stroke returns the paddle to the catch phase of the stroke. The recovery can include *feathering* the blade in the air during a forward stroke or slicing the blade through the water during a draw stroke. Feathering involves turning the blade parallel to the water during recovery. Feathering reduces wind resistance and conserves

Catch

- The catch, also called the *plant,* is the first phase of any stroke.

- Proper placement of the blade ensures that the stroke will be effective.

- How and where the blade is planted will depend on the stroke being used.

- Picture the blade being immobile in the water where you plant it, then notice that the canoe is being moved over the water past the paddle. The object is not to merely drag the paddle through the water.

Power

- The power phase of the stroke propels the canoe through the water.

- During a turning stroke, the power phase makes the canoe change directions.

- The side of the blade that is pushing against the water is called the *powerface* of the paddle.

- The *backface,* or *reverse face,* is the opposite, or following, side of the paddle.

energy over the course of a long paddle.

Two other terms you should know refer to the blade of the paddle. The *powerface* is the side of the paddle blade that pushes against the water during the stroke. The *backface* (or *reverse face*) is the other side of the blade. With straight-shaft paddles either side of the blade may serve as the powerface. With bent-shaft paddles the powerface is the side of the blade that pushes the water when the paddle is held so that the blade is bent forward. With paddles that have a scoop-shaped blade, the powerface is the side that does the scooping.

While a stroke is divided into different parts, the stroke is performed as a fluid combination of the parts. The plant flows into power, the blade exits and then recovers, to begin again.

Exit

- The *exit* phase is when the paddle is removed from the water.

- Timing of blade withdrawal affects the efficiency of the stroke. Removing the paddle late can create unnecessary resistance.

- How the blade is removed depends on the type of stroke.

- Exit sets the stage for the recovery phase of the paddle stroke.

Recovery

- The *recovery* phase returns the paddle to the start of the paddle stroke.

- The recovery phase can include feathering the blade to reduce wind resistance.

- Recovery can take place above water or in water, depending on the stroke.

- An efficient recovery allows the paddler to begin the next stroke.

FORWARD SWEEP

Sweep strokes are used to turn the canoe

A forward sweep stroke can be done on either side of the canoe. A forward sweep done on the right side of the canoe will turn the canoe to the left. A forward sweep on the left side of the canoe will turn the canoe to the right.

To execute a forward sweep on the left side, reach forward, planting the blade of the paddle parallel to the bow of the canoe. Your left arm will be straight, reaching out in front. Your right arm is bent, elbow near your ribcage. Keeping the left arm straight, rotate your torso, pulling on the paddle until it has made a half-circle motion and is now parallel to the stern of the canoe.

Keep an eye on the blade as you rotate. This is called *watching your work*. Repeating the forward sweep on the left side will cause the canoe to move in a circle to the right. Switch

Catch

- Hands remain in the standard position. Reach is extended by stretching out the arm.

- Reach forward and place the blade of the paddle parallel to the bow.

- Keep the outer arm straight. Keep the inner arm bent, held near the torso.

- The forward sweep will turn the canoe away from the paddle. A forward sweep on the right will turn the bow of the canoe to the left.

Power

- The blade of the paddle follows a 180-degree semi-circular path.

- The outer arm stays straight throughout the stroke. Concentrate on torso rotation.

- Watch your work. Follow the path of the paddle with your eyes.

sides to perform a forward sweep on the right side of the boat. This will make the canoe turn to the left.

Forward Sweep
- Keep outside arm straight.
- Reach, don't lean.
- Watch your work.
- Rotate torso!

Exit and Recovery

- Continue the sweep until the blade is parallel to the stern of the canoe.

- Slip the blade out of the water and swing the blade up to the bow to repeat the sweep.

- During the recovery phase, you can feather the paddle to reduce wind resistance.

- Feathering is turning the paddle parallel to the water so that it slices effortlessly through the air.

You aren't paddling to move the paddle *through* the water, you are paddling to move the canoe *over* the water! Every movement of the paddle in the water should affect the canoe. That is why some people call the start of a stroke the *plant*. Imagine that the paddle is stuck in place (planted) and that the canoe is moving past it.

Pivot Point in a Canoe

- Canoes do not turn like a car, with the front wheels leading the rest of the vehicle.

- Because a canoe rests flat on the water, it turns around the pivot point, which is in the middle of the canoe.

- While the bow of the canoe moves one direction, the stern turns the other way. This is difficult to notice at first because the canoe is also moving forward over the water.

- The pivot point allows you to easily spin the canoe 180 degrees.

SOLO I

REVERSE SWEEP
The reverse sweep turns the bow to the side you are paddling on

As its name implies, the reverse sweep is the opposite of the forward sweep. The paddler reaches behind, planting the blade parallel to the stern of the canoe. Then the paddler, keeping the outer arm straight, pushes forward on the paddle, making a big C-shaped arc. Performing a reverse sweep on the right side of the canoe will cause the bow to swing to the right. Doing a reverse sweep on the left will cause the bow to swing to the left. Repeating the reverse sweep several times will cause the canoe to make a circle going backward.

Practice the reverse sweep on both sides of the canoe. Many people develop a preference for paddling on one side or the other. Resist this temptation and work hard enough to become proficient and comfortable paddling all strokes on both sides of the canoe.

To pivot in place, combine a reverse sweep on one side of the canoe with a forward sweep on the other side.

Catch

- Your hands remain in the standard position. Reach is extended by stretching out the arm.

- Reach backward and place the blade of the paddle parallel to the stern.

- Keep the outer arm straight. Keep the inner arm bent, held near the torso.

- The reverse sweep will turn the canoe toward the paddle. A reverse sweep on the right will turn the bow of the canoe to the right.

Power

- The blade of the paddle follows a 180-degree semi-circular path.

- The outer arm stays straight throughout the stroke. Concentrate on torso rotation.

- Watch your work. Follow the path of the paddle with your eyes.

- Push vigorously with the outer arm. Imagine that the paddle is *planted* in the water and concentrate on making the canoe turn on the water, not merely moving the paddle through the water.

Reverse Sweep
- Look before you paddle!
- Keep the outside arm straight.
- Reach, don't lean.
- Watch your work.
- Rotate torso!

•••••••••••••• RED●LIGHT ••••••••••••

Always look behind you before paddling backward! It can be surprisingly easy to bump into another boat, a swimmer, the dock, or a tree while back paddling. Other craft can approach more quickly than expected. Also, your canoe can easily shift around due to moving water or wind, and it may not be where you thought it was in relation to objects or people. Always look!

Exit and Recovery

- Continue the sweep until the blade is parallel to the bow of the canoe.

- Slip the blade out of the water and swing the blade back to the stern to repeat the sweep.

- During the recovery phase, you can feather the paddle to reduce wind resistance.

- Feathering is turning the paddle parallel to the water so that it slices effortlessly through the air.

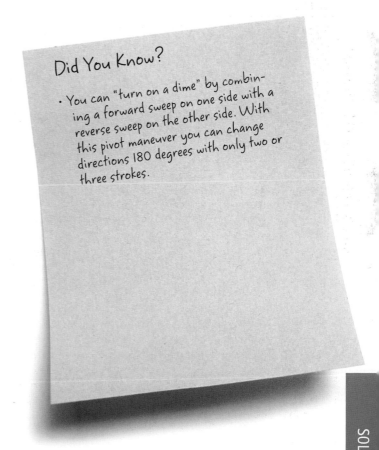

Did You Know?

- You can "turn on a dime" by combining a forward sweep on one side with a reverse sweep on the other side. With this pivot maneuver you can change directions 180 degrees with only two or three strokes.

SOLO I

FORWARD STROKE
The forward stroke propels the canoe forward

The forward stroke is sometimes called the *power* stroke. But this is not the brawny, far-reaching, froth-churning megastroke that people sometimes imagine. To be the all-day stroke that carries you miles across windy lakes or down sluggish rivers, the forward stroke must be energy efficient and create minimal resistance in the water.

The forward stroke is a fairly short stroke, only about 20 to 24 inches in length. A paddle blade that is straight up and down is using most of the force exerted on it to move the canoe forward. A paddle blade that is slanted in the water at the beginning of the stroke expends some of its force trying to lift the bow of the canoe in the air. A paddle blade that is slanted at the end of the stroke push is expending force trying to push the bow of the canoe down into the water. This is the advantage of a bent-shaft paddle on flat water: It directs most of the energy of the stroke into forward movement of the canoe, with

Forward Stroke: Catch

- Reach forward, placing the blade of the paddle alongside the canoe with the blade perpendicular to the gunwale.

- Do not overextend. The forward stroke is fairly short—20 to 24 inches.

- Insert almost the entire blade into the water. Do not sink the paddle up to the throat.

- This is also called the *plant*. Imagine the blade being planted—stuck firmly in place—in the water.

Forward Stroke: Power

- Propel the canoe over the water by rotating your torso. Your arms should stay in position and your shoulders twist.

- As you pull on the paddle, you will move the canoe past where the paddle was planted.

- Keep the stroke parallel to the gunwale and close to the hull without hitting or scraping the canoe.

- This is a short, powerful stroke, intended to keep you moving forward without tiring you out.

less effort from the paddler. However, bent-shaft paddles are difficult to steer with and are not to be used on whitewater.

The shaft of the paddle should be nearly vertical throughout the stroke. This keeps the blade near the edge of the canoe, maximizing efficiency. Keeping the shaft vertical also helps the paddler to use torso rotation to power the stroke. Your arms should remain mostly parallel throughout the stroke, and your torso and shoulders should rotate with each stroke. Although torso rotation may be cumbersome at first, it utilizes back and stomach muscles rather than just the arms.

Forward Stroke

- Keep the paddle vertical.
- Use 20- to 24-inch strokes.
- Keep strokes short and quick.
- Rotate torso!

Forward Stroke: Exit

- The blade remains perpendicular to the hull. Remove the paddle straight from the water at the end of the stroke.

- For a standard forward stroke, don't turn or twist the paddle.

- Remember that this is a short stroke. The exit is performed right as the paddle passes your hip.

- Do not draw out this stroke. The most efficient forward propulsion is achieved in 20 to 24 inches. After passing your hip, the blade starts to push up on the water, creating drag.

Forward Stroke: Recovery

- The recovery phase of the stroke returns the paddle to the beginning of the next stroke.

- As the blade leaves the water, swing the paddle smoothly forward, relying on torso rotation to provide the movement.

- *Feathering* is turning the blade parallel to the water so that it slices through the air with minimal resistance.

- In large waves, be cautious that the paddle blade clears the tops of the waves and doesn't get snagged and pulled down.

BACK STROKE

The back stroke is for stopping forward movement or for going backward

The back stroke is roughly the opposite of the forward stroke. It is used primarily for slowing down or stopping a forward-moving canoe. Hit the brakes! The back stroke is also used to move away from a dock, avoid other boats, or back out of narrow inlet.

Rotate back, plant the paddle behind you, and push forward.

This will slow or stop forward movement or begin pushing the canoe backward. Remember to look behind you!

You may notice that a simple back stroke doesn't simply move the canoe backward in a straight line. Any paddle stroke on the side of a canoe will also cause the canoe to turn a certain amount. A back stroke makes the bow of the canoe

Back Stroke: Catch

- If using the back, or reverse, stroke to move the canoe backward, glance behind to make sure you will not hit anything.

- Hand position on the paddle is the same as for the forward stroke.

- Reach back by rotating your torso and plant the blade just behind your hip. The blade is perpendicular to the hull, close to the canoe without touching or scraping.

- Insert almost the entire blade into the water. Do not sink the paddle up to the throat.

Back Stroke: Power

- Push forward forcefully on the paddle to move the canoe backward.

- Propel the canoe over the water by rotating your torso. Your arms should stay in position and your shoulders twist.

- As you push on the paddle, you will move the canoe past where the paddle was planted.

- Keep the stroke parallel to the gunwale and close to the hull without hitting or scraping the canoe.

swing to the side that you are paddling on. The turning motion is minimized by keeping the paddle vertical and close to the side of the hull. Moving the blade out away from the hull (as in a sweep) maximizes the turning motion of the canoe.

Back Stroke

- Look behind!
- Reach back, plant blade in the water.
- Push forward.
- Rotate torso!

Back Stroke: Exit

- The blade remains perpendicular to the hull. Remove the paddle straight from the water at end of the stroke. Do not turn or twist the paddle.

- This is a short, powerful stroke. The most efficient reverse propulsion is achieved in 20 inches. The

exit is performed soon after the paddle passes the knee.

- The back stroke moves the canoe backward *and* to the side on which the back stroke is done.

- The bow may hit something on the side on which you are paddling.

Back Stroke: Recovery

- The recovery phase of the stroke returns the paddle to the beginning of the next stroke.

- As the blade leaves the water, swing the paddle smoothly backward, relying on torso rotation to provide the movement.

- Feathering is not a concern with the reverse stroke. You will be doing far less reverse stroke than forward stroke.

- Direct your attention to how the canoe is moving and what your next maneuver will be.

SOLO I

59

STEERING THE CANOE

Confident and precise steering is required for a safe and pleasant trip

An inability to steer the canoe is the reason why many first-time paddlers never get into a canoe again. It is important to feel in control of your craft, and there are many techniques for making the canoe go where you want it to go.

Paddling using only the forward stroke will not keep the canoe moving in a straight line. When you forward stroke, the canoe will go forward, but the bow also turns away from the side you are paddling on. How can you compensate for this turning of the bow?

Using the paddle as a rudder is an effective way of turning the canoe. By placing the blade behind you vertically in the water and pushing out, you cause the canoe to turn to the

Steering with a Rudder: Step 1

- Reach behind you and turn the paddle blade vertical in the water. Push outward forcefully away from the canoe.

- Hold the rudder at a 45-degree angle until the bow has turned. This will turn the bow of the canoe to the side you rudder on.

- Be sure that the blade of the paddle is deep enough in the water.

- The rudder is effective in turning the canoe, but it is inefficient. It slows the forward motion of the boat dramatically.

Steering with a Rudder: Step 2

- By rotating back farther and holding the paddle at a "reverse angle"—tip of the blade pointing at the stern—the bow will move to the *opposite* side you rudder on.

- The upper arm will be pushed straight out, and the lower will be bent in

- and rotated behind you.

- Maintain a 45-degree reverse angle with the blade until the bow moves the desired distance.

- With a little practice, you can rudder the boat right or left without changing the side that your paddle is on.

side you are paddling on. Rudder on the left, and the bow turns to the left. Rudder on the right, and the bow turns to the right. The drawback to steering with a rudder is its inefficiency. Using a rudder really slows the forward movement of the canoe.

The J-stroke is a more efficient way of maintaining a straight line. The J-stroke is merely a forward stroke with the addition of a quick turn of the paddle and a gentle push away from the canoe. As you near the end of the forward stroke, turn the paddle so that the thumb of your grip hand is point-

ing down, then, using the throat hand, push the blade away from the canoe. Adjust the intensity of the push based on how much correction the bow needs to make to maintain a straight line.

The key to the J-stroke's efficiency is using the powerface of the paddle during the push phase of the stroke. This is why the wrist of the hand on the paddle grip is turned outward, leaving the thumb pointing down.

J-Stroke: Step 1

- Just before the end of a forward stroke, turn the blade so that it is parallel to the hull. Do this by turning your hand so that the thumb points down.

- A quick twist of your upper wrist will position the powerface of the blade so that it will be pushing against the water, away from the canoe.

- The key here is a *quick* change in the direction that the powerface is pointed. A slow, gradual transition will increase drag and slow the canoe more than necessary.

J-Stroke: Step 2

- Now push the blade away from the canoe with the throat hand. This pressure on the water will move the bow toward the paddle side.

- Adjust the amount of outward pressure according to how much you want the bow to turn.

- Use the J-stroke intermittently to keep your canoe on course.

- To steer the canoe opposite the side you are paddling on, use a partial forward sweep stroke. This way you can steer both directions from the same side of the canoe.

DRAW STROKE I

Draw strokes are used to move the canoe sideways across the water

The draw stroke is ideal for pulling the canoe sideways next to a dock or for "rafting up" with another canoe.

To perform the draw, turn the paddle parallel to the side of the canoe and reach out over the water. Reach out as far as you can. Prevent the canoe from tilting by shifting the weight in your hips toward the middle of the canoe. Plant the paddle vertically in the water and pull the canoe toward the paddle. A few inches before the canoe reaches the paddle, slice the

blade upward out of the water in the direction of the stern. Repeat the process until the canoe has been drawn across the water to where you want it.

See pages 63 and 64 for two variations on the recovery phase of the draw stroke. Use of the draw as a maneuvering stroke will be addressed on pages 68 and 90–91.

If you wait too long to begin the recovery, the paddle can get pulled under the hull of the canoe. If this happens, don't

Draw Stroke: Catch

- Hand placement on the paddle is the standard position, same as the for-ward stroke.

- Reach straight out from the side of the canoe. Reach with your arms, don't lean with your body.

- Be sure that the blade is parallel to the gunwale and plant the blade as far out as you can comfortably reach.

- Balance your weight be-tween your knees to allow as much reach as possible. Experiment to see how far your canoe can comfortably rock to the side.

Draw Stroke: Power

- Pull straight in with the lower arm. Pull with vigor so that you are moving the canoe sideways across the water.

- Again, focus on moving the *canoe over the water,* not the paddle *through* the water.

- This stroke is very effective for moving sideways on quiet water. It is often used to get closer to a dock or to move alongside another canoe.

try to force it back out! Just let go of the throat and the paddle will float up to the side. (Keep holding on to the grip!)

This stroke "draws" the canoe sideways across the water. It requires a bit of power to move the canoe broadside.

Draw Stroke: Exit

- When the canoe is inches from the paddle, slice the blade upward out of the water. Slice the blade in the direction of the stern.

- Push down with the grip hand, pull up with the throat hand. The paddle will now be parallel to the water.

- If the canoe gets too close to the paddle, the paddle can get wedged underneath the hull. Don't try to force the paddle free! Let go of the throat hand, and the paddle will float to the surface.

Draw Stroke: Recovery

- This version of the draw stroke is called the *out-of-water recovery draw stroke*. The exit and recovery phases of the stroke are combined.

- After slicing the paddle free from the water, reach back out to plant the blade again.

- Notice how your weight shifts in the canoe to compensate when reaching out and when pulling back on the paddle.

- Experiment to see how far your canoe can tilt but still glide sideways as you do the draw stroke.

DRAW STROKE II

The in-water recovery and the sculling draw add finesse to your canoe skills

Whereas the out-of-water recovery draw stroke is critical in crossbow maneuvering situations (covered on pages 62–63), the in-water recovery is a nice refinement for flatwater sideways movement.

Begin the draw stroke as described on page 62. When the canoe has been pulled almost to the paddle, quickly turn the blade 90 degrees and knife it back through the water out to the starting point. Return the blade to a position parallel to the canoe and then draw again. Repeat the in-water recovery draw until your craft has been moved where you want it to go.

The sculling draw is a particularly impressive stroke. With

In-water Recovery: Step 1

- The plant and power phases of the in-water draw are the same as the out-of-water draw.

- When the canoe has been pulled very close to the paddle, the exit phase consists of twisting the blade 90 degrees in the water.

- The blade, now perpendicular to the hull, is knifed out through the water to the plant phase.

- Now twist the paddle back so that it is parallel to the hull again. You are ready for the next power phase of the draw.

In-water Recovery: Step 2

- The key to an effective in-water draw is a smooth and controlled execution of the stroke.

- Begin very slowly and focus on each phase of the stroke. Experiment to learn the best place to twist the paddle 90 degrees for the exit.

- When knifing the blade back to the beginning of the stroke, keep the paddle perpendicular to prevent the blade from getting pulled sideways.

- Remember to keep your upper elbow low and near your chest. Don't risk shoulder dislocation.

minimal paddle movement, the canoe appears to glide magically across the water. The sculling draw is a continuous stroke performed without removing the blade from the water. When sculling, move the blade back and forth in a figure-8 pattern with the power face always pushing against the water. The angle of the blade creates the force that pulls the canoe across the water. Unlike the regular draw stroke, sculling requires that the paddle be held at an angle, slanting down from your shoulder. Keep your inner elbow low.

"Figure-8 pattern" describes the movement of the paddle in relation to the water. You are moving the paddle straight back and forth, just changing the angle of the blade.

Sculling Draw: Step 1

- Hold the paddle out from the side of the canoe at about a 45-degree angle.

- The blade will remain in the water while you make a continuous figure-8 movement with the paddle.

- With each pass of the paddle, twist the blade so that the powerface is pushing against the water.

- It is the pressure of the water on the powerface that pulls the canoe sideways.

Sculling Draw: Step 2

- The key to the sculling draw is an even, continuous pressure applied through a properly angled paddle blade.

- As the paddle is swept back and forth, twist the blade quickly to maintain constant pressure on the water.

- This is a more subtle stroke than the other draws, and an experienced paddler makes it look effortless.

- You can make it look effortless with a little practice and close attention to blade angle, pressure, and timing.

PUSHAWAY & PRY STROKES

These powerful strokes move the canoe sideways away from the paddle

Like the draw strokes, the pushaway and pry strokes move the canoe sideways. Unlike with the draw, the canoe is being moved away from the paddle, not toward it.

The *pushaway* is the opposite of the draw stroke. Plant the paddle parallel to the canoe, a few inches from the hull. Then forcefully push straight out using mostly your lower arm. The canoe will move *away* from the paddle. You may do an out-of-water recovery by dropping the grip hand and lifting with the throat hand, knifing the blade out of the water. You can also perform an in-water recovery by twisting the blade 90 degrees and pulling it back through the water to the starting point.

KNACK CANOEING FOR EVERYONE

Pushaway: Catch

- This stroke is used to move the canoe *away* from the paddle. It is the opposite of the draw stroke.

- Plant the blade parallel to, and only an inch or two away from, the hull.

- Be sure not to lean out toward the paddle—as you push this could lower the gunwale far enough to take on water!

- Your arms will provide the leverage, transferring the power from the blade pushing against the water to your knees (or feet and bottom), which will push the canoe sideways.

Pushaway: Power

- Push forcefully, using mostly your lower arm. This will move the canoe away from the paddle.

- If another pushaway is needed, you may do an in-water or out-of-water recovery to return the blade to the start of the stroke.

- Don't dislocate your shoulder—keep your upper elbow low!

- The pushaway is the sideways counterpart to the draw stroke. These two strokes allow you to move the canoe either direction from the same side of the canoe.

The *pry stroke* is a more powerful way of moving the canoe sideways away from the paddle. Rotate to the side of the canoe that the paddle is on. Slide the blade into the water alongside the hull with the throat touching the edge of the hull. The shaft of the paddle will be pointing away from you. By pulling the grip of the paddle toward you, the blade will push against the water, moving the canoe away from the paddle. You may then do an out-of-water or in-water recovery in order to repeat the stroke as necessary.

Pry: Catch

- The pry is a very powerful stroke that uses the paddle as a lever to move the canoe sideways away from the paddle.

- Slide the paddle into the water with the blade parallel to the hull. The handle points away from you, your upper arm straight.

- The throat of the paddle rests up against the hull of the canoe with the blade under the canoe.

- Do not lean toward the paddle. The pry stroke can put a lot of downward force on the gunwale.

Pry: Power

- To execute the pry, pull back forcefully on the paddle. This will push the canoe away from the paddle.

- Do not pinch your hand between the throat of the paddle and the gunwale of the canoe.

- In shallow water be careful that the tip of the blade does not catch on a rock. That could swamp your boat or break the paddle.

- The pry is very effective, but it can mar the finish of your canoe or dent wooden gunwales.

CROSS DRAW & THE PIVOT TURN

Use the cross draw to quickly move the bow, and to turn the canoe around

The *cross draw* stroke is a draw stroke (see page 90–91) done by crossing over the bow *without changing hand positions* on the paddle. This stroke can be done when paddling solo or from the bow in a tandem canoe. This quick stroke can help you avoid suddenly appearing rocks.

Rotate at the waist, swing the paddle over the canoe, reach out as far as you can, and pull toward the canoe. Keep your elbows low to prevent shoulder dislocation. The canoe will turn quickly to the side on which you do the draw.

The cross draw will feel a little awkward at first. It requires a lot of twisting at the waist and a far reach with the hand that is on the throat of the paddle. Be sure that your feet are

Cross Draw: Catch

- The cross draw allows you to powerfully turn the canoe away from the side you are paddling on.

- The cross draw requires some flexibility and agility and may feel a little awkward at first.

- Rotate at the waist and swing the paddle to the opposite side of the canoe *without* changing hand position.

- Keep your inner elbow low and pressed against your side. Reach out as far as you can and plant the blade in the water.

Cross Draw: Power

- After the blade is planted, pull forcefully toward the canoe. Your top arm punches out, your lower arm pulls in, and the blade is pulled toward the bow.

- This moves the canoe quickly to the side on which you perform the cross draw.

- This stroke can be done solo or by the bow paddler in a tandem canoe. Quick maneuvering can help you avoid rocks and make steering corrections in fast water.

- Practice the cross draw from both sides of the canoe to overcome any awkwardness.

pressed against the hull of the canoe or you might find that your bottom will spin in the seat as you pull toward you with the paddle.

On pages 52–55 you saw that you can pivot a canoe by combining a forward sweep on one side and a reverse sweep on the opposite side. You can also perform a pivot by doing a forward sweep on one side and a crossbow draw on the other side. This combination allows you to make a 180-degree turn quickly without having to change hands on the paddle.

Pivot Turn: Step 1

- To make a 180-degree turn without changing hand positions on the paddle, perform a forward sweep on one side of the canoe.

- Reach forward and plant the blade parallel to the bow.

- Keep your outer arm straight, watch your work, and sweep the blade in a large arc until it is parallel to the stern.

- Be sure to utilize torso rotation.

Pivot Turn: Step 2

- After completing a forward sweep on one side, perform a cross draw on the other side of the canoe.

- Repeat this combination of strokes until you have pivoted the canoe.

- Practice this pivot from both sides so that you

develop balanced paddling skills.

- Whenever turning or pivoting, remember to look first! You don't want to bang your canoe into another boat, a dock, or a swimmer's head.

SWITCH PADDLING & THE SOLO-C

Two more techniques for paddling in a straight line

The J-stroke is used to counteract the tendency of the canoe to turn to the opposite side as one forward paddles. An alternative to doing the J-stroke is to simply switch sides of the canoe. Known as the *Minnesota switch* or *power paddling* in tandem racing circles, it merely involves changing sides that one forward paddles on every six to eight strokes. Although the canoe does not maintain a perfectly straight line, this is an effective and powerful way to cover some distance while combating wind and waves. Switch paddling is typically a tandem canoe stroke but can be useful to the solo canoeist.

While canoeing solo you might find that the J-stroke requires too much effort to keep the canoe on course. A good alternative is the *Solo-C*. This stroke is a combination of a draw and a J-stroke. For the forward and J-strokes you begin with the paddle close to the hull. For the Solo-C, however, you plant the paddle as if you were doing a diagonal draw.

Switch Paddling: Step 1

- Switching sides is an alternative way to keep the canoe headed forward.

- Paddle forward on one side for three to five strokes and then quickly change sides and do the same number of forward strokes on the other side.

- The canoe does not go in a perfectly straight line, but it allows you to maintain forward momentum against waves and wind.

- When switching hands, eliminate any unnecessary and time-wasting movements.

Switch Paddling: Step 2

- At completion of the last stroke on one side, lift the paddle diagonally with the throat hand. This moves the throat of the paddle to the other hand.

- Turn the paddle with the new throat hand so that the blade is now pointing to the other side of the boat.

- As you are turning the paddle, move the new grip hand up to the grip.

- You are now ready to seamlessly begin forward paddling on the other side.

Then, following a C shape, pull the paddle under the canoe and end by pushing out gently at the end of the stroke.

At first, solo paddling can be more difficult and require more exertion than tandem paddling, but with a little practice the accomplishment and self-reliance of solo paddling can be yours.

Solo-C: Catch

- The Solo-C is an excellent alternative stroke for keeping the canoe traveling efficiently in a straight line.

- The Solo-C blends a draw stroke and J-stroke into one fluid motion. Your paddle will trace a big C in the water.

- Begin by reaching out and forward to perform a *diagonal* draw. Plant the blade so that it is at about a 45-degree angle to the canoe.

Solo-C: Power

- After the blade is planted, pull the paddle diagonally toward you. The blade will curve partly under the hull of the canoe.

- Continue forming a C shape toward the stern and finish by pushing the blade outward away from the canoe.

- Adjust the force of the ending push to keep the bow of the canoe moving in the direction you want to go.

- The exit and recovery phases of the Solo-C are similar to those of the J-Stroke.

HOLDING THE PADDLE
Correct hand placement and seating arrangements allow for effective paddling

The paddle is the steering and power mechanism for your canoe. Proper grip and hand placement allow you to comfortably maneuver and propel your canoe for long periods while minimizing fatigue and chance of injury.

Proper grip and hand placement on the paddle for tandem canoeing are the same as for solo paddling. (See pages 48–49)

The solo canoeist is solely responsible for the powering and steering of the craft. In tandem paddling, the tasks are divided between two people, but effectively sharing the work requires cooperation, communication, and practice.

The first decision is seating. The stern paddler sits or kneels at the back of the canoe. The bow paddler sits or kneels in the

Tandem Paddling

- Although most canoes have seats, learn how to paddle while kneeling. Kneeling increases stability by lowering the center of gravity.

- Most of the time in tandem canoeing the bow and stern will paddle on opposite sides of the craft.

- Note proper hand position and grip on the paddle: top hand wrapped over the grip, lower hand grasping the throat.

- Always wear a PFD when on the water! You never know when you will need it. Don't become a statistic!

Standard Seated Position

- For calm, flat water, sitting is just fine.

- Sitting in a canoe raises your center of gravity and makes the boat less stable than if you were kneeling.

- Sitting results in one point of contact with the canoe (your bottom on the seat)

- instead of three points while kneeling (bottom against front of seat and two knees).

- Be sure to wear protective footgear that will stay on your feet. It is often impossible to see what is under the water.

front. Most canoes come with built-in seats. Most paddlers choose to paddle from a seated position. However, the more traditional kneeling position offers several important benefits. Kneeling lowers your center of gravity and spreads your weight more evenly. This makes the canoe far more stable. Kneeling extends the reach of your paddle, improving maneuverability in moving water. Kneeling also increases the leverage and power of your stroke. However, kneeling can be rough on your knees and feet. Even if you do most of your paddling seated, know how to kneel. Kneeling improves your chances of suc-cessfully running any quick-moving water you encounter.

Among novice canoeists the stern paddler steers the canoe while the bow paddler provides most of the power. For experienced paddlers, steering is a shared task. Many canoeists develop a strong preference for paddling in either the bow or the stern. Become familiar with both! Your habitual stern paddler may be unavailable one day. Anyway, it is a great idea to change seats regularly to have a little variety and to experience both ends of the canoe.

Torso Rotation

- When learning to paddle, concentrate on using your large trunk muscles and not just your arms.

- With every stroke of the paddle your shoulders should twist and your torso rotate.

- Watch the zipper on your PFD. If it is moving back and forth as you paddle, then you are moving your torso.

- Your arms will bend some, but most of the power to propel the canoe should come from other muscles. Your arms hold the paddle in place while your torso provides the motion.

Torso Rotation and Position

- Note how the shoulders of both paddlers have turned during the course of the stroke.

- Torso rotation is equally important for stern and bow paddlers.

- Be sure to experience paddling in both the bow and stern of the canoe.

- Traditionally (it seems), in mixed canoes the woman will take the bow while the man is in the stern. Mix it up! It is good for everyone to be proficient in both places.

FORWARD SWEEP

Sweep strokes, which turn the canoe, are different in the bow and stern

A forward sweep stroke can be done on either side of the canoe. A forward sweep done on the right side of the canoe will turn the canoe to the left. A forward sweep done on the left side of the canoe will turn the canoe to the right.

A solo paddler does a full 180-degree sweep. Tandem paddlers split the stroke in half, and each does a 90-degree sweep.

To execute a forward sweep on the left side, the bow paddler reaches forward, planting the blade of the paddle parallel to the bow of the canoe. Your left arm will be straight, reaching out in front. Your right arm is bent, elbow near your ribcage. Keeping the left arm straight, rotate your torso, pulling on the paddle until it has made a quarter-circle movement and

Forward Sweep: Bow I

- The bow forward sweep allows the bow paddler to turn the front of the canoe away from the side that he is doing the sweep on.

- Lean forward and place the blade right next to the bow of the canoe.

- The blade should be fully submerged. The angle of the paddle shaft is about 35 degrees.

- Keep your outer arm straight as you reach as far as you can. Your inner elbow is tucked into your ribcage.

Forward Sweep: Bow II

- Keeping the outer arm straight, pull firmly back on the paddle.

- The bow forward sweep stops when the paddle is perpendicular to the canoe. This paddler was less efficient by paddling past about 90 degrees.

- The length of the stroke is 45 degrees—from the bow ("tip") of the canoe to the hip of the paddler—"tip to hip."

- Focus on using torso rotation. It takes some force to turn a loaded canoe in the water. Use all of your available muscles!

is now in line with your hip.

The stern paddler starts the forward sweep at the hip and, keeping the outer arm straight, forcefully pushes the paddle back until the blade is parallel with the stern of the canoe. The forward sweep will turn the canoe to the side opposite of the stroke. Repeating the forward sweep will bring the canoe around in a circle.

Focus on each part of the stroke while you are learning it. Learning each part carefully lets you combine the parts to create an effective stroke.
Catch: Paddle enters water positioned properly
Power: Stroke moves canoe over the water
Exit: Paddle leaves water smoothly to reduce resistance
Recovery: Paddle returns to start of stroke

Forward Sweep: Stern I

- The stern paddler begins the forward sweep at his hip and pushes the paddle back toward the back tip of the canoe: "hip to tip." Because the stern paddler in the photo is reaching far forward, his sweep will be less efficient. It is better to start with the paddle at 90 degrees.

- Stick paddle straight out from your side, outer arm straight, inner elbow tucked into torso.

- The blade is in the water. The shaft of paddle is on a 35 degree angle.

- The length of arc of the stern sweep is 45 degrees from "hip to tip."

Forward Sweep: Stern II

- Pull forcefully with the outer arm. The pressure of the blade against the water will make the bow of the canoe move away from the sweep.

- Keep the outer arm straight throughout the stroke, rotating your torso to pull on the paddle.

- Sweep the blade all the way back until it is next to the stern of the canoe.

- Repeat the forward sweep until the canoe has turned the desired amount.

REVERSE SWEEP

This sweep turns the canoe toward the side you are paddling on

The reverse sweep is performed exactly opposite of the forward sweep and has the opposite effect on the canoe. Again, the tandem reverse sweep is divided between the two paddlers.

The bow paddler thrusts her paddle directly out from the hip and, keeping the outer arm straight, pushes the blade in a 45-degree arc up to the bow. The stern paddler begins the reverse sweep by reaching back and planting the blade

parallel to the stern. The stern paddler then forcefully pushes forward until the paddle is in line with the hip. Repeat the reverse sweep until the bow has turned toward the paddle side of the canoe.

The sweep strokes are key to making course corrections and changing direction. The forward sweep may be inserted between forward strokes to maintain the desired direction of travel. Sweeps also permit pivot turns (pages 52–55).

Reverse Sweep: Bow I

- The reverse sweep turns the canoe toward the paddle.

- Plant the blade straight out from the hip. Keep the outer arm straight. Keep the inner elbow tuck into the torso.

- The blade is submerged, the paddle shaft at a 35-

degree angle from the water to the paddler's grip hand.

- The bow reverse sweep follows the 45-degree arc from the bow paddler's hip to the bow of the canoe: "hip to tip."

Reverse Sweep: Bow II

- Push forcefully on the paddle to turn the canoe's bow toward the blade.

- Keep the outer arm straight throughout the stroke and use torso rotation to provide the power.

- Repeat the reverse sweep until the canoe has turned the desired amount.

- The bow reverse sweep can be combined with a stern forward sweep on the opposite side of the boat to pivot the canoe.

Typically in tandem paddling, weight distribution and stability are maintained by stern and bow paddling on opposite sides of the canoe. This is a sensible general practice. However, some turning procedures, narrow passageways, or strong crosswinds make same-side paddling a desirable option. When same-side paddling is necessary, remain acutely aware of weight distribution. When extending your paddle always think *reach* instead of *lean*.

Reverse Sweep: Stern I

- The reverse sweep will turn the bow of the canoe toward the paddle.

- The stern paddler rotates back and plants the blade parallel to the stern of the canoe. Reach out as far as comfortably possible.

- Be sure that the outer arm is straight and that the inner elbow is tucked into the torso.

- The arc of the stern reverse sweep is the 45 degrees from the stern of the canoe to the hip of the paddler: "tip to hip."

Reverse Sweep: Stern II

- Rotating your torso, push the paddle firmly forward until it is parallel to the hip. Keep the outer arm straight throughout the stroke.

- The bow of the canoe should turn toward the side you are doing the reverse sweep on.

- Repeat the reverse sweep until the canoe has changed direction the desired amount.

- The reverse sweep is used to make major steering corrections and is combined with other strokes to pivot the canoe.

FORWARD STROKE

The forward stroke provides power to move the canoe forward

The forward stroke is sometimes called the *power stroke*. But this is not the brawny, far-reaching, froth-churning megastroke that people sometimes imagine. To be the all-day stroke that carries you miles across windy lakes or down sluggish rivers, the forward stroke must be energy efficient and create minimal resistance in the water.

The forward stroke is fairly short, only about 20 to 24 inches in length. A vertical paddle blade is using most of the force

exerted on it to move the canoe forward. A paddle blade that is slanted in the water at the beginning of the stroke expends some of its force trying to lift the bow of the canoe into the air. A paddle blade that is slanted at the end of the stroke push is expending force trying to push the bow of the canoe down into the water.

The forward stroke is performed the same way by both bow and stern paddlers. The shaft of the paddle should be nearly

Forward Stroke: Bow Catch

- Reach forward slightly and plant the blade just forward of your knee.

- The paddle should be vertical in the water. The grip hand should be almost directly above the throat hand.

- The paddle handle should not be angled and shouldn't scrape against the gunwale.

- The blade should be perpendicular to the hull to create the most forward movement.

Forward Stroke: Bow Power

- Using torso rotation, pull the blade backward. This will move the canoe forward.

- The path of the blade should be parallel to the hull. The blade should pass close to the hull but not scrape it.

- The closer to the hull the forward stroke is, the less the bow of the canoe will turn.

- The forward stroke should be about 20 to 24 inches in length. Several short, quick, forward strokes are more efficient than one overlong megastroke.

vertical throughout the stroke. This keeps the blade near the edge of the canoe, maximizing efficiency. Keeping the shaft vertical also helps the paddler to use torso rotation to power the stroke. Your arms should remain mostly parallel throughout the stroke, and your torso and shoulders should rotate with each stroke. Although torso rotation may be cumbersome at first, it utilizes back and stomach muscles rather than just the arms.

The forward stroke will move the canoe forward but will also turn the bow to the opposite side. Bow and stern paddling on opposing sides of the canoe will partially compensate for this effect. Steering is addressed on pages 82–83.

Forward Stroke
- Keep the paddle vertical.
- Use 20- to 24-inch strokes.
- Keep strokes short and quick.
- Rotate torso!

Forward Stroke: Stern Catch

- The execution of the forward stroke in the stern is identical to that in the bow.

- Use torso rotation. Your arms should remain roughly parallel to each other. Your chest and the paddle handle should stay mostly parallel.

- The forward stroke is fairly short, 20 to 24 inches. A longer stroke creates drag and is less efficient.

- Plant the blade close to the hull and pull straight back. This will move the canoe forward and minimize turning of the bow.

Forward Stroke: Stern Power

- Pull straight back. Lift the blade straight out of the water and swing forward to return to the catch phase.

- During the recovery phase you may *feather* the paddle by turning it parallel to the water. This allows the paddle to slice through air, creating less wind resistance.

- Over the course of several hours of paddling, feathering can make a difference in how tired you get, especially on windy days.

- A well-learned forward stroke will allow you to cross a lot of water efficiently.

BACK STROKE

The back stroke is for stopping forward movement or for going backward

The back stroke is roughly the opposite of the forward stroke. It is used primarily for slowing down or stopping a forward-moving canoe. Hit the brakes! The backstroke is also used to move away from a dock, avoid other boats, or back out of narrow inlet. Rotate back, plant the paddle behind you, and push forward. This slows or stop forward movement or begins pushing

the canoe backward. Remember to look behind you! You may notice that a simple back stroke does not simply move the canoe backward in a straight line. Any paddle stroke on the side of a canoe also causes the canoe to turn a certain amount. A back stroke makes the bow of the canoe swing to the side that you are paddling on. The turning motion is minimized by

KNACK CANOEING FOR EVERYONE

Back Stroke: Catch

- If using the back, or reverse, stroke to move the canoe backward, glance behind to make sure you will not hit anything.

- Hand position on the paddle is the same as for the forward stroke.

- Reach back by rotating your torso and plant the blade just behind your hip. The blade is perpendicular to the hull, close to the canoe without touching or scraping.

- Insert almost the entire blade into the water. Do not sink the paddle up to the throat.

Back Stroke: Power

- Push forward forcefully on the paddle to move the canoe backward.

- Propel the canoe over the water by rotating your torso. Your arms should stay in position and your shoulders twist.

- As you push on the paddle you will move the canoe past where the paddle was planted.

- Keep the stroke parallel to the gunwale and close to the hull without hitting or scraping the canoe.

keeping the paddle vertical and close to the side of the hull. Moving the blade out away from the hull (as in a sweep) maximizes the turning motion of the canoe. The back stroke is performed in the same way by both paddlers.

Back Stroke
- Look behind!
- Reach back, plant the blade in the water.
- Push forward.
- Rotate torso!

Back Stroke: Exit

paddle angle →

- The blade remains perpendicular to hull (see instructions on photo). Remove paddle straight from the water at end of stroke. Don't turn or twist it.

- This is a short, powerful stroke. The most efficient reverse propulsion is achieved in 20 inches. The exit happens soon after the paddle passes your knee.

- Remember that back stroke moves the canoe backward *and* to the side on which back stroke is done.

- The bow may hit something on the side on which you are paddling.

Back Stroke: Recovery

- The recovery phase of the stroke returns the paddle to the beginning of the next stroke.

- As the blade leaves the water, swing the paddle smoothly backward, relying on torso rotation to provide the movement.

- Feathering is not a concern with the reverse stroke. You will be doing far less reverse stroke than forward stroke.

- Direct your attention to how the canoe is moving and what your next maneuver will be.

STEERING THE CANOE
Steering is a cooperative effort, although the stern wields more influence

Using only the forward stroke will not keep the canoe moving in a straight line. When you forward stroke, the canoe will go forward, but the bow also turns away from the side you are paddling on. Even with bow and stern paddling on opposite sides, the canoe will turn away from the stern paddler. How can you compensate for this turning of the bow?

Generally, it is the job of the stern paddler to maintain a straight course. Using the paddle as a rudder is an effective way of turning the canoe. By placing the blade behind you, vertically in the water, and pushing out you cause the canoe to turn to the side you are paddling on. Rudder on the left, and the bow turns to the left. Rudder on the right, and the

Steering with a Rudder: Step 1

- Reach behind you and turn the paddle blade vertical in the water. Push outward forcefully away from the canoe.

- Hold the rudder at a 45-degree angle until the bow has turned. This will turn the bow of the canoe to the side you rudder on.

- Make sure that the blade of the paddle is deep enough in the water.

- The rudder is effective in turning the canoe, but it is inefficient. It slows the forward motion of the boat dramatically.

Steering with a Rudder: Step 2

- By rotating back farther and holding the paddle at a "reverse angle"—tip of the blade pointing at the stern—the bow will move to the *opposite* side you rudder on.

- The upper arm will be pushed straight out, and the lower will be bent in and rotated behind you.

- Maintain a 45-degree reverse angle with the blade until the bow has moved the desired distance.

- With a little practice, you can rudder the boat right or left without changing the side that your paddle is on.

bow turns to the right. Steering with a rudder slows the forward movement of the canoe.

The J-stroke is a more efficient way of maintaining a straight line. The J-stroke is merely a forward stroke with the addition of a quick turn of the paddle and a gentle push away from the canoe. As you near the end of the forward stroke, turn the paddle so that the thumb of your grip hand is pointing down. Then, using the throat hand, push the blade away from the canoe.

The key to the J-stroke's efficiency is using the powerface of the paddle during the push part of the stroke. This is why the wrist of the hand on the paddle grip is turned outward, leaving the thumb pointing down.

The J is performed only by the stern paddler. The bow paddler may occasionally help correct directional drift by doing a partial sweep, although this should be done in concert with the stern paddler's efforts.

J-Stroke: Step 1

- Just before the end of a forward stroke, turn the blade so that it is parallel to the hull. Do this by turning your paddle hand so that the thumb points down.

- A quick twist of your upper wrist will position the powerface of the blade so that it will be pushing against the water, away from the canoe.

- The key here is a *quick* change in the direction that the powerface is pointed. A slow, gradual transition will increase drag and slow the canoe more than necessary.

J-Stroke: Step 2

- Now push the blade away from the canoe with the throat hand. This pressure on the water will move the bow toward the paddle side.

- Adjust the amount of outward pressure according to how much you want the bow to turn.

- Use the J-stroke intermittently to keep your canoe on course.

- To steer the canoe opposite the side you are paddling on, use a partial sweep stroke. This way you can steer both directions from the same side of the canoe.

DRAW STROKES

Draw strokes move the canoe sideways across the water *toward* the paddle

The draw stroke is ideal for pulling the canoe sideways next to a dock or for "rafting up" with another canoe.

To perform the draw, turn the paddle blade parallel to the side of the canoe and reach out as far as you can over the water. Prevent the canoe from tilting by shifting the weight in your hips toward the middle of the canoe. This is especially important in a tandem canoe because you will be paddling on the same side. Plant the paddle vertically in the water and pull the canoe toward the paddle. A few inches before the canoe reaches the paddle, slice the blade upward out of the water in the direction of the stern. Repeat the process until the canoe has been drawn across the water to where you

Draw Stroke: Catch

- Hand placement on the paddle is the standard position, same as for the forward stroke.

- Reach straight out from the side of the canoe. Reach with your arms, don't lean with your body.

- Be sure that the blade is parallel to the gunwale and plant the blade as far out as you can comfortably reach.

- Balance your weight between your knees to allow as much reach as possible. Experiment to see how far your canoe can comfortably rock to the side.

Draw Stroke: Power

- Pull straight in with the lower arm. Pull with vigor so that you are moving the canoe sideways across the water.

- Again, focus on moving the *canoe over the water*, not the paddle *through* the water.

- This stroke is very effective for moving sideways on quiet water. It is often used to get closer to a dock or to move alongside another canoe.

want it. If you wait too long to begin the recovery, the paddle can get pulled under the hull of the canoe. If this happens, don't try to force it back out! Let go of the throat, and the paddle will float up to the side of the canoe.

See pages 64–65 in the solo section for details on the in-water recovery and the sculling draws. Both of these variations add a graceful finesse to your lateral movement.

Draw Stroke: Exit

- When the canoe is inches from the paddle, slice the blade upward out of the water. Slice the blade in the direction of the stern.

- Push down with the grip hand and pull up with the throat hand. The paddle will now be parallel to the water.

- If the canoe gets too close to the paddle, the paddle can get wedged underneath the hull. Don't try to force the paddle free! Let go of the throat hand, and the paddle will float to the surface.

Draw Stroke: Recovery

- This version of the draw stroke is called the out-of-water recovery draw stroke. The exit and recovery phases of the stroke are combined.

- After slicing the paddle free from the water, reach back out to plant the blade again.

- Notice how your weight shifts in the canoe to compensate when reaching out and when pulling back on the paddle.

- Experiment to see how far your canoe can tilt but still glide sideways as you do the draw stroke.

TANDEM II

PUSHAWAY & PRY

These strokes move the canoe sideways *away* from the paddle

The *pushaway* is the opposite of the draw stroke. Plant the blade parallel to the canoe a few inches from the hull. Then forcefully push straight out using mostly your lower arm. The canoe will move *away* from the paddle. You may do an out-of-water recovery by dropping the grip hand and lifting with the throat hand, knifing the blade out of the water. You can also perform an in-water recovery by twisting the blade 90 degrees and slipping it back through the water to the starting point.

The *pry stroke* is a more powerful way of moving the canoe sideways away from the paddle. Rotate your shoulders to the side of the canoe that the paddle is on. Slide the blade into the water alongside the hull with the throat touching the edge of the hull. The shaft of the paddle will angle away from the canoe. By pulling the grip of the paddle toward you, the blade will push against the water, forcefully moving the canoe away from the paddle.

KNACK CANOEING FOR EVERYONE

Pushaway: Catch

- This stroke is used to move the canoe *away* from the paddle. It is the opposite of the draw stroke.

- Plant the blade parallel to, and only an inch or two away from, the hull.

- Be sure not to lean out toward the paddle—as you push, this could lower the gunwale far enough to take on water!

- Your arms will provide the leverage, transferring the power from the blade pushing against the water to your knees (or feet and bottom), which will push the canoe sideways.

Pushaway: Power

- Push forcefully, using mostly your lower arm. This will move the canoe away from the paddle.

- If another pushaway is needed, you may do an in-water or out-of-water recovery to return the blade to the start of the stroke.

- Don't dislocate your shoulder—keep your upper elbow low!

- The pushaway is the sideways counterpart to the draw stroke. These two strokes allow you to move the canoe in either direction from the same side of the canoe.

In a tandem boat these strokes are used in conjunction with other strokes for quick steering. A pry combined with a forward sweep or a cross draw will permit you to evade rocks and other objects.

Pry: Catch

- The pry is a very powerful stroke that uses the paddle as a lever to move the canoe sideways away from the paddle.

- Slide the paddle into the water with the blade parallel to the hull. The handle of the paddle points away from you, your upper arm straight.

- The throat of the paddle rests up against the hull of the canoe with the blade under the canoe.

- Do not lean toward the paddle. The pry stroke can put a lot of downward force on the gunwale.

Pry: Power

- To execute the pry, pull back forcefully on the paddle. This will push the canoe away from the paddle.

- Do not pinch your hand between the throat of the paddle and the gunwale of the canoe.

- In shallow water, be careful that the tip of the blade does not catch on a rock. That could swamp your boat or break the paddle.

- The pry is very effective, but it can mar the finish of your canoe or dent wooden gunwales.

TANDEM II

PIVOTS
There are several ways to rapidly turn your canoe

Pivoting the canoe is an excellent demonstration of bow and stern paddlers working together to maneuver their craft in the water. Pivoting your canoe 180 degrees can be accomplished in several ways. Bow and stern paddlers can do draw strokes on opposite sides of the boat. Or one paddler can do a forward sweep on one side while the other paddler does a reverse sweep on the opposite side.

See pages 68–69 for the *cross bow draw* stroke. This stroke can be performed by the bow paddler while the stern paddler is performing a forward sweep on the opposite side. Experiment with different stroke combinations and see which ones work best for you and your partner. Different strokes may also perform differently depending upon wind and wave and current conditions. As in all tandem canoeing, communication between paddlers is key.

Learning to pivot on flatwater is the beginning of learning

Draw Pivot: Step 1

Draw Pivot: Step 2

- To turn the canoe, each paddler can do draw strokes on *opposite* sides of the canoe.

- Because the paddlers reach in opposite directions, the stability of the canoe is quite high.

- Paddlers may do either in-water or out-of-water recovery.

- The sculling draw can also be used to pivot the canoe. Experiment to see if it works best to have both paddlers do the sculling draw, or if one sculls while the other does a standard draw stroke.

- Draw pivot works best if the strokes are synchronized.

- Repeat the draw stroke until the canoe has been turned the desired distance.

- Combine other strokes to pivot your boat. Try a draw and a sweep or a sweep and a cross draw. How effective are a forward stroke and a draw?

- These different stroke combinations can be used for less dramatic turns than a full 180-degree pivot. Feel free to explore while paying attention to which strokes are most effective and efficient.

to steer and maneuver on fast-moving or whitewater. You will use the basic strokes introduced in Chapters 7 and 8 to become comfortable handling a canoe. If you try river canoeing you will build on these skills to perform ferries, sideslipping, and eddy turns.

Sweep Pivot: Step 1

- An effective way to spin the canoe is to combine a reverse sweep on one side with a forward sweep on the other.

- If the bow paddler does a forward sweep on the left side, the stern paddler does a reverse sweep on the right.

- Coordinate with your partner so that your strokes don't cancel each other out, leaving the canoe motionless.

- While learning to pivot, focus on stroke technique: torso rotating, outer arm straight, inner elbow tucked.

Sweep Pivot: Step 2

- Because paddlers are working on opposite sides, the canoe tends to be stable while pivoting.

- Be aware of how the canoe reacts when you shift from pivoting to forward movement.

- Two paddlers can spin a canoe quickly because canoes naturally turn from a central pivot point.

TANDEM II

CROSS DRAW

A powerful turning stroke performed in the bow of a tandem canoe

The *cross draw* stroke is a draw stroke (see pages 62–63) done by crossing over the bow *without changing hand positions* on the paddle. This stroke can be done when paddling solo or from the bow in a tandem canoe. This quick stroke can help you avoid suddenly appearing rocks.

Rotate at the waist, swing the paddle over the canoe, reach out as far as you can, and pull toward the canoe. Keep your elbows low to prevent shoulder dislocation. The canoe will

turn quickly to the side on which you do the cross draw. The cross draw is a powerful stroke and requires practice to become proficient. Because your hands remain in their original position on the paddle, the cross draw requires maximum torso rotation and arm reach. Improve your leverage by "locking" your legs and feet into the canoe. If seated, press your feet firmly against the inside of the hull and plant your bottom into the canoe seat. If kneeling, keep your knees apart

Cross Draw: Start Position

Cross Draw: Catch

- The cross draw is used by the bow paddler in a tandem canoe.

- The cross draw comes in handy for executing quick steering maneuvers, avoiding rocks, and helping pivot the canoe.

- When switching sides of the canoe, from forward stroke on one side to a cross draw on the other, *do not* change hand position on the paddle.

- Maintaining original hand position helps allow for the quick turning response of the cross draw.

- The cross draw allows you to powerfully turn the canoe away from the side you are paddling on.

- The cross draw requires some flexibility and agility and may feel a little awkward at first.

- Rotate at the waist and swing the paddle to the opposite side of the canoe *without* changing hand position.

- Keep your inner elbow low and pressed against your side. Reach out as far as you can and plant the blade in the water.

for stability and push against the edge of the canoe seat with your bottom.

The cross draw is often executed by the bow paddler in conjunction with a sweep or pry performed by the stern paddler.

Cross Draw: Power

- After the blade is planted, pull forcefully toward the canoe. Your top arm punches out, the lower arm pulls in, and the blade is pulled toward the bow.

- This moves the canoe quickly to the side on which you perform the cross draw.

- This stroke can be done solo or by the bow paddler in a tandem canoe. Quick maneuvering can help you avoid rocks and make steering corrections in fast water.

- Practice the cross draw from both sides of the canoe to overcome any awkwardness.

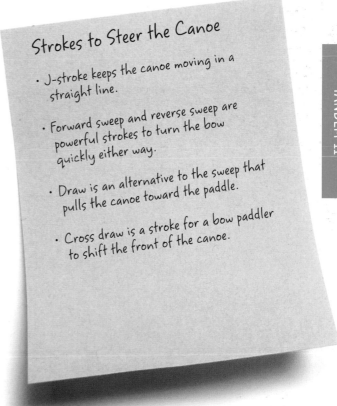

Strokes to Steer the Canoe

- J-stroke keeps the canoe moving in a straight line.

- Forward sweep and reverse sweep are powerful strokes to turn the bow quickly either way.

- Draw is an alternative to the sweep that pulls the canoe toward the paddle.

- Cross draw is a stroke for a bow paddler to shift the front of the canoe.

TANDEM II

SWITCH PADDLING

A good way to maintain direction while working your way across a windy lake

The J-stroke is used to counteract the tendency of the canoe to turn to the opposite side as one forward paddles. An alternative to performing the J-stroke is to simply switch sides of the canoe. Known as the *Minnesota switch* or *power paddling*, this stroke merely involves changing the side that one forward paddles on every six to eight strokes. Although

the canoe does not maintain a perfectly straight line, this is an effective and powerful way to cover some distance while combating wind and waves. Switch paddling is typically a tandem canoe stroke but can be useful to the solo canoeist.

When using the Minnesota switch, experiment to see after how many strokes you want to switch sides. Designate which

Switch Paddling: Step 1

- Switching sides is an alternative way to keep the canoe headed forward.

- Paddle forward on one side for six to eight strokes and then quickly change sides and do the same number of forward strokes on the other side.

- The canoe does not go in a perfectly straight line, but it allows you to maintain forward momentum against waves and wind.

- This stroke is sometimes called the *Minnesota switch* or *power paddling*.

Switch Paddling: Step 2

- At completion of the last stroke on one side, lift the paddle diagonally with the throat hand. This moves the throat of the paddle to the other hand.

- Be sure to coordinate switching sides between the bow and the stern.

- In-sync switch paddling is more efficient and keeps the canoe moving forward with the greatest momentum.

- The canoe will not move in a perfectly straight line, but switch paddling will effectively get you across the water.

paddler will call the switch. Many teams find that it works best for the stern paddler to call the switch because it is easier for the bow paddler to hear the stern than the other way around.

Pay attention to your technique while switching paddle hands. Part of the effectiveness of switching comes from changing sides without losing time or momentum. Blend your hand switch into the recovery phase of the last forward stroke before you change sides. Unnecessary or inefficient movements can really add up over the course of a full day of paddling.

Switch Paddling: Step 3

- Turn the paddle with the new throat hand so that the blade is now pointing to the other side of the boat.

- As you are turning the paddle, move the new grip hand up to the grip. You are now ready to seamlessly begin forward paddling on the other side.

- When switching hands, eliminate any unnecessary and time-wasting movements.

- In most cases, you and your partner will paddle six to eight strokes per side.

Switch Paddling: Step 4

- For switch paddling to be effective, the bow and stern switches must be simultaneous.

- This is usually accomplished by having one paddler call the switch. Often it is easier for the bow paddler to hear the stern paddler.

- A little practice will help you determine the cadence of the switch. In some wave and wind conditions, you may switch every three strokes.

- In very windy conditions, you may find it best to paddle on one side longer than on the other.

TANDEM II

CHANGING POSITIONS

Need a different perspective? Change places without having to land the canoe

An experienced paddler should be equally proficient in the bow and stern. In order to practice both roles, it is a good idea to be able to change positions while out on the water. Some paddling authorities advise against changing positions while afloat, believing that many capsizes occur during "unnecessary" movements by the paddlers. However, moving around is normal, and practicing lets you learn how to move without mishap. Learning to change positions requires clear communication and careful movements by both paddlers and develops paddler confidence.

Two approaches to changing places are the *leapfrog* method and the *side-by-side* method. Both require that you keep

Changing Positions: Step 1

- Be sure that you are in a safe spot for changing places. Consider wind, current, waves, and objects that your canoe might hit.

- Decide which paddler will move first. Both paddles should be stowed flat on the bottom of the canoe. It is very easy to trip over

- a paddle leaning against a thwart.

- The first paddler slowly rises to a squatting position, one hand on each gunwale.

- The bow person will need to turn in place so that she is facing backward.

Changing Positions: Step 2

- The nonmoving paddler needs to remain stationary, leaning forward with one hand on each gunwale.

- The first paddler moves to the middle of the canoe and kneels down, tucking her head low.

- The less room the first paddler takes, the easier it is for her partner to climb past her.

- After the first paddler is fully situated, the second paddler leaves his place and moves to the other end of the canoe.

your weight low and balanced in the canoe. In the leapfrog method, one paddler moves to the middle of the boat and kneels down as low as he possibly can. The second paddler then climbs over the first, keeping hands on the gunwales and weight distributed between his feet. Smaller paddlers can pass each other in the middle of the canoe.

Whichever method you use, you must follow some guidelines. Be aware of your surroundings. Change places only in a safe spot. You don't want to run into an object or be blown by high winds when neither paddler is in place. Only one person moves at a time. You must communicate and be in agreement on how you will change places and the order you will follow. The paddler who is not in motion should stabilize the boat by lowering her weight as much as possible and providing counterweight when required. Take your time. Rushing this procedure may put you in the water. Be patient with your partner. It can take a few moments to get situated in a new spot and be ready for the next step.

Changing Positions: Step 3

- The second paddler, moving slowly and with feet spread and one hand on each gunwale, straddles the first paddler.

- After the second paddler gets situated in his new spot, the first paddler moves to the other spot and settles in.

- Both paddlers then grab their paddles and set off! It is always nice to see the water from another perspective.

Changing Positions: Step 4

- Switching seats is easy and fun. It just takes a little planning, communication, agility, and practice.

- Nearly everyone is able to change spots. Be sure to take your time and don't rush it.

- Changing positions is a good way to remember that your partner is experiencing a different trip than you are, even if he or she is only 8 feet away.

- Changing positions is also a good way to practice all the strokes needed for tandem paddling.

DROWNING

Minimize the risk of serious accident through preparation and planning

Canoeing is a water sport and carries with it the potential of drowning. The likelihood of drowning can be *greatly* reduced by maintaining a proper respect for the power of water. Moving water can exhibit awesome force. Water carved the Grand Canyon and has washed away cities, yet a person can drown in only a few inches. Do not fear water but do respect

its power by taking proper precautions and staying alert.

Most states' boating regulations require that there be one PFD on board for each person. Although the law considers it optional to *wear* a PFD, common sense and reasonable caution dictate the importance of wearing a PFD whenever you are on the water! Capsizing is a time of chaos and confusion.

First Line of Defense

- Always wear a properly fitted, fastened PFD when on the water.

- A PFD that is too big or not fastened may not keep your head above the water.

- It is worth the money to have a comfortable, reliable

life jacket. There are many design options available.

- The PFD is always worn on top! Wear jackets or rain gear under your PFD. Anything over your PFD is likely to float around your face and head or entangle your arms.

Learn to Swim

- Although knowing how to swim is not required for a safe canoe outing, it greatly enhances your sense of comfort and your ability to respond to emergencies.

- Encourage all children in your family to become confident swimmers. It will make them safer, will

contribute to your peace of mind, and help everyone have more fun on hot days.

- Swimming ability is no substitute for wearing a PFD! No one can swim if he or she is unconscious.

- PFDs also provide insulation against hypothermia.

There is no opportunity to don your PFD after your canoe has flipped over. It will likely be floating out of reach. If you are knocked unconscious, a properly fitted and fastened PFD will keep your head above water.

Avoid alcohol while paddling. Drinking slows reaction times, increases the likelihood of making mistakes, and impairs judgment. The majority of paddling fatalities involve alcohol.

Knowing how to swim will enhance your comfort level in and around the water. Swimming ability decreases panic and allows you to assist other paddlers and to retrieve gear.

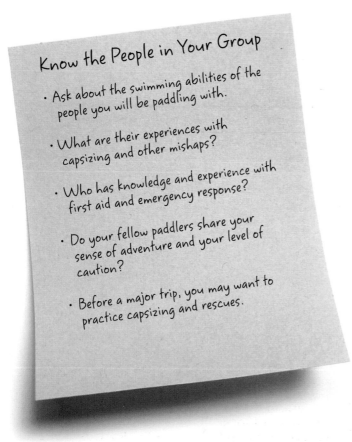
GREEN ● LIGHT

In calm water, while wearing a PFD, practice flipping your canoe. Notice how you react. Practice exiting the canoe without hitting your head on the gunwale. Learn to keep hold of your paddle during capsize. Also try keeping hold of the canoe. Just bob in your PFD and learn to trust that it will keep you afloat. Begin to anticipate how you will respond during an unplanned capsize.

Ready to Respond

- Keep a throw bag or properly coiled throw rope near at hand in your canoe. Secure it against falling out or floating away.

- Practice tossing the throw rope to a floating "victim." Toss the rope so that it lands behind the victim but close enough to grab.

- There may be knots on the ends of the rope to enable holding on.

- Have no loops that are big enough for a hand, neck, or foot to go through. Never tie yourself to a throw rope.

HAZARDS

HYPOTHERMIA

A low body-core temperature, losing more heat than is produced, can be fatal

Hypothermia is a condition in which the body's internal temperature has been lowered enough to cause illness. Hypothermia does not require bitterly cold conditions. A poorly dressed, wet paddler can begin to exhibit signs of hypothermia on a day with temperatures in the 50s, especially if there is wind. Hypothermia is dangerous. It can develop with little warning and quickly affect judgment and reasoning. The individual can have difficulty performing tasks, become withdrawn and apathetic, experience sluggishness and disorientation, unconsciousness, and eventually cardiac and respiratory failure.

A person experiencing mild hypothermia will shiver, com-

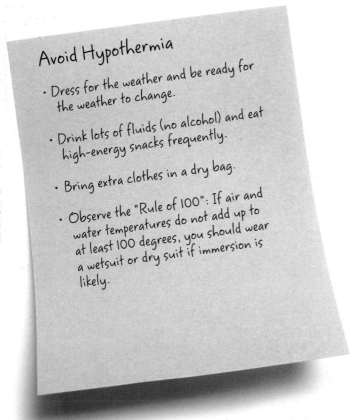

Avoid Hypothermia

- Dress for the weather and be ready for the weather to change.

- Drink lots of fluids (no alcohol) and eat high-energy snacks frequently.

- Bring extra clothes in a dry bag.

- Observe the "Rule of 100": If air and water temperatures do not add up to at least 100 degrees, you should wear a wetsuit or dry suit if immersion is likely.

Clothing

- Select clothing that can be layered and will still insulate if it gets wet. Fleece, polypropylene, and other synthetic fibers are often good choices.

- Wool is an excellent insulator but can be heavy when wet. Avoid cotton clothing and down jackets—no insulation when soaked!

- Bring good rain gear— jacket and pants. These can also serve as wind protection. The wind can whisk away body warmth very rapidly.

- Don't forget a warm hat. Consider a wetsuit on cold days if immersion is likely.

plain of being cold, have difficulty using his or her hands, and display attitude changes: withdrawal, apathy, or irritability. Respond by getting the person warm, dry, and out of the wind. Replace wet clothing. Give him warm drinks and food. NO ALCOHOL! Build a fire to help him warm up.

Symptoms of moderate to severe hypothermia include mental confusion, violent shivering, slurred speech, stumbling, unresponsiveness, decreased pulse and breathing, cessation of shivering, and physical collapse. This is a very fragile state; treat the person gently. End exposure by covering the person and getting him or her out of the wind. Remove wet clothing and place the victim in a sleeping bag or blanket with another person to rewarm the victim's core temperature. Arrange for medical attention and evacuation immediately.

Untreated hypothermia can progress very rapidly. If someone gets immersed on a cool day, respond quickly. Keep the person engaged through conversation and continually monitor his or her mental and physical status.

If you suspect that someone is not doing well, *insist* on a break to get warmed up and rested. Doing so may save a life.

First Aid Kit

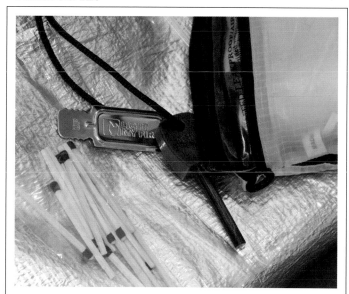

- Basics: Band-Aids, gauze pads, gauze roll, tape, soap or antibiotic ointment, aspirin (or acetaminophen or ibuprophen), tweezers, safety pins.

- Include an emergency blanket (it retains heat and blocks the wind), matches in a waterproof container, and a firestarter.

- Pack in a small dry bag or in a wide-mouth plastic water bottle (watertight, crushproof, buoyant).

- Include a small booklet of first aid instructions. It provides guidance and reassurance during a mishap.

Food

- Bring lots of high-energy snacks: trail mix with nuts, dried fruit, and chocolate pieces.

- Power bars, crackers and cheese, oranges and apples, and cookies will get eaten and provide energy.

- A Thermos of hot chocolate or sweet tea will keep you warm and lift spirits.

- Or bring a small stove and pot to heat water for cocoa, tea, or soup.

STRAINERS, DAMS, & WATERFALLS

A capsize can happen anywhere, but these features can make it dangerous

An unplanned capsize is rarely fun, but strainers, dams, and waterfall magnify the hazards. A strainer is an object, usually a fallen tree or logjam, that lies in the water. A person or boat can get swept under the branches or trunk of the tree and get snagged underneath. The power of the moving water can make it impossible to free yourself. Never attempt to go under a log or downed tree! Grab on, climb over, pull yourself to shore, or wait for help.

A sweeper is a tree that has fallen over the river with branches extending down toward or into the water. If you attempt to paddle beneath a sweeper, the dangling branches may be sturdy enough to "sweep" you out of the canoe. A big

Strainer

- A strainer is an object that lies in the water and can trap things underneath it.

- The power of the current can easily suck capsized paddlers underneath to get snagged on branches.

- Never try to pass underneath a tree, log, or other object in swiftly moving water! If you get snagged, the current can keep you there.

- Climb over any strainers or make your way to the shore to get around downed trees.

Sweeper

- Similar to a strainer, a sweeper is a tree near the water that has branches dangling down into the current.

- If the branches are sturdy enough, they can pull paddlers from the canoe and sometimes pull a canoe under the current.

- Carefully assess any branches you pass underneath. Avoid getting snagged.

- Debris, spiders, snakes, or other things can be knocked from branches into your boat.

enough sweeper may act like a strainer and pull bodies or boats under the surface of the water.

There are tens of thousands of dams on America's rivers. Most of them are small "low-head" dams, and many of them are not marked on maps. Dams can be hard to see and possess an extremely dangerous hydraulic. Water from a dam pours nearly straight down, creating a "hole" that has a recycling current. That current will keep things like people and boats in the hole. Avoid dams! Check maps carefully and keep an eye out for a straight horizon line across a river. Always land on the bank well above the dam to assess the conditions and locate a portage route.

Waterfalls are a naturally occurring hazard similar to dams. Like dams, falls and ledges create holes. Keep alert for a straight horizon line and be prepared to portage. Read the map carefully but remember that not every threatening feature will be noted. Do not assume that dams and falls will be announced with signs.

Dam

- Low-head dams are dangerous and have earned the nickname "drowning machines."

- Water pours over a dam, creating a hydraulic. The water forms a recycling current that can trap boats and people. (Dam pictured doesn't have a pool below, but many do.)

- Because of the concrete apron on the sides of spillways, there is not an "escape valve" for the hydraulic.

- Do not enter a hydraulic to rescue a person or a boat. The recycling current of the hydraulic is too strong to fight against.

Waterfall

- A waterfall can have a hydraulic similar to a low-head dam.

- Check maps carefully but also always look ahead while paddling on streams and rivers.

- Waterfalls and dams can be recognized by the straight horizon line they create across the river. Trees beyond the horizon line will appear too short.

- Always get off the river well above the horizon line and scout out the dam or waterfall. Be ready to portage around falls, dams, or rapids.

OTHER NATURAL HAZARDS

Rocks, rapids, and lightning can pose significant risks, so be aware!

More frequent than the challenges presented by dams and waterfalls are those presented by rocks and rapids. A canoe may be scraped by a rock or broken in half or wrapped around a boulder. The severity of damage that can be inflicted by rocks depends on the volume and speed of the water and your skill and experience in maneuvering a canoe.

Rocks at, or just below, the water's surface sometimes appear from nowhere. Remember that the rocks aren't moving, but you are. There is no substitute for keeping your eyes peeled for rocks and signs of rocks and knowing how to steer around them. Hitting a rock head on can damage the canoe and can throw paddlers off their seats.

Rivers flow because gravity pulls water downhill. Water flows more rapidly at *rapids* because the riverbed drops quickly in a short distance. Rivers tend to be shallower at rapids because the same amount of water has to cover a

Rocks

- Rocks are a common component of most paddling trips. Learn to anticipate where rocks will be and know how the avoid them.

- Be prepared to execute a forceful sweep, cross draw, or pry to steer around suddenly appearing objects in the water.

- Watch for surface ripples that may indicate submerged rocks.

- Try to minimize hitting or scraping rocks. Any encounter with rocks will scrape or dent your canoe to some extent. The less contact, the longer your canoe will last.

Rapids

- Rapids might be defined as lots of rocks in fast-moving water.

- Rapids are rated on an international scale of difficulty (see pages 134–35) ranging from 1 to 6. Most novices can easily manage ratings 1 and 2.

- It is wise to stop and scout any 2+ rapids before paddling through them. Scouting allows you to plan a route.

- Portage any rapids that you feel uncomfortable running. Rapids and portage trails are often noted on topo maps and water trail maps.

greater distance. The result is more rocks and faster water than on flatter parts of the river. The same stretch of rapids can be very different at different times, depending on the volume of water in the river. Water levels can change quickly for a couple of not-so-obvious reasons. It may be sunny where you are but storming upstream. In some locales this can create flash floods. Other rivers can experience dramatic level changes due to water being released from behind dams. Some dams release on a daily schedule. Other dams release water unannounced.

Lightning can kill. If you see lightning or hear thunder, it is best to get off the river. Sitting out in a canoe during a storm leaves you very exposed. It's a good idea to wait at least twenty minutes after the last flash or rumble before resuming paddling.

Thunderstorms

- Get into the habit of checking the most reliable weather forecast available before heading out onto the water.

- Keep an eye on the clouds and be alert for any rapid changes in wind speed, wind direction, or temperature.

- Being on the open water makes you a target for lightning. Find a place on shore, away from tall, isolated trees.

- Wait at least twenty minutes after the last flash of lightning or rumble of thunder before returning to the water.

Dangers to Be Prepared For

- Capsizing and swamping: Practice!

- Drowning: Wear a PFD!

- Strainers and sweepers: Pull over before them!

- Rocks, rapids, dams, and falls: Stay alert!

- Sunburn, bug bites, falls: Wear sunscreen and insect repellant; walk carefully!

- Hypothermia: Dress properly, know the signs, have fluids and snacks, extra clothes, and a blanket!

- Heat exhaustion: Get into the shade; drink lots of water!

SUNBURN, FALLS, & BELONGINGS
These threats may be less than catastrophic but can still ruin a trip

Wear a hat and loose-fitting clothing to protect skin from the sun. Use sunscreen! The sun is more intense when you are paddling because the sun is reflected up off the water as well as coming straight at you. Even well-tanned and dark-skinned people can suffer sunburn. Be careful to cover all exposed skin: face, ears, back of the neck, top of the feet, top of the head. Severe sunburns are painful and can make movement difficult. Don't ruin your trip by not protecting your skin. If you do get sunburned, keep the burn covered, apply lotion or sunscreen to moisturize the burnt area, and drink lots of water.

It's easy to trip and fall on a canoe trip. Trails are uneven, rocks are plentiful, and you are often carrying a heavy load that obscures your view. The middle of an 80-yard portage is no place to twist an ankle or break a wrist by landing on it wrong. Slow down, take your time, and look ahead. It is

Sunburn

Falls

- The sun is more intense when you are on the water. It reflects off the water as well as hits you directly.

- Wear loose-fitting clothing and a broad-brimmed hat. Apply sunscreen to any exposed skin.

- Mild sunburn is uncom-

fortable. Severe sunburn can blister and become infected. Burnt skin can inhibit movement and ruin an otherwise perfect trip.

- Sunglasses protect your eyes and reduce glare off the water, allowing you to more easily see submerged rocks.

- Avoid a twisted ankle, bruises, a broken wrist, or other fall-related injuries.

- Look before you step! Glance down the trail before setting off with a canoe over your head or a heavy pack on your back.

- Be cautious stepping into the water. It can be impossible to see rocks, dropoffs, or other objects.

- Landing sites are often muddy and covered with wet rocks. Take your time and know where you are stepping.

always better to be late than to be injured and late.

No one intends to capsize, but even the most experienced paddlers sometimes do. Plan ahead so that when that fateful moment occurs you won't regret it for the rest of the trip. Glasses sink fast. Secure eyeglasses or sunglasses with a strap or cord. If glasses are critical for you to see well, stow an extra pair in your pack. Cameras and binoculars are ruined by immersion in water. Keep them within reach in a small dry bag clipped to your seat or thwart. Secure car keys in a zippered pocket. Tie all bags and packs to the thwarts of the canoe. Tie

down the spare paddle. In a capsize, anything not tied down will sink or float away. This includes shoes and water bottles.

When you get into a gear bag during a trip, always be sure to re-close it securely and make sure it is tied into the canoe.

Losing Things

- Objects are easily lost on canoe trips. If you have something extremely valuable or irreplaceable, don't take it canoeing!

- Leave jewelry at home. Secure any items you need to bring with you. Use an eyeglass strap!

- Keep cameras and binoculars in a small, *closed* dry bag when not in use.

- Put car keys in a zippered pocket. A second set of car keys with another paddler in your group is good insurance against getting stranded at the take-out.

Plan Ahead

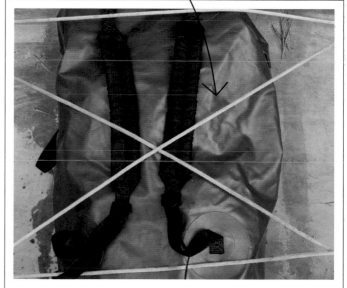

- Pack your gear carefully. Be sure that dry things stay dry by packing them in sturdy plastic bags inside fastened dry bags.

- Secure bags to thwarts with rope, carabiners, or bungee cords. Tie down your spare paddle, or you might not have it when needed.

- Anything not secured will sink or float away in the event of a capsize.

- Any electronic device you "must" have with you (phone, electronic car key ring) must be in a dry bag, or else you may be replacing it.

BOATS, BUGS, & SNAKES
Here are a few more hazards to keep on your "radar screen"

Your canoe is no match for a motor boat, yacht, oil tanker, or Jet Ski. Almost any motorized craft is bigger, heavier, and faster than your canoe. On rivers and other smaller waterways, boats customarily pass oncoming traffic on the right. Follow this convention. However, some motor boats and Jet Skis zip around very erratically, so the best policy is to "drive defensively." Your best strategy is to stay visible. If you are not sure that another craft has seen you, wave your arms and paddles.

If you will often be paddling on waters with motorized boats, consider buying a brightly colored canoe. At night, always outfit your boat with a light that can be easily seen.

Because large ships maneuver and stop so slowly, they do not yield to smaller craft. It is your responsibility to stay out of their way. Do not underestimate the speed of a large ship or boat. Don't try to race a ship. If you are crossing a shipping channel, always cross *behind* a ship, never in front.

Motor Boats and Ships

- Drive defensively! Your canoe cannot outrun a yacht, fishing boat, or oil tanker.

- Large ships have the right-of-way because they cannot stop or turn quickly.

- Stay visible and steer clear of motorized craft. When two craft approach each other, it is customary (and in some cases the *law)* to pass on your right.

- When it is dark, make sure you have a visible light source on your canoe. Most states require some kind of light on all watercraft at night.

Jet Skis

- Small motorized personal craft (Jet Skis) can move very quickly and seem to appear from nowhere. Keep your eyes and ears open!

- Be prepared to wave your arms and paddles if you aren't sure that the other person has seen you.

- Consider purchasing a brightly colored canoe and PFDs. You will be easier to see.

- Err on the side of caution. It is better to avoid a collision than to argue about who is at fault.

Bring insect repellant. Few biting bugs are lethal, but there are fewer experiences more annoying than suffering swarms of biting flies while you are trying to enjoy a relaxing paddle. Some people are highly allergic to bees, wasps, or other insects. If someone in your party is highly allergic, make sure she has appropriate medications (Benadryl, EpiPen, or other prescription medicine) to counteract a sting.

Most snakes are not poisonous, and most poisonous snakes go out of their way to avoid humans. However, smart paddlers will research the area they will be canoeing and be aware of poisonous snakes that live in the region and be able to identify them. Some snakes will hang out in branches of trees and occasionally get knocked into a passing canoe that sweeps underneath the tree. Don't panic. Do not kill a snake. Scoop the snake out with your paddle.

Insects

- Bring insect repellent. Mosquitoes and black flies can test the patience of the most stoic paddler. Few bites are lethal, but some people are highly allergic to bee and wasp stings.

- Bring appropriate medicines for people with known allergies. Benadryl can help with moderate allergic reactions. Highly allergic paddlers should arrange to bring EpiPen or other doctor-recommended antidote.

- You might consider an antibiotic anti-itch cream for your first aid kit to reduce discomfort from bites.

Snakes

- Most snakes are harmless! Most poisonous snakes avoid humans as much as possible.

- Research ahead of time to learn what poisonous snakes inhabit the area you will be visiting. Read up on their behaviors so you can respond appropriately.

- If you do encounter a snake, try to avoid it. Snakes just want to be left alone.

- If a snake does happen to drop into your canoe from a tree, just scoop it out with a paddle.

SELF-RESCUE: SWAMPED CANOE

Be prepared to manage a swamped or tipped-over canoe

There are numerous methods of dealing with a swamped or capsized canoe. The method you select will be influenced by several factors. *Where are you?* Are you on a slow-moving river, a roaring creek, a glassy pond, a large, choppy lake? *Who is there?* Are you alone? Do you have a paddling partner? Are there other canoes nearby? *What rescue techniques are you trained in?*

Self-rescue is dealing with a capsized or swamped ca-

noe solo or with your partner if you are in a tandem canoe. *Swamping* is water entering a canoe. A canoe may be totally or partially swamped by waves washing over the side. A *capsize* is when a canoe turns over, often dumping paddlers and gear into the water.

Depending on the amount of water, a partially swamped boat can be bailed out. Bailers can be improvised from cups or tin cans, but the most useful is made by cutting the bot-

Canoe to Shore

- The first task after swamping your canoe is to empty out the water.

- Sometimes you can bail out the water, but in a full swamping you will usually need to get the canoe to shore in order to drain the water.

- Grab the canoe by the gunwale and swim or walk it to shore. Avoid getting tangled in the painters if they are dragging in the water.

- Make sure to grab your paddle and any other gear and stow in the canoe.

Drain the Canoe

- Find a suitable spot on shore to drain the canoe. Turn the canoe from the side or tilt from the end to allow water to escape.

- If the shore is not clear enough to get the whole canoe up onto it, turn the canoe upside down and rest the bow or stern deck plate on a log, rock, or patch of shore.

- Then raise the other end, allow water to drain, then turn the canoe upright.

KNACK CANOEING FOR EVERYONE

tom of an old plastic bleach bottle, leaving the cap on, and tying a tether cord through the handle. If you have shipped more water than you can bail, you will have to get the canoe to shore or to water shallow enough to stand in while draining the boat. You can swim to shore and pull the canoe behind you, or you can paddle the swamped canoe to shore.

Once to shore or shallow water, turn the canoe upside down to drain the water. Lift one end of the canoe to break the air seal. Solo paddlers can position one end on the shore and lift the other end to drain the water. Tandem paddlers can lift

the canoe above the water to drain it, turn the canoe right side up, and then set it back down. Keep track of paddles and other gear while draining your boat; they can float away.

Enter a Swamped Canoe

- An alternative way to get your swamped canoe to shore is to paddle it instead of dragging it.

- Getting into a swamped canoe and staying in can be a little tricky. A swamped canoe tends to spin, and sudden movements will start the canoe rotating.

- With the canoe upright, push the nearest gunwale low enough so that you can roll into the canoe.

- Then slowly shift your weight so that the canoe rights itself and remains level.

Hand Paddle a Swamped Canoe

- After entering the swamped canoe, you can use a paddle or your hands to move the boat to shore.

- Sit or kneel in the middle of the canoe. Sitting in the seat will raise the center of gravity too high.

- You might find hand paddling more effective than using a paddle. It is easier to keep the canoe balanced when you are paddling on both sides at once.

- Paddling a swamped canoe can be very slow going, but it's good experience to have.

SELF-RESCUE: REENTRY
How to reenter a canoe from the water without swamping

Perhaps you lose your balance and fall out of the canoe, or maybe it's a hot day, and you jumped overboard to cool off. How can you get back in without dragging the canoe all the way to shore or filling it with water?

Place yourself at the center point on the side of the canoe. Reach over the gunwale and place both hands on the bottom of the canoe (or grab the center thwart with one hand if necessary). Push with your hands and kick your legs un-

til your hips are over the gunwale. Roll onto your back and then swing your legs into the canoe. This is not a particularly graceful move, but it is not as difficult as it looks (after a little practice). Be careful about hitting your head on the thwart, gunwale, or hull of the canoe.

Practicing this exercise will teach you a lot about the stability of your craft. How far can it lean before tipping over? How does changing hand placement affect the response of the

Solo Reentry: Step 1

- If you fall out of your canoe or jump out to swim, you will want to get back in while bringing minimal amounts of water with you.

- The solo reentry is not a graceful maneuver. But the goal is to get back into the boat.

- This is one of the few moves that requires much physical force, but it is easier than it looks.

- Position yourself at the middle of the canoe.

Solo Reentry: Step 2

- Reach over the gunwale and place both hands on the bottom of the canoe.

- You will need to pull the gunwale down to make it low enough to get your body over.

- Place your hands as far across the bottom of the canoe as you can to keep the gunwale from tipping too far.

canoe to your weight as you lean over the gunwale?

You may never need the solo reentry, but doing it will build your confidence and self-reliance and enhance your understanding of your craft.

Solo rentry is all about weight placement. You will have to lower the gunwale far enough to get over it, but not so far that the canoe swamps.

Solo Reentry: Step 3

- Kick your feet and push with your hands until your hips are over the edge of the gunwale.

- Throw your head and torso as far into the middle of the canoe as you can.

- Some people find that they need to grab the center thwart to have enough leverage to get over the gunwale.

- As you tumble yourself into the canoe, be alert not to whack your head on the thwart.

Solo Reentry: Step 4

- Now roll onto your back and swing your legs into the canoe.

- You're in!

- Look to see how much water you brought in with you. With a little practice, the amount of water will be surprisingly small.

- Being able to reenter a canoe on your own is a great confidence builder. It increases self-reliance and enhances your general comfort level whenever you are on the water.

CAPISTRANO FLIP

Empty your canoe in deep water without pulling it to shore

The Capistrano flip is a self-rescue technique for emptying a swamped canoe in deep water. It is performed by two or more people wearing PFDs. The swamped canoe is turned upside down. The paddlers place themselves under the canoe. After lifting a gunwale to break the air seal, kick three times and quickly push the canoe up and over. This maneuver requires coordination and strength, but even if not completely successful it can remove enough water to permit bailing.

The paddlers can then reenter the canoe. See pages 114–15. The Capistrano flip works best with canoes that have good buoyancy. If the Capistrano flip is not effective with your boat, be prepared to utilize other methods of self-rescue. These may include paddling or swimming the swamped canoe to shore where it can be drained. If another canoe is nearby, its occupants can help with a canoe-over-canoe rescue (pages 116–17).

Capistrano Flip: Step 1

- The Capistrano flip can be performed by two paddlers in deep water to clear most of the water from the canoe.

- Begin by turning the canoe upside down. The two (or more) paddlers position themselves underneath in the air pocket.

- Each paddler grasps a gunwale with each hand. Decide which direction you are going to lift and toss the canoe.

Capistrano Flip: Step 2

- Begin by breaking the air seal by lifting one gunwale.

- Paddlers then kick three times and push the canoe up into the air.

- When the canoe is as high as you can get it, flip up one side to turn the canoe over.

- This will leave the canoe, floating right side up, nearly empty of water, with you holding onto the gunwale.

If you swamp or capsize in deep water and are unable to perform a self-rescue, it is usually best to stay with your canoe. It will provide floatation, and it is easier to spot by rescuers. If you are with another paddler, huddle together to conserve heat. A solo paddler should assume the HELP (Heat Escape Lessening Posture) position. Fold your arms against your chest, cross your legs, and keep still until assistance arrives. If you will be paddling in deep, cold water, dress accordingly. Wear layers of insulating clothes, a wetsuit or dry suit, and a cold weather hat that will stay on your head.

Capistrano Flip: Step 3

Capistrano Flip: Step 4

- This maneuver requires strength, coordination, and agility.

- However, even a poorly executed Capistrano flip can remove significant amounts of water from a swamped canoe.

- A partially emptied canoe is easier to paddle and move than a full one.

- If you are unable to pull off a Capistrano flip, be prepared to swim your canoe to shore. If another canoe is nearby you can request a canoe-over-canoe rescue (pages 116–17).

- A properly fitted PFD makes this move much easier.

- Canoes with lots of built-in floatation are easier to flip in this manner.

- Supplementary floatation bags can be purchased. Large inner tubes or blocks of Styrofoam can be rigged to fit in the canoe and contribute buoyancy. Additional floatation also displaces water that could fill the boat.

- With a fully loaded canoe that swamps, you may have no option except to swim it to shore to empty the water.

RESCUES

TANDEM REENTRY
How to get back into the canoe without swamping

A tandem reentry is very similar to a solo re-entry with the addition of a second person to support and stabilize the canoe. After performing a successful Capistrano flip or when reentering after a cooling swim, one paddler pulls down on the gunwale while the other paddler enters from the opposite side. The entering paddler places her hands on the floor of the canoe and then pushes and kicks until her hips are over the gunwale. The supporting paddler should allow the

gunwale to lower enough to make it easier for the entering paddler to get across the gunwale. The entering paddler then rolls onto her back and swings her legs into the boat. The first paddler then moves to either the bow or the stern and, kneeling, provides counterweight while the second paddler enters the boat. The first paddler may need to lean forcefully away as the entering paddler pushes down on the canoe to lift herself in. The first paddler will then need to skillfully read-

First Paddler Enters

First Paddler In

- The second paddler waits in the water and supports the canoe by pulling down on the gunwale opposite the first paddler.

- The first paddler to reenter the canoe grabs on to the gunwale or reaches over the gunwale to place hands on the bottom of the canoe.

- The first paddler then kicks her feet and pushes with her hands to raise her torso and hips into the canoe.

- The first paddler rolls into the canoe on her back while the second paddler adjusts the amount of counterpressure on the gunwale.

- The first paddler swings her legs into the canoe and then moves to her place in the bow or stern.

- The first paddler's job now is to counterbalance the canoe while the second paddler gets in.

- The first paddler kneels in the bow or stern and leans heavily away from the side that the second paddler enters on.

- Lean forcefully but be ready to ease up and shift weight back to the center.

114

just her weight as the second paddler enters. You don't want to reswamp the boat at this point!

This method of entry is also used as part of a canoe-over-canoe rescue. The rescuers provide stabilizing support from their canoe that is opposite the entering paddler.

Second Paddler Enters

- As the first paddler leans away, the second pushes on the inside bottom of the canoe, kicks with his feet.

- When high enough, the second paddler lifts his torso and hips over the gunwale and then rolls onto his back and swings his legs into the canoe.

- The first paddler shifts her weight to accommodate the second paddler.

- These steps flow together into a continuous maneuver. Heaving oneself into a canoe is seldom graceful but is effective after a couple of practice tries.

Getting under Way (Again)

- After both paddlers are back in the boat, move carefully to get situated and ready to go.

- Don't be in too much of a rush, or else you might end up back in the water.

- Gather your paddles and be sure you have everything.

- Even very experienced paddlers sometimes dump unexpectedly. After you are back in the canoe think about what happened and how to avoid *that* in the future, laugh at yourself, and start paddling.

RESCUES

CANOE-OVER-CANOE RESCUE
How one canoe can assist a capsized canoe

If a second canoe is in the vicinity, this is the classic technique for rescuing a capsized or swamped canoe. The rescuing canoe approaches the victims and assesses the situation. Rescuers gather paddles and other gear while reassuring the victims. Have one victim grab onto the bow or stern of the rescuing canoe. This provides stability and gives the victim a task. The swamped canoe is then positioned upside down and perpendicular to the rescuing canoe. The second victim

can be directed to the far end of their boat. The second victim pushes down on his end of the canoe while the rescuers reach underneath the other end, lift the gunwale, and lay the deck plate of the swamped canoe across their own gunwale. The swamped canoe is slid across the rescuing canoe, allowed to drain, turned upright, and then slid back into the water. The rescued canoe is placed parallel and stabilized while the victims reenter their craft.

The Approach

- The rescuing canoe approaches the swamped paddlers.

- Question paddlers to make sure they are conscious and not seriously injured.

- Gather paddles or other floating gear. Position the

rescuing canoe in a "T" position with the swamped canoe.

- If there are two paddlers in the water, have one of them grab the bow or stern of the rescuing boat. Position the other paddler at the end of the swamped canoe.

The Lift

- The bow and stern paddlers of the rescuing canoe kneel on the bottom of their canoe facing each other.

- One of the rescuers reaches out to grab the swamped canoe under the deck plate.

- The other rescuer leans away to counterbalance the canoe.

- As the rescuer lifts the canoe, have the paddler in the water push down on the end of the canoe to help raise the other end.

This rescue can work flawlessly if the water is not rough and if the victim's canoe is not loaded with gear. In those cases, it may be preferable to tow the swamped canoe to shore, where it can be drained.

Empty the Canoe

- Slide the rescued canoe over the rescuing canoe and let the water drain out.

- After the canoe is drained, turn the canoe so that it is upright. Spin the canoe carefully to maintain the balance of your canoe.

- Then slide the canoe back into the water, being careful not to hit the paddler(s) in the water.

- Turn the empty canoe parallel to the rescuing canoe.

Paddlers Reenter

- Stabilize the rescued canoe while the paddlers reenter the boat one at a time.

- Return paddles and other gear to the rescued paddlers.

- Be sure that the rescued paddlers are okay. Reassess for any injuries. If the weather is cool, be alert for symptoms of hypothermia.

- If everyone is okay, push off and enjoy the rest of your trip.

RESCUES

EXTENSION RESCUES

Rescue a struggling swimmer or paddler without putting yourself at risk

Be prepared to assist a struggling paddler or exhausted swimmer. While on a canoe trip it should be unnecessary to leap into the water like a lifeguard to offer assistance. You should have objects to reach with, ropes to throw, and a canoe available to paddle out to an exhausted or unconscious person. The Boy Scout mnemonic—Reach, Throw, Row,

Go—displays the order in which assistance should be provided. Assess the situation before committing yourself. The primary consideration in any emergency or rescue situation is to not create more victims who need help. Provide help in a way that will not put yourself in the same condition as the victim.

Reach

- In order to assist a struggling swimmer or paddler in the water while minimizing risk to more people, follow this order: reach, throw, row, go.

- If the person is close enough, extend a hand, paddle, or other object; pull her to the dock or canoe.

- Be sure that you are stable and locked in position. A frantic swimmer can easily pull a rescuer off balance.

- Talk to the victim to reassure her and give her directions on how to help you.

Get to Shore

- After pulling the victim to the canoe, have her hang on. If she is incapable, have one paddler hold her while the other paddles to shore.

- A panicked swimmer may try to climb right into your canoe! Anticipate this panic and do not let her swamp your boat!

- Remember rule number one for rescuers: Do not create more victims.

- Respond quickly but don't make more mistakes by rushing or panicking yourself.

For water rescues, reach to the person with your hand, a paddle, or other object. Make sure that you are planted and can't be pulled in. If the person is too far to reach, then use a throw rope or bag to pull her in. You might also toss her a seat cushion or PFD. If the person is beyond the reach of a rope, is panicking, or is unresponsive, paddle out to retrieve her. Be extremely aware that a person who thinks she is drowning will grab onto you or your canoe wildly and possibly cause a capsize. Be prepared to counterbalance and to keep the victim from swamping your boat.

After rescue, assess victims for injuries, signs of hypothermia, or symptoms of shock. Victims may be in denial, in withdrawal, or combative. Calm and assure victims. Arrange for medical attention if necessary.

Capsizes and other incidents can happen to anyone. Reduce the chance of needing rescue by planning ahead, being prepared, staying aware of your surroundings, and not taking unnecessary risks.

Throw: Step 1

- Keep a throw bag or coiled throw rope near at hand so that you can assist troubled swimmers who are too far to reach by extension.

- Try to throw the rope so it lands behind the swimmers. Avoid hitting them in the face.

- When reeling in a swimmer, pull the rope in hand over hand. If on shore, stand with one leg behind to provide support.

- When in a canoe have a stern paddler back paddle to hold the canoe in place.

Throw: Step 2

- Never tie yourself to a throw rope or wrap the rope around yourself!

- You can tie knots in the ends of the rope to make it easier to hold on to but do not use loops.

- If you miss your target on the first try, carefully recoil the rope as you pull it in. A tangled rescue rope will only waste time.

- Practice tossing a throw rope occasionally. This will keep you confident and will ensure that the coiled rope is ready for action.

PONDS & SMALL LAKES
Flatwater canoeing provides plenty of options for paddling enjoyment

A large pond or a small lake is an ideal place to learn canoeing basics. On a smaller body of water, it is easier to avoid big waves and motorized boats. Often the water will be warmer than in a really large lake. This is a good place to learn your paddling strokes and experiment with capsizing and rescues.

Swimming and fishing can be very pleasant activities, even if the shoreline is visible all the way around. Ponds also provide a laboratory for hands-on nature study of plants, insects, fish, mammals, birds, reptiles, and amphibians and how they interact in and around the water.

Even though a pond seems like a controlled environment,

At the Lake

- A canoe is a great source of entertainment and transportation while spending time at a cottage or summer house.

- An early morning paddle to go fishing while the mist is still rising is always a special experience.

- Push off from shore on a clear night to paddle around under a full moon or to get an unobstructed view of the stars and meteor showers.

- You can paddle across the lake or down the shore to visit neighbors rather than driving the car.

Swim!

- A canoe makes a great place to swim from. The canoe can be a floating "home base" on a lake.

- Take all standard precautions while swimming: An adult should supervise. Have PFDs in the boat, if not wearing them while swimming.

- Carefully assess the underwater conditions before anyone jumps in. Check for rocks and other objects under the surface.

- Many swimming spots are shallow, so wear shoes to protect feet from broken glass and other hazards.

follow the same standard safety precautions you would on a big lake. Always wear your PFD. Maintain constant supervision of children. It takes only a few inches of water and a minute or two to drown. Keep an eye on the weather. A thunderstorm can blow in quickly, and lightning can strike anywhere. Biting insects might be more prevalent than on a larger body of water. Don't forget the sunscreen. Sunburn is always uncomfortable. Discourage going barefoot unless you have carefully inspected the underwater areas. Broken glass, torn soda cans, rebar, fish hooks, sharp sticks, and rocks can be anywhere.

Even though a float on the local pond is not far away, plan ahead. Have a basic first aid kit with you. Bring plenty of water and make sure everyone stays hydrated. Lunch or snacks will keep people energized.

Bring binoculars and nature guides. Ponds and small lakes are a great place to watch birds and turtles.

Family Outing

- A small lake on a calm day is a perfect place for a family canoe with children of any age.

- A calm lake is great for practicing paddling basics and learning how to work together as a team to propel the canoe across the water.

- Children naturally love water, and family canoeing is a great way to instill lifelong love and respect for our lakes and rivers.

- Keep an eye out for jumping fish, basking turtles, and birds of all sorts.

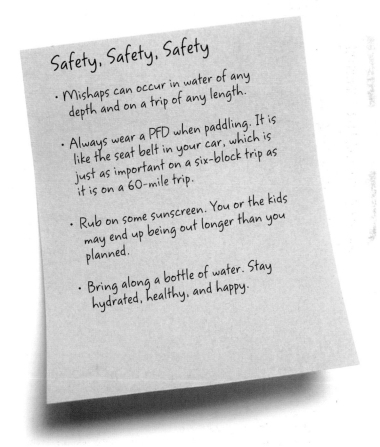

Safety, Safety, Safety

- Mishaps can occur in water of any depth and on a trip of any length.

- Always wear a PFD when paddling. It is like the seat belt in your car, which is just as important on a six-block trip as it is on a 60-mile trip.

- Rub on some sunscreen. You or the kids may end up being out longer than you planned.

- Bring along a bottle of water. Stay hydrated, healthy, and happy.

FISHING BY CANOE

Fishing and canoeing are a natural combination of great outdoor activities

The key to an enjoyable canoe fishing trip is to keep equipment to a minimum. You already have plenty to carry. Bring a rod, reel, a small selection of lures, a stringer, and maybe a net. When selecting a rod and reel, look for something lightweight and compact but not too flimsy. Rods that break down into three or four sections are easiest to pack. If you

already have a two-piece rod, you might consider a plastic or aluminum tube to prevent breakage. A piece of PVC pipe can be adapted to this purpose. Small bungee cords work well for securing the rod to the thwarts while portaging.

Use an anchor to keep your canoe in place while still fishing. A bag made from nylon mesh filled with 10 to 12 pounds

Fish by Canoe

- A canoe is a fabulous way to fish. It is lightweight, manageable by one person, quiet, and allows access to waterways that many motor boats can't navigate.

- Solo canoeing and fishing go well together: solitude, space, and less tangling of lines.

- Keep equipment to a minimum. Be selective about the gear you bring, and you'll spend more time fishing and less time carrying stuff and fooling with tackle.

- Establish a system for keeping gear secure in case you capsize.

Fishing Canoe

- Any canoe can be fished from. But there are models designed for the serious canoe fisher.

- Because fishing requires some moving around in the boat and attention focused on landing the fish when you hook it, stability is important.

- Noise detracts from a fishing trip and scares away the fish. Pick a boat that you can paddle quietly and that absorbs the noise from impact with objects.

- Pole brackets and other accessories on the market can be added to the canoe you already have.

of rocks works well. Leave the rocks behind when you head home or hit the portage trail. Bring the bag with you and use local rocks. Twenty feet of $^3/_8$-inch cord will serve as an anchor line, or tie the anchor to the end of the painter.

You can accessorize your canoe with rod holders, seat backs, and drink holders. If you are buying a canoe primarily for fishing, consider a sporting model designed for fishing or hunting. They are stable, roomy, and quiet.

Selection of lures is guided by personal preference and the targeted fish. A variety of spinners and small spoons is usually adequate. For live bait suggestions, inquire locally. Follow all regulations! All states and provinces require a fishing license. These can be obtained at bait shops, sporting goods stores, resorts, and many gas stations.

Tandem Fishing

- Tangle-free tandem fishing requires communication and an awareness of each other's fishing styles.

- Consider how you cast. You don't want to hook your partner's head or clothing. And you don't want your partner to hook you.

- Tandem paddlers will usually fish on opposite sides to minimize tangling lines.

- Being in a canoe allows you to maneuver easily to retrieve snagged lures. Discuss this with your partner before paddling to rescue your lure.

Fishing Gear Storage

- Buy or devise a soft-sided "tackle box" that hangs from the canoe thwart or seat.

- This keeps lures and pliers handy but secure from loss during capsize.

- Get into the habit of zipping the bag closed or snapping shut the buckle when you don't need access to it.

- Fishing rods are easily broken. An aluminum rod case or a piece of PVC tubing can be tied to the thwarts for storing rods during portages.

HUNTING & NATURE WATCHING

A canoe lends itself to many aspects of hunting, nature photography, and observation

The processes of nature watching and hunting share many similarities up to the point of pulling the trigger: studying the lives and histories of animals, stalking quietly, observing carefully and patiently. Canoes with their shallow draft greatly increase access to obscure weed-choked reaches of lakes and wetlands.

Because these activities utilize the canoe as a vehicle for other interests, initial stability is a main consideration. Select a canoe whose tippiness won't distract from zeroing in on a heron through binoculars or sighting a mallard.

Many hunters use a canoe as a gear transport more than as a shooting platform. However, capsize is always a possibility.

Freedom of Movement

- A canoe allows for good positioning while hunting waterfowl. The shallow draft permits access to wetland backwaters and sloughs.

- When selecting a canoe for hunting, your need for stability is the first priority. A tippy canoe is harder to hunt from and is more likely to capsize.

- Paddling speed is of less concern than maneuverability while hunting.

- If hunting alone, consider the weight of the boat. How heavy of a craft can you manage on your own?

Capacity and Comfort

- A tandem canoe can easily carry two hunters and lots of equipment.

- Be sure to coordinate who is shooting and in what direction. Try to shoot so that the recoil is in line with the keel.

- A spacious canoe, with seat cushions and seat backs, can be more comfortable than a blind.

- Select a PFD that you can shoot in. Practice raising your gun while wearing your PFD. Don't let the stock catch on the padding. Remember a PFD for your dog!

Keep track of your gear. Invest in a floating gun case and use a shotgun leash while shooting. In the event of capsize, you won't lose your gun in the muck below you. In order to still sit in the stern seat, solo hunters should employ ballast in the bow of the canoe. A cooler full of sand is about the right weight. If you buy a camouflage canoe or go to the trouble to paint it yourself, don't neglect the paddles. When shooting from the canoe, fire so that the recoil is in line with the long axis of the boat. This will minimize the risk of capsize or swamping related to gun recoil.

Remember that it is the hunter's responsibility to obtain all required permits and licenses and to follow regulations regarding bag limits.

Photographers will want to follow similar precautions as hunters in regard to their equipment. Keep camera gear you are not using in watertight dry bags or boxes. Keep the camera strap around your neck. A gentle bump into a log can be enough to send your SLR flying. Binoculars and water also tend not to mix well. Keep them near at hand in dry bag that is strapped to your seat or the closest thwart.

Nature Observation

- Because your attention will be on the birds and other animals you want to watch, select a canoe that is stable.

- Pick a canoe that is quiet. Avoid aluminum if possible.

- After considering stability and noise, pick a craft that is easy for you to steer. You will want to be able to access remote, marshy areas.

- Because you may be sitting still for long periods, consider bringing a Crazy Creek chair or installing seat backs.

Viewing and Photographing

- Take great care to secure optics against incurring water damage or getting dropped into the water.

- Keep binoculars on a strap! A gentle but unexpected bump into a log can cause a person to drop what he is holding.

- Have a dry bag or other storage system organized so that you can easily stow binoculars or cameras when not in use.

- Be prepared to observe startled animals. You can easily surprise mammals and birds when paddling silently through the weeds.

BIG LAKES & CANOE SAILING

A large lake provides challenges and opportunities of a greater scale than a small lake or pond

There is something particularly satisfying about floating a long way from shore or paddling the shortest distance to the next portage across a big lake. However, a large lake is susceptible to choppy water and large, wind-driven waves. A large lake can go from glassy smooth to large breakers in a brief time as the weather shifts and the wind increases. On large bodies of water it is imperative to constantly monitor the wind and to watch for any signs of changes in the weather. You do not want to be a mile from shore as the clouds blacken and thunder begins to rumble.

If you plan to spend time on large water, you will want to investigate canoe covers. These fasten to the gunwales and

Big Water

- Extreme caution is the most important consideration when canoeing on one of the Great Lakes or other very large body of water.

- The water can change from glassy smooth to crashing waves in a brief time.

- Constantly assess wind speed, wind direction, temperature, and cloud conditions. A shift in any of these can precede a change in wave conditions.

- Know where you will go if the conditions worsen and be sure to get off the water while it is safe.

Spray Cover

- An open canoe is easily swamped in big waves.

- A lot of water can be kept out of your boat by using a spray cover. Spray covers are of various designs but stretch from gunwale to gunwale with openings for the paddlers.

- A spray cover will also keep out rain and reduce wind resistance.

- A spray cover can be dangerous. Be absolutely sure that the spray cover will not trap or entangle paddlers in the boat.

thwarts to cover the canoe except for holes for the paddlers. Canoe covers can keep out rain and waves. A cover can be dangerous in a capsize if it entangles the paddler.

When paddling in waves, cut through or across the waves. Do not get caught parallel in the troughs of waves. It is extremely easy to swamp.

If you are out on a big lake with the wind at your back, it can be very exciting to harness that wind power with a sail. Most canoe sailing is an improvised affair. Hold up a tarp or tent fly with your arms so that it catches the wind. You can also tie the cloth to canoe paddles or poles. Be cautious about tying poles or a mast to the canoe; a side gust of wind might be enough to capsize the boat. Never tie sail lines to a person or wrap them around any body parts. These could easily tangle and lead to drowning.

Another option is a sail kite. This can provide significant pull in even a mild breeze.

Improvised Canoe Sailing

- If traveling with the wind, use its power to your advantage.

- Improvise a sail by wrapping a tarp or rain fly around a couple of paddles or other uprights.

- The bow paddler holds the uprights apart, catching the wind, while the stern paddler steers.

- If you tie a "mast" in place, be alert for sudden gusts or changes in wind direction. Let go of the sail to prevent the wind from blowing the canoe over onto its side.

Planned Canoe Sailing

- Maximize your wind power with a sailing rig conversion kit.

- Canoe conversions can be simple or elaborate. Rigs range from a mast, bracket, and sail to a rigging deck, leeboard, rudders, additional floatation, and stabilizer outriggers.

- Any additional gear adds weight, takes up space, and must be carried at some point. And extensive canoe sailing requires experience and practice.

- Be sure that any sailing gear you bring fits with your abilities and the goals for your trip.

RIVERS & CURRENTS
A river is moving water pulled downhill by gravity

Learning how to paddle and control a canoe on flatwater is excellent preparation for learning to maneuver on moving water. When you are canoeing on a lake, the wind can impact your paddling, but most of the canoe's movement comes from your paddle pushing and pulling against the water. On a river, the water itself is moving. The paddler needs to know how to interpret and then respond to moving water to assure a safe and successful canoeing experience.

The movement of water is known as *current*. The speed of current is impacted by three components: the amount of water, the width of the river, and the gradient (steepness) of the river. The more water, the narrower the channel, and the steeper the riverbed, the faster the water will flow.

The *primary* current is the general direction that the river is flowing. The primary current, however, moves at different speeds, depending on what level in the river it is at. This is

Big River

- A river is a stream. The term *stream* denotes "the flow of water within any natural channel." So a small creek and a large river are both streams.

- Streams that can be canoed span a large spectrum from narrow, rocky seasonal creeks to wide, massive rivers like the Ohio, Missouri, and Mississippi.

- Each kind of river has its own pleasures, distinct character, and types of hazards.

- Large rivers can carry large boats and ships and sometimes have dams and locks.

Wild River

- Smaller, more remote streams are often sought out by paddlers looking to "get away from it all." Attractions include fewer people, greater immersion in nature, and faster water.

- Although there aren't cargo ships to dodge, there are hazards to take into account. Rapids and whitewater require special skills and experience to paddle safely.

- Watch for rocks, ledges, and other obstacles.

- There are small, quiet, flatwater rivers, and there are small, raging, turbulent waterways.

known as *laminar* flow. The slowest-moving water is next to the bottom due to friction with the riverbed. The fastest-moving water is just below the surface. The surface water is slowed slightly by friction with the air. The speed of the current also varies from side to side. This is the *linear* flow. Water nearest the bank is slower due to friction than water in the unobstructed center of the channel.

The primary current is affected by obstacles, including bends in the river. The water on the outer part of the bend flows faster than water on the inner part of the bend. This is very important to remember because the outer part of a bend is where there are most likely downed trees or other objects in the river.

The effect of objects (rocks) in the middle of the current is discussed in the section "Reading a River."

Moving Water

- How the current behaves depends on where it is in the river and the obstacles it encounters.

- Along a straight section of river, the water flows fastest in the middle and slowest along the sides.

- Rivers flow where they have cut a channel from the rock and earth. Most rivers rarely flow in a straight line for long.

- As water flows around a bend, the speed of the current is different at different places in the river.

Outside Bend Moves Faster

faster slower

- The current flows more quickly and more powerfully on the outside bend than the inside bend.

- Because current is faster and stronger on the outside bend, that is where your canoe will naturally be pulled.

- On slow, shallow rivers, stay on the outside bend to avoid getting grounded.

- On faster rivers, be very cautious of the outside bend. The faster outer current can undercut the bank and bring trees and boulders down right into the natural path of the faster current.

READING A RIVER

Learn to avoid scrapes and collisions by knowing what certain water features mean

Reading a river is viewing water movements and knowing how they may impact your canoe. As you know, current is moving water. When moving water hits obstacles, it behaves in certain ways. The behavior of the water can provide clues about the location and depth of rocks and how your canoe will respond to the current around those rocks.

Imagine a smooth stretch of river that has an even, sandy bottom on a windless day. Even though the water is moving, the surface will be smooth and flat. Now imagine a large boulder has been placed in the river just underneath the surface. The water will no longer be smooth and glasslike. Ripples will begin to bubble out *downstream* of the boulder.

Obstacles

- Rocks are the most common obstacle you will encounter in rivers. River rocks vary from the size of a pea to that of a semitrailer.

- It is best to avoid colliding with, scraping past, or dragging over rocks of any size.

- Rocks at, or just under, the water's surface can often be observed by the behavior of the water at that point.

- An underwater rock creates a V in the water with the closed end of the V pointing upstream.

Downstream Vs

- Two parallel rocks will create a pattern of three Vs in the water. Each rock will produce an upstream V.

- Between the two rocks there will appear a smooth-looking V pointing downstream.

- This smooth downstream V is where you want to aim your canoe for a smooth passage, *if there is not a third rock waiting at the end of the V.*

- A shallow section of river with lots of exposed rocks is known as a *rock garden*.

From upstream the water will form a V shape, with the rock near the point of the V. A V pointing at you indicates an object you should always avoid!

Two rocks parallel in the current will create two upstream Vs and a chute between them. This chute will look like a smooth V pointing *downstream*. This chute is often an excellent path between two obstacles. But always beware of additional rocks that might be hidden in the downstream turbulence.

Depending on the volume and speed of the current and the size and depth of the rock, the surface water will create different patterns. An obstacle near or above the surface will create a V. Water passing over a rock below the surface can create a small wave *downstream* of the rock. This rounded wave is called a *pillow*. For paddlers, "pillows" are filled with rocks.

Water flowing over a ledge or large rock can create a large trough just past the object called a *hole*. The wave that follows the hole is called a *standing wave, haystack,* or *roller*.

Eddies

eddy

- Eddies are the relatively calm waters behind a large rock or other obstacle.

- As water rushes past the rock, some water flows back upstream to fill in the space left behind the object.

- The upstream current, below the obstacle, provides a resting spot for your canoe while descending rapids or paddling upriver.

- The border between the stronger downstream current and the upstream current is called the *eddy line*.

Dams, Ledges, and Falls

- Low-head dams, large rock ledges, and waterfalls present a significant threat to the canoeist.

- These features can be recognized by the *horizon line* created by the lip of the dam or ledge. A flat-flowing river moves into the distance without interruption.

- If you see a "line" stretching across the stream, immediately pull to the bank to scout out the drop.

- Water dropping over an edge often creates a *hole* or *hydraulic*, a recirculating current that traps people and objects.

HAZARDS OF MOVING WATER

Moving water is extremely powerful and must be treated with respect

Much of the danger of moving water is due to the fact that it is moving. Moving water will take with it anything that is not secured. Moving water will take dirt with it, eroding banks and allowing trees to fall into the water, creating strainers (see page 100). There is danger when moving water encounters objects that are not moving: large rocks, bridge abutments, tree trunks, and ledges. Part of the danger is your canoe slamming into an unmoving object. The second danger of unmoving objects is the way they affect the current of the water. Water flowing over ledges, rocks, and dams creates holes.

Water flowing around rocks creates eddies. An *eddy* is

Strainers

- Strainers are objects in the water that pull the water underneath them.

- Strainers are usually downed trees or logs, but large rocks can also suck the current underneath.

- Paddlers in the water and even canoes can get pulled under strainers. People can get snagged underneath a strainer and drown.

- *Never* try to swim under a log or downed tree! If you see a strainer, paddle or swim away from it at full force.

Flood Waters

- Flood waters are extremely dangerous for paddling. High water levels create very strong and unpredictable currents.

- High water can also bring lots of debris of all sorts with it. Running into, or getting hit by, a log can easily lead to a capsize.

- Flood waters are also often very polluted with eroded soil, animal waste, and agricultural runoff—not the kind of water to risk a capsize in.

- Flood waters are especially dangerous, but rivers can be hazardous at any water level.

formed when the current rushes past an obstacle so fast that some of the water is pulled back upstream to fill in the space behind the obstacle. Sometimes you can observe calmly floating sticks or other debris caught in an eddy. Depending on the size and speed of the current, eddies can be of little consequence to the paddler, a major threat, or a great help (see "Braces & Eddy Turns," pages 142–43). In a very powerful current, the danger of any eddy lies along the *eddy line,* the border between the main downstream current and the calmer upstream movement behind the object.

Water rounding a bend in the river moves faster on the outside of the bend. Your canoe will tend to stay in the faster current. However, the outside bend is a common location of strainers. Strainers can be deadly and must be avoided! Paddle or swim away from a strainer at full speed.

Moving water is dangerous because of *inertia*. Canoes tend to respond slowly in moving water, so you must begin steering earlier and using more force than if you were on still water.

Capsize Position

- If you capsize in rapids, turn on your back with your feet pointing downstream.

- Keep your head upstream to protect it from rocks. Use your feet and hands (or paddle if you held on to it) to ward off rocks.

- Swim toward the bank at

an upstream angle. This will move you through the current like a ferry (see page 138).

- Don't try to stand in fast-moving water; your foot can get trapped between rocks, and the current can hold you under.

Moving Water Is Powerful

- Moving water can really pack a punch! Modern canoes are strong and durable but can be crushed or broken in half by the river.

- A swamped canoe that gets pinned underneath rocks or a log with the current pouring into it can be nearly impossible to pull loose.

- Carefully select paddling routes with water conditions that are within your skill and experience zone.

- If you are harboring any concerns about safety, pick a different spot or different day to paddle.

INTERNATIONAL SCALE OF RAPIDS

Rapids are classified on the following scale to rate their intensity and difficulty

Rapids are defined as a "river section with steep, fast flow around obstructions." This bare-bones definition ignores the heart-pounding excitement that the paddler begins to feel upon observing even moderate "flow around obstructions." Rapids should always be approached cautiously. The amount of water on a given day affects how tame or threatening the drop can be. Also, rivers change, and rocks move. Some rapids are so difficult that they must be portaged around. Some are so calm that you hardly think twice about zipping through them. Some are in the middle. Should we run them? Should we portage? The following International River Rating Scale provides a somewhat objective way of describing rapids.

Class I Rapids

- Easy. Fairly smooth water with some waves, obstructions but easily negotiated.

- Class I rapids are suitable for paddlers with some moving-water experience. The route is easily recognizable.

- There may be human-made obstruction like bridges or pier pilings.

- Class I rapids are usually easily handled. But note that moderate to high water levels from storms, spring thaw, or dam releases can substantially increase the difficulty rating of any rapids.

Class II Rapids

- Moderate. Medium-quick water with wide, clear channels that are evident without scouting.

- Maneuvering may be required, but rocks, medium-sized waves are easily missed by trained paddlers.

- River speeds may exceed vigorous back-paddling speed. Watch for occasional ledges and inconveniently placed rocks.

- Err on the side of caution. If unsure of approach, pull over and scout rapids. If you or your partner is uncomfortable running the rapids, then portage.

Class I: Easy. Smooth water. Waves are small; and the route is easily recognizable. There may be human-made difficulties like piers. River speed is less than hard back-paddling speed.

Class II: Moderate. Medium to quick water with frequent rapids. Waves up to 3 feet clear passages. Maneuvering required. River speed may exceed hard back-paddling speed.

Class III: Difficult. High, irregular waves with clear passages that require complex maneuvering. Advance scouting required. This is the limit of an open canoe.

Class IV: Very difficult. Intense, powerful, and turbulent. These are long and powerful rapids with boiling eddies. Powerful and precise maneuvering required. Cannot be run in canoes without decking or floatation bags.

Class V: Extremely difficult. Long, violent rapids that follow each other without interruption. River is filled with obstructions, gig drops, holes, and boiling eddies. Should be attempted only by expert paddlers in whitewater canoes.

Class VI: Extraordinarily difficult, limit of navigability. Paddlers face a constant threat of death. Navigable by only the very best canoeists under carefully controlled conditions.

Class III Rapids

- These are difficult rapids with lots of large, irregular waves. Holes and drops of 3 feet or more require complex maneuvering.

- Scout Class III rapids before running because routes can be difficult to determine.

- Because it can be easy to swamp due to large waves, Class III is the limit for open canoes. Be prepared to deal with wet paddlers.

- Consider having a canoe cover and extra floatation for running Class III rapids.

Class IV Rapids

- These are very difficult rapids. Class IV rapids are intense, powerful, turbulent, unpredictable, and dangerous.

- These rapids often include large, unavoidable holes and very big waves. These conditions require powerful and precise maneuvering.

- Class IV rapids are suitable only for highly skilled paddlers with extensive whitewater experience. Attempted only by kayaks or decked whitewater canoes with extensive floatation.

- Risk of injury is significant. Water conditions make rescues difficult.

RAPIDS, PARALLEL SIDESLIP

Quickly moving water requires caution and the ability to react quickly

Most beginning paddlers will want to stick to Class I rapids, and intermediate paddlers won't go wrong staying with Class II rapids. Class II rapids are about the roughest you should try running with a loaded wilderness canoe.

It is important to remember that the ratings given to rapids in guidebooks and on maps correspond to the river's normal flow. Changes in water level affect the ratings. During the spring thaw or after major storms the increased volume of water might make what is usually considered Class I rapids comparable with Class III. During a long, dry spell, Class IV rapids might be slowed to a trickle.

Whatever the ratings might be, do not try running rapids

Class V Rapids

- These are extremely difficult, long, obstructed, violent, and very dangerous rapids.

- Features include big drops, large holes, constricted routes, undercut shorelines, and rocks. Boats may be easily pinned.

- Swims are dangerous, and rescues are difficult, even for experts.

- Proper equipment, extensive whitewater experience, and solid rescue skills are essential for survival.

Class VI Rapids

- These are extraordinarily difficult, extremely powerful, and difficult rapids. Should be attempted by only the most highly skilled and experienced paddlers.

- Injury or death is a strong possibility.

- Class VI rapids are considered runnable but only by the best of paddlers under the best of conditions.

- *No* rapids should be taken for granted. Don't run rapids that you don't feel confident you can handle. It is better to portage than get injured or worse.

that make you overly anxious. If you feel like you can't easily afford to capsize, then you should portage. Comfort with running rapids comes with experience and practice, but rapids remain potentially dangerous for all paddlers. The water is always moving, and conditions are always changing. Your canoe is also moving, and thus the situation is always shifting. Rocks don't move, but it sometimes seems that way! Do not slip into a false sense of security when it comes to moving water and don't take anything for granted.

Parallel Sideslip: Step 1

- This is a maneuver to shift the canoe sideways in slower currents. The parallel sideslip is useful for evading a rock or other obstacle.

- The bow paddler does a draw stroke while the stern paddler does a pry stroke.

- Or the reverse: The bow paddler does a pry while the stern paddler does a draw.

- Which combination you use depends on the desired direction of lateral slip. The draw is done on the side to which you are moving.

Parallel Sideslip: Step 2

- The bow and stern paddlers simultaneously use turning strokes so that the canoe moves across the water while remaining parallel to the current.

- The bow paddler initiates sideslipping when he or she sees a rock straight ahead.

- The bow paddler does a draw, pry, or cross draw, and the stern paddler responds by doing a pry or draw to keep the boat parallel.

- With a little practice, sideslipping will become a nearly automatic response to looming obstacles.

FORWARD & BACK FERRYING
The back ferry will slow the canoe while moving it sideways

A ferry is a maneuver that allows the paddler to cross the current without getting swept downstream. The ferry uses the water's energy deflected off the side of the canoe. This force, balanced against upstream paddling, results in movement of the boat across the current. Ferrying is useful for positioning the canoe in the correct channel at the start of a set of rapids and for avoiding an obstacle just downstream.

The keys to successful ferrying are boat angle and speed.

The slower the current, the greater the angle of the canoe. The faster the current, the smaller the angle created by the canoe. To ferry, point the upstream end of the canoe slightly toward the shore you are headed toward. Holding that angle, paddle upstream into the current. There are upstream (forward) and downstream (back) ferries.

In the forward, or upstream, ferry, the bow of the canoe is pointed upstream, and the paddlers use forward strokes. The

Back Ferry: Part 1

- Back ferrying is angling the boat to the current in such a way so that when you back paddle the force of current will move the canoe sideways.

- The back ferry is very useful for maneuvering sharp bends where there is a strainer or rock.

- The current will want to keep the canoe in the faster outside bend.

- The back ferry will allow you to stay in control and to keep to the inside bend and miss the obstacle.

Back Ferry: Part 2

- Just before the bend, you need to shift the canoe so that it is at about a 30-degree angle to the current.

- Shift the canoe so that the stern is closer to the inside bank and the bow is pointing toward the center of the river.

- This shift is most easily accomplished with a pry done by the stern paddler.

- As soon as the 30-degree angle is established, both paddlers begin back paddling.

bow paddler provides power while the stern paddler maintains the proper angle. The maximum effective angle is about 45 degrees and less if the current is fast. The forward ferry is useful for paddling upstream. It allows the paddlers to shift to the slower current streams and to "eddy hop," moving from the sheltered area of one boulder to the next.

For the back, or downstream, ferry, the bow paddler begins vigorously back paddling. The stern paddler then does a pry or draw to shift the stern of the canoe in the direction that he wants to move laterally. This shift should angle the canoe about 30 degrees. Then the stern paddler joins the bow paddler in back paddling. Back paddling will limit downstream drift, while the current will push on the angled canoe, moving it laterally across the current.

Back Ferry: Part 3

- Back paddling slows the forward movement of the canoe.

- Because the boat is at an angle, the current pushing on the angled side of the boat causes the canoe to move sideways.

- This sideways movement keeps the canoe to the inside of the bend.

- Continue to back paddle until the current pushes you around the inside bend, missing the obstacle. The stern paddler uses a back sweep or other steering stroke as necessary to maintain an effective angle.

Back Ferry: Part 4

- After rounding the bend, both paddlers do draw strokes to straighten out the canoe and align it with the downstream current.

- Ferrying requires a little practice to learn how to find and maintain the proper angle.

- Forward ferrying is easier to perform because you are looking upstream and can judge the angle more easily.

- Back ferrying is more useful when headed downriver. It slows the canoe while moving it sideways.

LANDING WITH A BACK FERRY

A back ferry allows you to land stern first in fast water

When landing a canoe in swift currents, use a back ferry to push the stern (upstream) end of the canoe against the shore first. If you land bow first, the current is more likely to grab the stern end and swing it downstream. To land with a back ferry, the bow paddler does a pry to pop the bow away from the bank. Both paddlers then back paddle forcefully to move the stern toward the bank so that the stern paddler can reach out and grab hold of the shore.

The back ferry is also very useful for staying on the inside bends of fast-moving rivers. You will remember that rivers run fastest on the outside bend. This faster-moving water can undercut the bank, bringing down trees and other obstacles right in the path of the main current. So the back ferry is a smooth way to keep to the inside bend and avoid strainers and boulders that tend to appear in the outside bend. Outside corners also collect logs, sticks, and other debris from

Back Ferry Landing: Step 1

- Landing stern first, while still facing downstream, seems counterintuitive. We are used to just nosing the bow right up onto the bank.

- However, landing bow first in fast water can allow the current to grab the stern and swing it rapidly out into the channel.

- This is particularly bad if the canoe hits a rock and swamps or gets pinned.

- Before landing, shift the canoe angle so that the stern is closer to the shore.

Back Ferry Landing: Step 2

- The stern can be angled toward shore by the bow paddler doing a pry to push the bow away from the bank.

- Both paddlers then back paddle to move the canoe near the shore.

- The angle of the canoe, with the bow pointing out, allows the current to help move the boat sideways to the shore.

upriver. As you approach a curve, push the stern of the canoe to the inside of the bend and back paddle. As you round the curve, a moderate draw or pry will realign your canoe so that it is pointing downstream.

In theory, ferries are simple. You align your canoe at a slight angle to the current and then propel the boat against the current. In reality, it takes a lot of practice to keep your canoe under complete control while ferrying. Practice your first ferries on slow-moving current. Proper angle is key. With too wide an angle to the current, you get swept downstream.

With too narrow an angle, your sideways movement is nonexistent. As with all new maneuvers, practice, experiment, and observe what works for you and what doesn't.

Back Ferry Landing: Step 3

- The stern paddler reaches out first to grab on to the shore. In the excitement, remember to *reach* and not lean.

- After the stern paddler grabs on, the current will push the bow parallel to the shore.

- When the bow paddler grabs on to the shore, don't pull too hard. This can push the stern out into the current.

- The bow paddler helps keep the canoe in place while the stern paddler keeps the stern of the canoe near the shore.

Back Ferry Landing: Step 4

- Practice the back ferry and back ferry landing in slow currents before you really need it in fast ones.

- The back ferry allows for the graceful, controlled negotiation of strong currents.

- The back ferry combines the proper angle of the boat to the current with upstream paddle strokes. The stern is angled in the direction you want the canoe to move.

- This slows the canoe in the water and moves it sideways using the power of the current.

BRACES & EDDY TURNS

Braces are paddle movements to prevent capsize and help with eddy turns

The *low brace* is used to stabilize the canoe during turns and to keep it from capsizing in big waves. To perform a low brace, reach far out with the blade laid nearly flat on the water and push down hard. If you are capsizing, a powerful downward push will help you regain balance. The push should be fast and smooth. If the canoe is moving forward, raise the leading

edge of the blade so that it is at an angle to the oncoming water. Pushing down on the paddle will stabilize the canoe.

A *high brace* is a useful recovery stroke when the canoe is leaning away from your paddling side, and it is used when entering or leaving eddies. Position yourself and the paddle as if you were about to do a draw stroke; however, your up-

Low Brace

- The low brace is used to stabilize a canoe during sharp turns and to prevent capsizing.

- Reach far out on the side that the canoe is leaning and push down forcefully with the blade.

- The push should be fast and smooth. The force of the blade against the water will right the canoe.

- Don't hesitate to reach far out over the water to push down on the paddle. The low brace is like reaching out to steady yourself when you stumble.

High Brace

- The high brace is very useful for entering and leaving eddies.

- Reach out as far as you can. Your upper arm will be high in the air. Plant the blade deep in the water and hold it there, and the canoe will spin around the paddle.

- To prevent a capsize on your nonpaddle side (the canoe is rolling away from the side you are paddling on), lean out far as if doing a draw.

- Plant the paddle and pull on it to right the canoe.

per arm is high in the air, and the paddle blade is fairly deep in the water.

Instead of pulling the canoe toward the paddle, as in a draw stroke, hold the paddle's position in the water where you planted it. This should turn the canoe around the paddle. Think of the paddle as a pole that you grab while running past, and it spins you around.

An eddy is a good place to rest and to scout your next move. However, the differential between the main current and the back current of the eddy can be tricky to negotiate.

An *eddy turn* is the most effective way to enter an eddy. As the canoe passes the obstacle, the bow paddler reaches out toward the eddy with a high brace. The stern paddler then joins in with a vigorous forward sweep. This combination will turn the canoe into the eddy below the object. The canoe will now be in a calm spot, facing upstream.

Eddy Turn: Part 1

forward sweep
current
high brace
eddy

- Use an eddy turn to pull into the calm water behind a large obstacle.

- The key is to cross the current differential at the eddy line quickly.

- One combination is for the bow paddler to do a high brace on the side of the canoe near the eddy right after passing the obstacle.

- The stern paddler then does a strong forward sweep to push the boat over the eddy line.

Eddy Turn: Part 2

- The combination of the high brace in the bow and a forward sweep in the stern pushes the canoe over the eddy line while the current spins the stern downstream.

- The canoe is now resting in the calm eddy pool, facing upstream.

- This provides a resting spot and a place to plan the approach to the next set of rapids.

- If paddlers are on opposite sides of the canoe, the stern paddler can perform a low brace while the bow paddler performs a pry.

PEELING OUT OF EDDIES

An eddy peel-out is the best way to exit an eddy and reenter the main current

The edge of the eddy, where there is a differential between the main current (rapid movement downstream) and the eddy current (slow upstream movement), is called the *eddy line*. When leaving an eddy, *peeling out*, it is important to lean downstream. Leaning upstream is almost always a precarious move; as you lean upstream, the gunwale is pushed down toward the water. As the gunwale nears the water, the current is pushing the hull farther downstream; this can lead to an amazingly fast capsize.

Because you are facing upstream in an eddy, angle the bow out into the current. As the bow crosses the eddy line, the bow paddler does a high brace and leans downstream. The

Peeling Out Using a High Brace

- Enter the current at a 45-degree angle.

- As the bow crosses the eddy line, the bow paddler does a high brace on the downstream side of the canoe.

- If peeling out to the right, a high brace is done on the right side. If peeling out to the left, a high brace is done on the left.

- As the bow paddler braces, the stern paddler does a forward sweep on the side opposite the brace.

Back in the Current

- The bow paddler leans downstream as the canoe crosses the eddy line.

- As the canoe crosses into the strong downstream current, the canoe pivots from the force of the water and from the direction provided by the brace and sweep.

- The maneuver ends when the canoe is parallel to the main current.

- The bow paddler forward paddles, while the stern paddler does a low brace if needed to keep the canoe balanced.

stern paddler does a strong forward sweep, and the current then pivots the canoe so that it is facing downstream.

The eddy turn is the best way to leave an eddy. Paddling out of the lower end of the eddy is possible in weak currents but difficult if the downstream current is strong. Also small rocks and gravel often accumulate at the downstream end of an eddy.

In an alternative peel-out, the stern paddler performs a low brace while the bow paddler performs a pry stroke. Which peel-out you do depends on which side of the canoe you are paddling on and which side of the eddy you wish to exit. If you exit to the right, and the bow paddler is paddling on the right, the bow paddler will do a high brace and the stern paddler will do a forward sweep on the left. If the canoe is exiting left, and the bow paddler is paddling on the right, the bow paddler will do a pry while the stern paddler does a low brace on the left side.

Peeling Out Using a Low Brace

- Forward paddle with some speed across the eddy line with the canoe at about a 45-degree angle.

- The stern paddler performs a low brace on the downstream side of the canoe.

- The bow paddler helps push the canoe into the current with a pry or a cross draw.

- As the canoe crosses the eddy line, the current spins the canoe downstream. Both paddlers forward paddle, being ready to maintain balance.

Scout the Rapids!

- Take all rapids seriously! Rocks and moving water deserve your respect.

- If you have *any* doubts about how to approach a set of rapids, land the canoe and investigate. Land well above the rapids. If you wait too long, you may get swept in.

- Study the rapids from shore and look for channels, obstacles, holes, and eddies. Develop a plan for how you will maneuver.

- Most rapids will have portage trails. If you are unsure about your skills, portage.

CANOE ON THE OCEAN?

Approached with caution, coastal regions can be safely paddled in a canoe

Canoes were among the original oceangoing vessels, allowing their occupants to travel vast expanses of water to migrate to new territory, to fish, and to conduct trading expeditions up and down continental coasts and among distant islands.

Today paddling is mainly a leisure-time activity undertaken for adventure, relaxation, and enjoyment. The vast majority of

ocean paddling is done along coasts and bays, in estuaries, and among nearby islands. Although most coastal, ocean, or sea paddling is done in kayaks, canoeing is a very viable activity as long as proper care is exercised at all times.

Perhaps even more than when canoeing on rivers, one must maintain total respect for, and awareness of, the power

Ocean Canoe

- Canoeing on the ocean requires proper equipment, paddling skills, experience, knowledge of ocean conditions, and, most important, caution and respect.

- Select a canoe designed for waves and wind. Install additional floatation to displace water and keep the boat afloat during capsize.

- Install a secure-fitting spray cover to keep out waves, rain, and splashed water.

- Select where and when you paddle very carefully. Anticipate all likely conditions and be sure to remain within your abilities.

Inflatable Canoes

- Quality inflatable boats are difficult to puncture and impossible to sink when they are intact.

- They can be "bounce-land-ed" through surf and rocks that would likely damage other materials.

- Inflatable boats take on less water than a rigid craft and thus recover from capsize easily. However, there is less room for equipment.

- Inflatable canoes are lightweight. They are portable, folding to fit into a duffle bag. With a good pump it takes only ten to fifteen minutes to inflate them.

of water. Part of the power of oceans comes from the immense quantity of water. Another part of the power of the ocean is the constantly changing conditions on the surface. Many factors impact the water at any given point: tides, currents, waves, winds, the nature of the coastline, and the topography of features underneath the surface. These factors combine to create what might be very calm conditions at one moment and extremely rough and violent conditions a few hours later.

Whereas it is possible and enjoyable to paddle for a short time on very calm water in an open canoe, it does not take very much wind or wave activity to swamp a small open boat. Oceangoing canoes should be outfitted with a securely fitting spray cover. Make sure that paddlers will not get tangled in the spray cover during capsize.

Additional floatation is also recommended. Inflated floatation bags will keep displaced water from entering the boat and will help keep the canoe afloat. Canoes can also be built, or retrofitted, with outriggers to maintain stability.

Outrigger Canoes

- Outrigger canoes originally were developed by people in Malaysian southeast Asia to migrate eastward to Polynesia and New Zealand and westward to Madagascar.

- Outriggers are lateral support floats attached to one or both sides of a canoe.

- Outriggers provide great stability, with less inefficiency than making a single-hull canoe wider.

- Outrigger canoes can be paddled quite fast and in rougher waters than a standard canoe. Outrigger canoe racing has become a popular international sport.

Ocean Paddling Instructions

- Numerous paddling schools and instruction opportunities are available up and down both coasts of the United States.

- Most coastal paddling schools focus on sea kayaking, although many of the basic skills—knowledge of tides and currents, weather, chart reading and navigation, trip preparation—are applicable to canoeing.

- Many paddling clubs also offer instructional classes and trips, as well as socialization with other avid paddlers.

OCEAN PADDLING
Coastal canoeing opens up a whole new world for paddling

There are three broad levels of competence in ocean paddling. The first level is the novice. The novice should go on open water only when it is calm and under supervision of a more experienced paddler.

The second level is the proficient paddler. These paddlers have been guided and instructed in how to handle their canoe on the sea under reasonable conditions. Proficient paddlers know that their boat is seaworthy and has basic equipment for comfort and safety. Proficient paddlers know how to self-rescue if capsized, can negotiate small waves, and are able to launch and land in a number of circumstances.

The third level is the advanced paddler. This paddler has a high degree of skill in surf. He or she can plan and lead open-water expeditions under adverse conditions and has extensive knowledge of weather and coastal navigation.

The demands of coastal paddling can be quite different

Coastal Canoeing

- Coastal paddling provides access to many exciting experiences and locations not available inland.

- Paddling on the ocean requires that you exercise extreme caution and awareness at all times.

- Acquire proper training or go with experienced coastal paddlers. Don't paddle alone on coastal waters.

- Research the areas where you will be and bring adequate gear and safety equipment. Stay aware of the weather and water conditions and be prepared to respond to changes.

Ships and Harbors

- Canoes are small compared with most motor boats, and they are very small compared with ships.

- When paddling in harbors, it is your responsibility to stay out of the way of ships. Stay clear of any large craft. They can travel deceptively fast.

- Make yourself as visible as possible. Buy brightly colored PFDs and a brightly colored boat.

- Consider putting reflective tape on your canoe and PFDs. Have headlamps or other bright lights for when conditions are dark or overcast.

from those of river and lake canoeing. The space involved is much larger and might require additional safety equipment. A GPS unit can help with navigating and staying found. A VHF marine radio permits one to request emergency assistance and to frequently check weather broadcasts. Strobe lights, flares, and EPIRBs (Emergency Position Indicating Radio Beacons) can also guide rescue efforts to your location. These technologies can be added to the whistle and signal mirror that you should already have.

The ocean is big, so make yourself as visible as possible. Buy a brightly colored boat and brightly colored PFDs. Add high-visibility reflective tape to increase your ability to be seen.

Safe sea travel requires a familiarity with nautical charts, compasses, and navigation. Acquire large-scale charts and study them beforehand. Some paddlers also bring along the corresponding topographic maps for the shore they are paddling along. Also be sure to consult tide and current tables.

Arctic Canoeing

- Paddling expeditions are possible anywhere there is open water.

- Alaskan and Arctic trips are for skilled paddlers with the proper gear and experience level to deal with extremes.

- Numerous outfitters lead guided trips to these more remote and extreme locales.

- Glaciers, sea lions, polar bears, and whales are among the amazing phenomena to be witnessed on a Far North paddle.

Charts

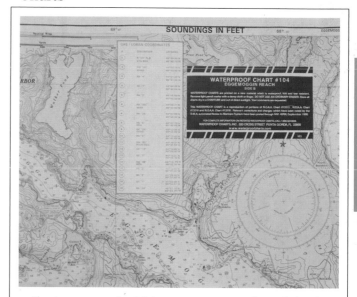

- Charts are maps that highlight marine features and are designed for navigation.

- Charts contain a great deal of detailed information that is important for the coastal paddler, including rocks, islands, and buoys.

- Charts show water depths at average low tide levels and may be drawn in feet, fathoms (6 feet), or meters. The intertidal area is indicated by a different color.

- Charts give information about shores. There are contour lines for landforms and symbols for radio towers or other structures.

TIDES

The pull of the sun and moon causes the oceans to be in constant motion

Tides are the cyclical rising and falling of the surface of the Earth's oceans. Tides are caused primarily by the gravitational forces of the sun and moon, although the sun's impact is only about one-fourth that of the moon's.

The moon attracts the water nearest it, producing a "bulge" of ocean on the side of the Earth closest to the moon and a bulge on the opposite side of the Earth, farthest from the moon. These bulges create *high tides*. The space between the bulges creates *low tides*.

Because the moon takes twenty-four hours to revolve around the Earth there are two high tides and two low tides each day, with six hours between the highest and lowest

Tidal Currents

- Tidal currents are the flow of water due to the movements of the tides.

- Tidal currents are fairly predictable because they are caused by the gravitational pull of the moon.

- The power of tidal currents is most affected by the makeup of the coast. Islands, rocks, and channels create different conditions than on a long strip of gravel beach.

- Currents can be predicted by using current tables. Tidal currents for some areas are depicted visually on *tidal charts*.

Tide Tables

DATE	HIGH TIDE TIME	HT (ft)	TIME	HT (ft)	LOW TIDE TIME	HT (ft)	TIME	HT (ft)
1 T	12:15	7.4	11:03	9.3	5:11	3.6	6:04	-0.7
2 F	12:47	7.6	11:46	9.1	5:56	3.3	6:39	-0.5
3 S	1:18	7.8	12:26	8.8	6:37	3.1	7:11	-0.2
4 S	1:46	7.9	1:05	8.4	7:17	2.8	7:40	0.3
5 M	2:14	8.0	1:45	7.8	7:58	2.6	8:08	0.9
6 T	2:41	8.0	2:27	7.1	8:40	2.5	8:35	1.6
7 W	3:08	8.0	3:14	6.4	9:26	2.3	9:02	2.2
8 T	3:37	8.0	4:12	5.8	10:18	2.2	9:31	2.9
9 F	4:10	7.9	5:30	5.2	11:19	2.0	10:03	3.5
10 S	4:51	7.9	7:16	5.1	12:29	1.7	10:49	4.1
11 S	5:44	7.9	9:00	5.3			1:40	1.3
12 M	6:47	8.0	10:00	5.8	12:06	4.5	2:42	0.8
13 T	7:52	8.3	10:39	6.2	1:38	4.5	3:33	0.2
14 W	8:52	8.8	11:11	6.7	2:51	4.3	4:17	-0.4
15 T	9:46	9.2	11:41	7.2	3:49	3.9	4:57	-0.8
16 F	10:37	9.6			4:39	3.3	5:36	-1.1
17 S	12:12	7.8	11:26	9.7	5:28	2.7	6:12	-1.0
18 S	12:43	8.3	12:15	9.5	6:16	2.0	6:49	-0.7
19 M	1:16	8.8	1:06	9.1	7:05	1.4	7:26	-0.2
20 T	1:50	9.1	1:59	8.3	7:57	0.9	8:03	0.6
21 W	2:26	9.4	2:58	7.5	8:52	0.5	8:42	1.5
22 T	3:06	9.4	4:05	6.6	9:52	0.4	9:24	2.5
23 F	3:51	9.2	5:28	5.9	10:59	0.3	10:14	3.3
24 S	4:44	8.9	7:08	5.7	12:14	0.3	11:21	3.9
25 S	5:49	8.5	8:43	5.9			1:32	0.2
26 M	7:04	8.1	9:49	6.3	12:52	4.2	2:41	0.0
27 T	8:17	8.3	10:34	6.7	2:21	4.1	3:39	-0.2

- Tidal changes can happen approximately every six or twelve hours, depending on the region.

- There is a vast amount of variation in times and heights of tides in different locations. To find out the time and water levels of different tides, use local tables.

- Tide tables can be found online, in local newspapers, at libraries, and at Coast Guard stations and marinas.

- Remember to combine tide information with other factors affecting paddling conditions, such as tidal currents, winds, and weather.

points. The tide is about fifty minutes later each day due to the moon's twenty-eight-day revolution around the Earth.

The strip of seashore that is submerged at high tide and exposed at low tide is the *intertidal zone*.

Although the strength of the current is related to the size of the tides, topography of the waterways is more important. Islands and channels direct incoming water into constricted pathways and can make the tides in these spots flow much more rapidly. Islands, bays, and peninsulas can create circling eddies and cross currents.

The times of high and low tides can be learned by consulting tide tables for the area of the coast you will be paddling.

The timing and strength of currents are predicted with annual tables published by the National Oceanic and Atmospheric Administration (NOAA). These tables give predictions for slack and the times and speeds of maximum currents. *Slack* is the period of least activity when the currents slow down and turn the other direction. Slack is the safest time to paddle when the currents are hazardous.

High Tide

- High tide is the maximum height reached by a rising tide, also called *flood tide* or *high water*.

- High tides are *diurnal*, happening twice each day, twelve hours apart. In areas where this happens, tide tables may differentiate between *higher high water*

and *lower high water*.

- *Slack water*, or slack tide, is the period during which no appreciable tidal currents are flowing.

- Slack water usually happens near high tide and low tide when the direction of the tidal current reverses.

Low Tide

- Low tide is the minimum height reached by a falling tide, also called *ebb tide* or *low water*.

- Low tides are *diurnal*, happening twice each day, twelve hours apart. In areas where this is happens, tide tables may differentiate between *higher low water*

and *lower low water*.

- Low tide can expose rocks and other obstacles that might be less threatening during higher water.

- Always be sure to camp above the reach of high tide. Be sure that all boats are securely tied.

COASTAL HAZARDS

Ocean canoeing presents additional hazards for the paddler to be prepared for

Ocean waters are constantly in motion due to tides. This constantly moving water interacts with the topographic features of the coastline and the ocean floor to create powerful currents. When the wind and increased wave action are added to this situation, the challenges presented to a small craft can be very serious.

There are various conditions and types of water movements to be aware of in addition to standard waves. *Reflection waves* are waves that bounce back after hitting a pier, wall, or other large surface. Reflection waves collide with the incoming waves, creating destabilizing wave patterns. When reflection waves are strong, they can cause *clapotis*—a high,

Lakes versus Oceans

- On a lake, if the wind doesn't blow, the water will be calm.

- The waters of oceans are constantly in motion due to tides, currents, and weather many miles away.

- On smaller lakes, the water temperatures may be fairly warm. Ocean waters and the Great Lakes can be frigid even in midsummer.

- Oceans are salt water. You must bring adequate amounts of drinking water with you.

Tide Rips

- Tide rips are stretches of turbulent water caused by one current flowing into or across another current.

- Most tide rips are manageable with good paddling skills and balance. Other rips produce waves that any paddler should avoid.

- In calm weather, rips sound like river rapids and appear as a dark patch on the surface, sometimes flecked with white breaking waves.

- In windy weather, tide rips can be camouflaged by wind sounds and whitecaps, making them harder to see from a distance.

vertical, broken wave. This can be a challenging condition in which to keep a small boat from capsizing.

A *weather tide* occurs when waves are made steeper, larger, and closer together by wind blowing against an opposing current. Seas are usually much rougher when the wind and current oppose each other.

Other hazards include tide rips, tide races, and surf. Surf is created by breaking waves on the shore. Surf can present major challenges to safely launching or landing a canoe. Seek out spots with minimal surf. Large surf can toss a boat

and its occupants around effortlessly. If the surf seems stronger than your ability level, wait for a calmer day. Smaller surfs can sometimes be found near an island or along a point of land or peninsula.

Tide races are formed by the incoming or outgoing tide being forced through a channel or other constriction. Tide races can cause major eddies, whirlpools, and other unusual current features.

Tide Race

- A tide race is created by a fast-moving tide passing through a constriction. This can form waves, eddies, and hazardous currents.

- The constriction can be caused by a passage where the sides narrow or by an underwater obstruction.

- A *rip current* is a strong surface flow of water returning seaward.

- Rip currents can occur on any beach with breaking waves. Rip currents can be recognized by unusually calm waters, caused by the channel of water flowing out.

Surf

- Surf is waves breaking upon the shore or other shallow area.

- Avoid large surf for landing your boat. You can often find much smaller surf and a safer place to land in an area protected by a point of land or an island.

- Stay well outside the surf line while paddling because larger waves can break farther out. This can occur quite intermittently and unexpectedly.

- Waves can break in any shallow place, not just near shore.

COMMUNICATIONS

Stay informed of the weather and be prepared to signal for emergency assistance

Your first responsibility is to remain aware of the weather and how it is likely to impact your canoeing experience. Paddling on the ocean puts you at huge risk. Wind and storms can turn calm seas into raging cauldrons. However, these changes are somewhat predictable, based on weather conditions and forecasts. At a minimum, check the forecast before setting out and plan your trip to conclude during predictable favorable conditions. For trips more than a few hours, take a marine weather radio and listen for updates frequently.

Handheld marine VHF (very high frequency) radios have a range of 5 to 10 miles at sea level. They are generally the most effective emergency signaling device. Most VHF trans-

Weather Radio

- Marine forecasts for twenty-four hours focus on wind speeds and directions.

- Forecasts can include size of waves and swells, visibility limits due to fog or drizzle.

- "Light and variable" means wind speeds of 5 to 15 knots. Winds greater than 15 knots can be difficult for paddling.

- A small craft advisory is issued for expected winds between 21 and 33 knots; a gale warning is issued for winds stronger than 33 knots; and a storm warning is issued for winds of over 47 knots.

Signal Mirror

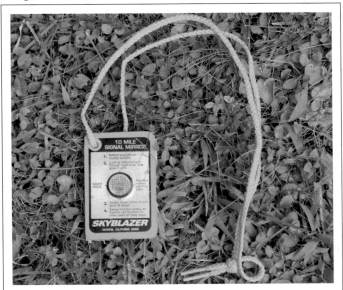

- Although any mirror will reflect the sun, a signal mirror permits accurate aiming of the flashes.

- If there is a hole in the mirror, sight through the hole and hold a thumb at arm's length so that its tip covers your target.

- Adjust the mirror so that you can see the flash on your thumbnail. Keep moving the mirror back and forth to flash across your thumb.

- Stop flashing when an aircraft is approaching because the flash blinds the pilot.

ceivers include weather channels. The Telecommunications Act of 1996 permits recreational boaters to use a VHF marine radio and EPIRB *without* having an FCC ship station license.

An EPIRB transmits emergency signals for twenty-four to thirty-six hours, indicating your location on the sea. These signals are monitored by the Coast Guard. EPIRB units range in cost from $200 to $1,500. EPIRBs must be registered with the Coast Guard. This enhances the Coast Guard's ability to respond to actual emergencies and to assess accidental or hoax emergency signals (about 90% of EPIRB activations).

Other technologies for attracting attention and assistance include whistles, mirrors, strobe lights, flares, smoke canisters, and dye markers. Always carry an accessible whistle while paddling on open water. It can alert people to your position in fog or in the dark. A signal mirror can be very effective in helping rescue pilots to locate you on sunny days. Smoke canisters can be shot into the air on overcast days to indicate your position. Flares provide a very bright and visible indicator of your position for a brief period of time.

Strobe Light

- Coastal paddlers are required to have flares or a battery-operated strobe light when paddling at night.

- A strobe light is a flashing white light that can be seen for 1 mile or more on open water.

- Strobes are for emergency use only. Models come in various sizes and have various ways of being attached to PFDs.

- Select a strobe that is waterproof and corrosion resistant and will flash for at least eight hours.

Ocean Canoeing Safety

- Do not exceed your capabilities!

- Know the tide schedule and be aware of local currents and conditions.

- Know the weather forecast and stay alert to changes in the weather.

- Take proper equipment and emergency signaling gear.

- Ocean water tends to be cold! Wear a wetsuit or other appropriate protection from hypothermia.

- Be prepared for the unexpected. Have a plan for landing if conditions become threatening.

ROPE & TWO HALF HITCHES
Careful selection of rope and the knots used gets the job done right

When buying rope, select nylon rope of ¼- to ⅜-inch diameter. Most ropes are now made of nylon or plastic (polypropylene). Plastic rope tends to become brittle and less pliable over time. Nylon remains flexible and holds a knot better than plastic. Avoid clothesline or other cheap cord. It might hold a canoe tied up to a dock, but don't trust it to keep the canoe on top of your car at 60 miles an hour. Nylon rope coils easily, is less likely to rot, and works well as an emergency throw rope.

The needs for rope on a canoe trip are many. You should have 12- to 20-foot painters attached to the bow and stern. Painters are used to secure the boat to a car for transport or to tie to a dock or tree. Painters are also used to line the canoe upstream or through rapids (see pages 226–27).

Ropes, or straps, are necessary for transporting a canoe by car. Ropes are also necessary to hang food bags, secure gear into the canoe, set up a tarp, and dry wet socks. It's a good

Types of Rope

- Select strong, durable, pliable rope for painters, tie-downs, and throw ropes.

- For canoeing purposes, woven nylon rope ⅜-inch in diameter works very well.

- Buy enough rope for two 12- to 15-foot painters, two

10-foot tie-down ropes, a 50-foot throw rope, and a couple of 20-foot lengths to tuck into your pack.

- Whenever you cut nylon rope, melt the ends with a flame to prevent fraying.

Two Half Hitches: Step 1

- The *working end* of a rope is the part of the rope that gets moved around to tie the knot.

- The *standing end* of the rope stays still or gets tied to the object.

- Use two half hitches to attach a rope to an object.

Pass the working end of the rope around the object you are tying the rope to.

- Wrap the working end of the rope around the standing end of the rope. This creates a hole. Pass the working end through the hole.

idea to have a 50-foot coil of rope near at hand to use as a throw rope. Keep a small coil of thin nylon cord in your day pack. It will often come in handy.

····················· GREEN ● LIGHT ·············

Take care of your rope! It will tie (and untie) easier and stay stronger if it is kept clean. Prevent fraying by melting the ends of the rope with a flame. Take time to melt the ends any time you cut a rope. Avoid using tape to prevent fraying. It will come off and will make the end of the rope sticky.

Two Half Hitches: Step 2

- After passing the working end through the hole, the working end is wrapped around the standing end.

- The working end must wrap around the standing end in the same way both times. If the working end wraps *over* the standing end on the first wrap, it must wrap over

- on the second wrap also.

- If the working end is wrapped under the standing end, it must wrap under both times.

- After the second wrap, the working end passes through the hole created by the wrap.

Two Half Hitches: Step 3

- Tighten the knot firmly against the object. Two half hitches can work loose if not made quite tight.

- Leave a tail of at least 2 inches on the working end. If the tail is too short, the knot can come loose.

- This knot is useful for tying rope to the canoe, tying a painter to a tree or post, and attaching the rope to a canoe rack.

- Two half hitches can also be used to finish off the trucker's hitch instead of a quick release knot.

BOWLINE
The classic sailor's knot that won't slip when under pressure

You will be able to meet nearly any knot-tying challenge with the four knots presented in this book. There are three main tasks for knots: tying a rope to an object, tying a rope to another rope, and securing gear.

There are three criteria for a good knot. It is easy to tie. It does the job. It is easy to untie.

Learning to tie knots and remembering how to tie them require practice. There is nothing intuitive about knots. Useful knots do not appear in nature; they are human designed and must be learned and practiced. However, after you have learned these knots and know when to use them, they will serve you well.

Two half hitches (see pages 156–57) are used to attach a rope to an object. They can be used when tying a canoe to a car rack. They are used to tie a painter to a tree. They can also be used to finish off a trucker's hitch.

Two half hitches (see pages 156–57)

Bowline: Step 1

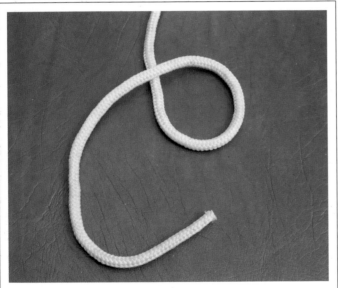

- The bowline creates a very secure nonslipping knot at the end of the rope.

- Twist the working end to create a loop about 1½ feet from the end of the rope.

- When making the loop, lay the working end over the standing end of the rope.

- This loop is often referred to as the *rabbit hole*.

Bowline: Step 2

- The working end is passed up through the loop and around the back of the standing end of the rope.

- The working end is also called the *rabbit*, and the standing end is also called the *tree*.

- A mnemonic device: The rabbit comes out of its hole, then goes around the tree and back down its hole.

The bowline creates a loop that will not slip when weighted. It can be an alternative to two half hitches when tying a rope to an object. The bowline can also be used in rescue situations. It can be tied around a person's chest without fear of crushing her when the rope is pulled. The bowline can be used anytime you want a secure, nonslipping loop on the end of the rope.

The bowline (pronounced "bull-in") knot provides a non-slipping knot that is easy to untie because it doesn't jam or cinch.

Bowline: Step 3

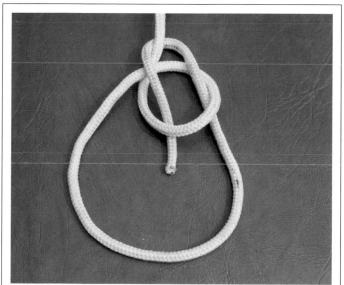

- After the working end passes up through the loop and around the back of the standing end, it passes down through the loop.

- It is important that the initial loop is twisted in the right direction.

- If twisted properly, the loop tightens down on the working end, creating a nonslipping knot.

- If the loop is twisted the wrong way, the knot falls apart as it is tightened.

Bowline: Step 4

- After the rabbit has gone "back down its hole," carefully tighten the bowline.

- Make sure that there is a tail of at least 2 inches to keep the working end from slipping back through the knot.

- The size of the final loop is determined by how far up the working end you make the original twist.

- The bowline can be a stand-alone loop or be tied around an object.

TRUCKER'S HITCH
This is a versatile knot for tying a load in place

This knot is also called a *power hitch, pulley hitch,* or *power cinch.* Whatever it is called, it is a phenomenally useful knot, most often used to secure canoes on the top of transport vehicles.

Passing the working end of the rope through the pulley loop allows for a lot of pressure to be applied while tightening the rope. It is easy to maintain that pressure while finishing off the hitch with a quick-release knot or two half hitches.

This knot is called the *pulley hitch* because it doubles the force of pulling on a straight rope. Be careful to not apply too much pressure to a Kevlar or other fragile hull.

The pulley loop and the quick-release knot allow for easy adjustments to be made to achieve the desired snugness for the load.

The trucker's hitch can be used to secure gear bags in the canoe and to give an adjustable knot on tents and flies. Use

Trucker's Hitch: Step 1

- Secure one end of the rope to the canoe rack with two half hitches. Pass the rope over the canoe.

- Form a loop in the rope about 2 feet above the bar that the loose end of the rope will be tied to.

- Grasping the rope just below the loop, push the rope upward so that a bend of the free end of the rope can be pushed through the loop.

Trucker's Hitch: Step 2

- After pushing the bend through the loop, hold onto to the bend and tighten the loop.

- This creates a quick-release loop in the rope. If the loop is in the wrong place, pull firmly on the free end of the rope to untie the loop.

- Retie the quick-release loop in the spot where you need it.

in place of the more traditional *taut-line hitch*.

A good knot is easy to tie, easy to untie, and does the job.

Trucker's Hitch: Step 3

Trucker's Hitch: Step 4

- Keeping the quick-release loop intact, pass the working end of the rope under the canoe rack.

- Then pass the working end of the rope through the quick-release loop.

- This creates a pulley that allows you to place a great deal of tension on the rope.

- Pull down firmly on the working end and hold the rope in place at the quick-release loop with your thumb.

- While holding the tension, grasp the free end of the rope just below your thumb. Wrap the free end around the part of the rope just before it passes through the loop.

- Make a bend in the free end and push the bend through the loop you just created.

- Snug up the loop to create a quick-release knot. Maintain the tension with your thumb and forefinger while tightening the loop.

- The trucker's hitch can also be finished with two half hitches for a more secure knot.

SHEET BEND

This is the knot for tying two pieces of rope together

Forget the "granny" knot! The sheet bend is far more elegant, easier, and effective than layering overhand knots until the ropes will hold. The sheet bend works for connecting any two pieces of rope, especially ropes of different diameters.

When tying ropes of different diameters, make the initial loop with the larger rope. The smaller rope will then pass through and around the loop and pass under itself to create the "locking" feature of the knot.

To untie a sheet bend, loosen the knot by pushing the four ends toward each other. After holding a heavy load any knot can become stiff. Try bending the knot back and forth to loosen it. Resist the temptation to slip a knife or other sharp edge into a stiff knot. It should be unnecessary, and a metal edge can abrade the fibers and weaken the rope for future use.

When tying two particularly slippery ropes (polypropylene) together, leave long "tails" on each rope and secure the sheet

Sheet Bend: Step 1

- Use the sheet bend to tie two ropes together. It works well with ropes of different diameters.

- With one rope, the larger if they are different sizes, form a bend near the end of the rope.

- Pass the second rope up through the loop made by the bend.

- Wrap the second rope around the bend, going underneath both parts of the first rope.

Sheet Bend: Step 2

- Pass the working end of the second rope underneath itself, forming an X over the bend of the first rope.

- Keeping the X in place, snug the knot by pulling on all four of the ropes.

- Then tighten the knot by dropping the tails and pulling firmly on the two other ropes.

- Loosen the sheet bend by pushing all four "ends" of the rope together toward the knot.

bend with two half hitches with each end of the rope.

You can also tie a quick-release sheet bend by looping the end of the second line under itself rather than pulling the end straight through. Experiment with this variation only after you have mastered the standard sheet bend.

When not using a rope, it is important to keep it neatly coiled. Even short pieces of cord are more easily stored and accessed if they are kept coiled. Coiled ropes won't get tangled or knotted, will be ready to use when needed, and lend an air of professional expertise. Like a good knot, effective coiling requires a little practice.

To coil a rope for rescues, tie it off at the top of the coils so that it will unravel smoothly when thrown.

Coil a Rope

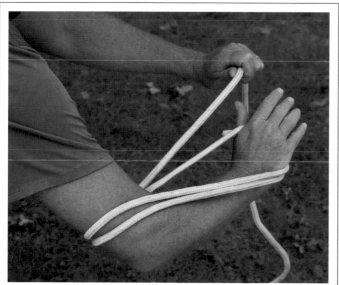

- Keep ropes of all lengths neat, untangled, and ready to use by coiling them.

- Before coiling, run the rope through your fingers to make sure there are no knots.

- Hold an end of the rope in one hand. Slide the other hand out along the rope to measure the size of the loop. Hook the loop of rope on the fingers of the first hand.

- Keep the first hand still. This prevents the loops from getting tangled.

Secure a Coiled Rope

- After the rope is coiled, wrap the last foot or so of rope around the middle of the coils.

- Tuck the tail of the rope under the last wrap and pull tight.

- To keep a coiled rope ready to throw as a safety line, secure the coil by wrapping the last foot of rope through the coils at the top.

- This keeps the rope in a rounder shape for throwing, but care must be taken to prevent snarling during storage.

MAPS & CHARTS

Having a good map and knowing how to read it are indispensable for staying found

Maps are an important part of the planning phase of any canoe trip. Carefully consulting maps can help you to determine what to expect while paddling and to assess whether a particular trip is within your skill and experience range.

Different maps provide different kinds of information. The United States Geological Survey (USGS) creates and makes available to the public a variety of topographic maps covering all parts of the country. These maps are available in different scales and thus vary in their usefulness to the paddler. Generally, you will want the most detailed maps you can get. A map with a scale of 1:250,000 means that 1 inch on the map represents 250,000 inches on the ground (1 inch = 4

Map of a Lake

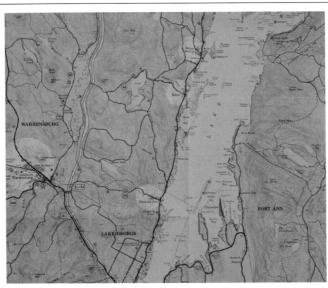

- Pay close attention to the scale of the map. There is usually a bar graph somewhere on the map illustrating the distance represented by an inch or other unit of measurement.

- Use islands and shoreline features to keep track of your location.

- Bays, inlets, streams, and campsites provide good clues to your location.

- Frequently check what you see against your map. A large island might *look* like the shoreline of the lake.

Maps for Canoeing

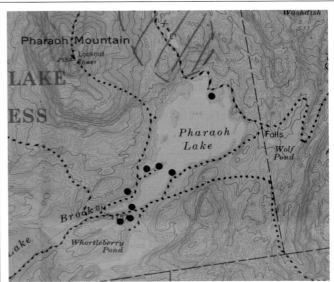

- Good canoeing maps indicate campsites and portage trails. Contour lines indicate land features and help pinpoint your location.

- Water levels indicated on maps should be treated cautiously. Levels change; low water may reveal "islands" that aren't on the map.

- What appears on the map as a thick blue line between two lakes may be a rock-lined dry creek bed when you get there.

- Maps are essential for planning and staying found, but be prepared to adapt.

miles). On a map with a scale of 1:50,000, 1 inch represents 4,166 feet, or about ⁴/₅ of a mile. An inch on a scale of 1:24,000 represents 2,000 feet, or a bit more than ¹/₃ of a mile.

A *topographic* map indicates the elevation of land by using contour lines. The difference in elevation between lines will be indicated at the bottom of the map. Contour lines that are close together indicate steep hills, whereas spaced-out contour lines indicate flatter terrain. This can be extremely valuable information when assessing the gradient of rivers and the steepness of portage trails.

Maps should be studied for the location of dams, falls, and rapids. Some maps will clearly indicate these features, some will not. Many canoeing maps also show the location of portages and campsites.

Maps contain a lot of information, but even the most accurate maps can't show everything. Also physical features can change dramatically over time. Rivers change course, dams and bridges can be built or removed, campsites and trails can disappear. The water level in lakes and rivers can vary immensely and may be quite different from what is shown on your map.

River Map

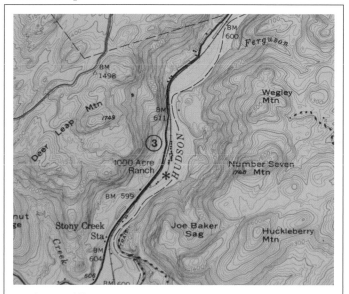

- When paddling a river, maps are important for anticipating rapids, dams, or other challenges.

- The contour lines can help you estimate the gradient of the river and the nature of the banks and surrounding countryside.

- Water trail, or paddling, maps often point out features like portages, campsites, parking areas, and restaurants.

- Find out how recent your map is and when possible talk with someone who has been on the river recently.

Coastal Charts

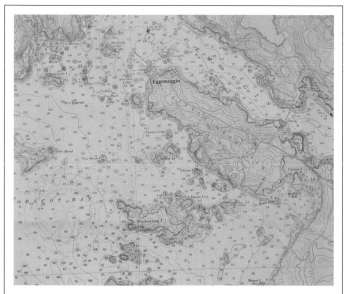

- Charts are maps of waterways that are designed for navigation. They focus on water and coastlines, giving very little information about the adjoining land.

- Charts show water depths, shoreline features, tidal ranges, rocks, navigation aids like lights and buoys.

- Charts should be supplemented by the appropriate tide table for your area.

- Consult *U.S. Coast Guard Pilots* for detailed information regarding currents, tides, seasonal weather patterns, and other factors affecting navigation.

COMPASSES

An essential on any wilderness trip, the compass will keep you oriented

A compass can be exceptionally useful on an overcast day when the lakeshore all looks the same or when you want to cross a large lake in a straight line. The value of a compass is that it always points to magnetic north. With that information and a map, you can keep track of where you are and determine what direction you want to go.

The Earth's magnetic field flows northward like a prevailing wind. The compass needle aligns with this flow and shows the direction toward magnetic north. One thing to keep in mind is the potential of magnetic disturbance from objects that contain iron or steel (knives, stoves, batteries, etc.) or that generate electromagnetic fields (radios). These objects

Hiker's Compass

- For most of your paddling needs, a hiker's compass will work beautifully.

- It is lightweight and easily carried in a pocket or on a lanyard around your neck. It can also be attached to a thwart so as to be easily referenced.

- The hiker's compass has a rotating housing set on a rectangular base. The movable housing assists with taking a bearing.

- The base often includes ruler markings, which can be very useful in estimating distances on the map.

Marine Compass

- A marine compass does not have a movable housing or base.

- Direction is indicated by a rotating card inside the glass dome. The card is marked with directions and degrees.

- Because a marine compass is attached to the boat and has large, easy-to-read numbers, it is convenient to use while paddling.

- However, it is more expensive, heavier, and harder to use outside the boat for route planning or hiking.

can cause the needle to point in the wrong direction. Check the potential disturbance of objects by moving them close to the compass and watching to see if the needle moves. Usually a few feet is an adequate distance to prevent objects from influencing the compass. Be aware that power lines and steel structures like bridges might also disturb the compass needle.

In addition to having a north-pointing needle, a compass is a circle divided into 360 degrees. North corresponds to 0/360 degrees, east is 90 degrees, south is 180 degrees, and west is 270 degrees. The other degree readings indicate the directions out from the center of the compass. These degrees can be used to determine and follow a direction of travel, even if landmarks are obscured by fog or darkness. But it can be tricky to maintain a straight line by following only a degree heading.

It takes some practice to become proficient in applying compass bearings to on-the-water navigation, but it is an important and invaluable skill on any wilderness trip.

Parts of a Compass

- The needle indicates magnetic north.

- Housing with degree markings divides a circle into 360 degrees and allows you to maintain a direction of travel.

- Base, direction-of-travel arrow indicates the directional bearing the compass is pointed.

- The ruler along the base of the compass allows you to accurately measure distances on the map.

Taking a Bearing

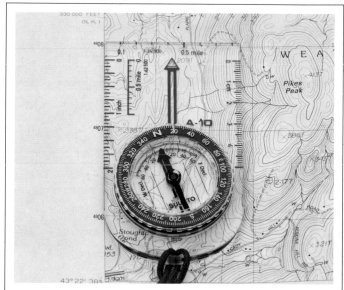

- Point the direction-of-travel arrow at your target destination.

- Turn the compass housing until the north-pointing needle is lined up with the 0/360 degree mark.

- The degree indicated at the base of the direction-of-travel arrow is your bearing.

- This is your bearing from your starting point. If you stay in a straight line and follow the bearing, you will end up where you started. If you get off course, the same degree heading will point to a different spot.

MAP & COMPASS

Combine map and compass to enhance your navigational ability to "stay found"

Maps are easier to read if they are oriented to your surroundings. Use the compass to determine north and then turn your map to correspond. This can make it easier to correlate land forms with symbols on the map.

Maps are usually oriented so that the top of the map is north. Note that this is *geographic,* or actual, north and not magnetic north. Magnetic north is several hundred miles away from true north. Consequently, there is a difference between "north" on your compass and "north" on your map. This difference is called *declination*. On nautical charts this difference is called *variation*. The imaginary line that passes through both magnetic and true north is called the *agonic*

Orient the Map

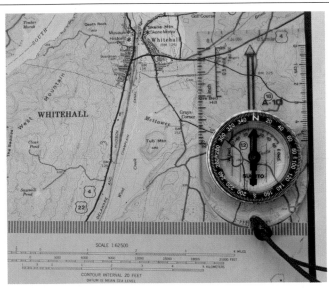

- On almost all maps the top is north but check the compass rose to be positive.

- Turn the housing of the compass to align the direction-of-travel arrow and the marking for north, 0/360 degrees.

- Lay the compass on the map so that the edge of the compass base lines up with a longitude (north-south) line on the map.

- Turn map and compass so that the needle is aligned with the 0/360-degree marking. The map is now oriented to the north.

Declination

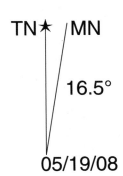

- Declination is the difference between true north and magnetic north. Your compass points magnetic north, but maps are oriented to true north.

- The difference in declination is represented on maps by a diagram showing the degrees between magnetic north and true north, giving a direction of east or west.

- If declination is east, subtract that number from your compass bearing for true north.

- If declination is west, add that number to your compass bearing for true north.

line. On this line declination is zero. The difference between magnetic north and true north becomes greater the farther you are from the agonic line. In the United States the agonic line runs diagonally through eastern Wisconsin to the gulf coast of Florida.

Declination is determined by how far east or west of true north is from magnetic north. For example, the declination in Oregon is about 20 degrees east, and in Vermont declination is about 15 degrees west. To account for this difference, look at your map for the declination for the place you are in. If the declination is *west,* add those degrees to your compass bearing to get true north. If the declination is *east,* subtract those degrees from your compass bearing to get true north.

In the far west or northeast of the United States, declination can impact the accuracy of your navigation, although, in general, if you keep careful track of where you are on the map and stay oriented to your physical surroundings, you won't have any problems.

Taking a Bearing from a Map

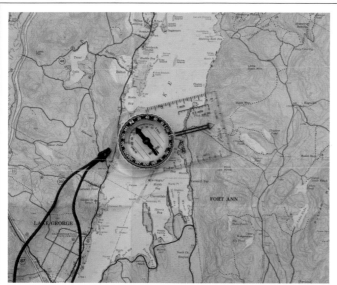

- If it is foggy or if landforms are confusing, you may not be able to see exactly where you are headed.

- You can determine your bearing, the degree reading you want to go, by combining your map and compass.

- Orient map to north. Place the middle of the compass on your current location. Turn the direction-of-travel arrow to point at your destination while keeping the needle aligned with the 0/360-degree marking.

- Follow the bearing indicated at the base of the direction-of-travel arrow.

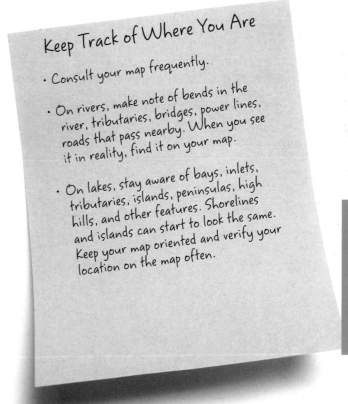

Keep Track of Where You Are

- Consult your map frequently.

- On rivers, make note of bends in the river, tributaries, bridges, power lines, roads that pass nearby. When you see it in reality, find it on your map.

- On lakes, stay aware of bays, inlets, tributaries, islands, peninsulas, high hills, and other features. Shorelines and islands can start to look the same. Keep your map oriented and verify your location on the map often.

NATURAL THREATS

Potential hazards lurk everywhere, but most can be avoided with common sense

The purpose of focusing on the hazards of canoeing is not to instill fear or to overemphasize the dangers involved. By being cognizant of the hazards, you can avoid them in most cases. In the event that the weather turns nasty or a mishap occurs, you are best able to respond when you have anticipated this occurrence and planned ahead.

Avoiding dangerous weather is the first step. Check the forecast for where you are headed. Consider any weather forecast longer than two days out unreliable. Be prepared for dramatic changes in temperature, storms, and wind. While out paddling keep one eye on the weather. Be alert for changes in wind speed and direction. Notice the first signs of

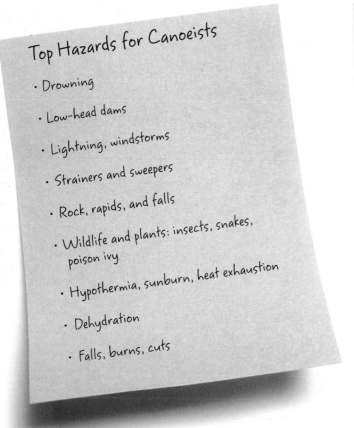

Top Hazards for Canoeists

• Drowning

• Low-head dams

• Lightning, windstorms

• Strainers and sweepers

• Rock, rapids, and falls

• Wildlife and plants: insects, snakes, poison ivy

• Hypothermia, sunburn, heat exhaustion

• Dehydration

• Falls, burns, cuts

Be Ready for Extremes

- Even the most careful outdoors person can get caught in threatening weather. In high winds, tornadoes, or thunderstorms, seek the best shelter available.

- Avoid solitary tall trees and assess whether other trees or branches might get knocked down by the wind.

- If adequate shelter is not available in a lightning storm, minimize your power of attraction by squatting or sitting as low as possible.

- Decrease your conductivity by sitting on a foam pad.

COIDs (clouds of impending doom) and be ready to get off the water. Lightning is not something to gamble on.

Consult the list of ten essentials (see below) and carry this gear with you. Depending on anticipated conditions, you may wish to supplement with an emergency blanket, material for ground insulation (foam pad), and signaling devices like whistles, mirrors, or flares.

If you do get caught in an electrical storm, paddle to shore *immediately*. Get out of your canoe and avoid tall trees that might attract lightning. If in the open, crouch or sit to lower your height.

Be alert for wildlife. Bears will be attracted to food. Keeping your camp clean and food off the ground in a bear bag will minimize their visits. If a bear does appear, make noise! Scream, shout, bang pots together, stand tall and spread your arms to appear more threatening. If you encounter bears, moose, or other large animals with young, move away immediately. Do not approach the young and do not come between a mother and her young. Mothers do not tolerate any perceived threat to their offspring.

The Ten Essentials

- Full water bottle
- Extra food
- Extra clothing, including rain gear
- Waterproofed matches
- Candle or other firestarter
- First aid kit
- Pocketknife
- Map of the area
- Compass
- Flashlight with extra batteries

Handy Emergency Supplies

- Supplement your standard first aid kit with other handy items in your gear.

- A pocketknife or multitool is indispensable. Candles are excellent to start fires, and their glowing light inspires hope and confidence in a grim situation.

- An emergency blanket, although lightweight and small, contains heat and blocks the wind.

- Bring extra matches. Have waterproofed matches in several spots among your equipment. A small coil of light nylon cord has more uses than can be listed.

FIRST AID FOR CUTS
Cuts and scrapes are common injuries

For scrapes, irrigate the injury with clean water, washing out any dirt or grit. Cover with gauze and a bandage.

With any cut that is bleeding, the first priority is to apply pressure to stop the bleeding. With a very small cut, a Band-Aid may be adequate. With a larger cut, use gauze, a clean cloth, or your hand if there is nothing else to press firmly on the wound and maintain pressure. Firm, direct pressure will stop almost all bleeding. As gauze or cloth becomes blood soaked, quickly remove your hand, add more cloth or gauze on top, and replace your hand to resume the pressure. It may take fifteen minutes or longer for the bleeding to stop. If possible, elevate the injury. Do not remove the cloth or gauze to see if bleeding has stopped! If bleeding appears to be halted, tie the dressings in place with gauze strips or tape.

After bleeding has been controlled, treat to prevent infection. *Wash your hands.* Use clean latex or rubber gloves if

Deep Cuts

- Try not to get too alarmed by a little blood. With small cuts, bleeding helps clean dirt out of the wound.

- Don't panic if you see what seems like a lot of blood. Blood is a message that you need to do something.

- What you need to do is stop the bleeding. The first priority with major wounds is always to stop the bleeding.

- Apply direct pressure immediately.

Direct Pressure

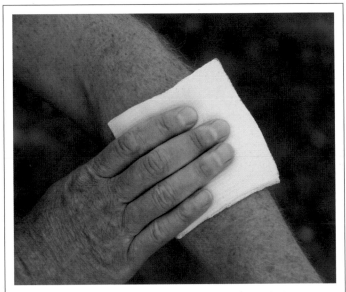

- Do not allow severe bleeding to continue while rummaging around for a sterile dressing or gloves.

- Use a bandanna, other clothing, or your bare hand if necessary. When a sterile dressing is available, place it directly over the wound.

- If the dressing becomes soaked with blood, place additional dressings on top of the old ones and continue direct pressure.

- Don't stop! It may take a little while. Direct pressure stops the bleeding in nearly all instances. Elevating the wound helps slow bleeding.

available to reduce risk of contamination of the wound and to protect the caregiver. *Wash in and around the wound* to remove bacteria and foreign matter. Any dirty wound should be irrigated with large amounts of water. *Cover with a sterile dressing* and bandage in place. *Change the dressing daily.* Monitor the wound for infection: foul- smelling pus, redness around the wound, swelling, fever, considerable pain.

Make sure the person receives medical attention promptly. Minor wounds can be treated, and the trip can continue. Large, gaping wounds will require evacuation and immedi-

ate medical care. Err on the side of caution. Do not risk infection or permanent injury just to finish a canoe trip.

Direct pressure will stop almost all bleeding. Elevate the wound to help slow bleeding.

Tape Dressing in Place

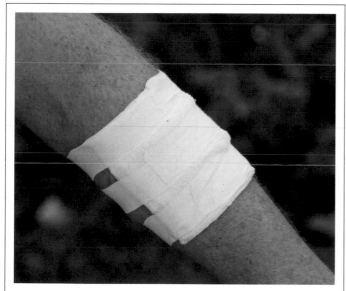

- Don't lift dressings to see if the bleeding has stopped! This might cause bleeding to start again. Add additional dressings or absorbent material as needed. Maintain direct, firm pressure.

- If the bleeding seems to have stopped, add a little more dressing and then

tape securely in place.

- Wrap a layer of gauze around the limb before taping to protect skin or when the dressing is removed.

- After taping, assess areas below the wound to make sure that the dressing hasn't cut off all circulation.

Tie Dressing in Place

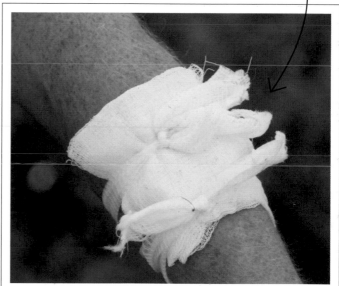

- If you don't have tape, the dressing can be tied in place using gauze rollers, strips of cloth, or elastic wrap.

- Be sure to check areas below the dressing for circulation. Press on the skin with the tip of your thumb or finger. Hold it for a second and release.

- The skin will be pale and should return to normal color as the blood refills that area.

- If the skin stays pale, you may need to loosen the dressing to allow blood to circulate.

FIRST AID FOR BURNS

When stoves, fires, and candles cause burns, respond according to the burn's severity

Minor burns that do not form blisters involve only the first layer of skin. There is reddening of the skin, mild pain, and slight swelling. These burns can be treated by immersing the burned part in cold water at once. No other treatment is necessary. The patient may take aspirin for pain.

A *partial-thickness burn* involves the top layers of skin. There is blistering, moderate pain, and moderate swelling.

A *full-thickness burn* involves damage to all layers of skin and to underlying tissues; tissues may appear white or charred. Pain may be severe or absent if nerve endings have been killed by the burn.

To treat these major burns, cool the burn at once with copi-

Burns

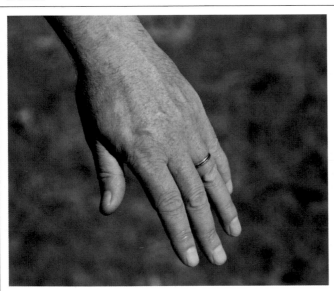

- Burns range from superficial, involving only the top layer of skin, to life threatening.

- Life-threatening burns include partial-thickness burns covering more than 10 percent of the body and full-thickness burns covering 5 percent of the body.

- Burns suffered while outdoors are commonly caused by fires, stoves, cooking accidents, candles.

- Some of the worst burns occur when a tent catches fire with someone inside. Do all cooking outside. Do not allow open flames or smoking in tents.

Cool the Burn

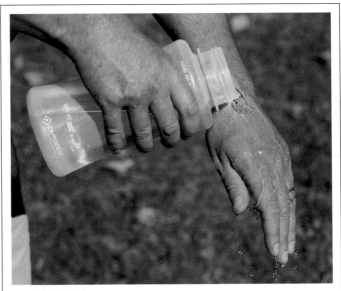

- The first task is to stop the burning. Pour lots of cool water on the burn.

- The burned area can be immersed in cold water if the burn is superficial or partial-thickness with unbroken blisters.

- Remove burned clothing. Small pieces of adhered cloth should not be removed. Do not break blisters. Broken blisters are more likely to become infected.

- Remove rings or other jewelry from the burned area.

ous amounts of clean, cool water. Remove all rings or other jewelry from the burned area. Carefully wash the burned area with a sterile gauze pad, soap, and sterile (boiled and cooled) water. Spread a thin layer of antibiotic ointment over the wound and cover with a dry, sterile dressing.

Pain can be relieved by wrapping the burned area with additional layers of dressing to exclude air. Elevate the burned extremity. Assess the patient and look for signs of shock.

ZOOM

Shock is a life-threatening condition that can result from a large burn, major bleeding, dehydration, or severe allergic reaction. Signs of shock include weak, rapid pulse; pale, cold, damp skin; a drop in blood pressure; confusion, weakness, or loss of consciousness. Have the person lie down with feet elevated. Maintain body warmth with a blanket. If conscious, give sips of water. Treat wounds. Be very gentle. Keep the person calm.

Clean the Burned Area

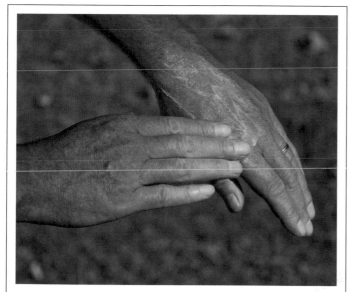

- After the burn has been cooled, wash the affected area with a gauze pad, soap, and clean water.

- For a partial-thickness burn where there is an open wound, use a sterile gauze pad and sterile water.

- Water can be sterilized by boiling for one minute. Water must be cooled to body temperature before using.

- After washing the burned area, apply a thin layer of antibiotic ointment.

Protect

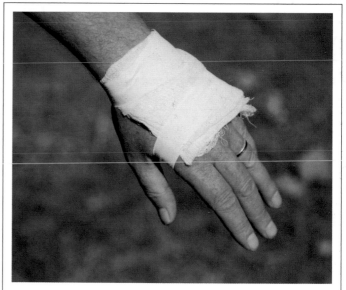

- Cover the wound with a dry, sterile dressing and tape in place.

- To lessen pain, add more dressing to keep air from the wound. If the burn is on an arm or leg, keep that area elevated.

- Change the dressing every day. If the patient has suffered a major burn, arrange for medical attention immediately.

CARING FOR HYPOTHERMIA

Stay alert for signs of hypothermia; it can be subtle but extremely dangerous

Hypothermia is a serious condition that can gradually develop, and can prove deadly. Hypothermia occurs when the body is creating less heat than it is losing, and the core body temperature starts to drop.

Hypothermia can result from immersion in very cold water and the person cannot get into dry clothes, or reduce their exposure to wind and cold air. Hypothermia can also occur gradually in more moderate weather. Wet clothing and brisk winds can pull away heat without the person fully realizing it.

A person experiencing mild hypothermia will shiver, complain of being cold, have difficulty using their hands, and display attitude changes: withdrawal, apathy, or irritability. Respond by

Contributing Factors

- The condition of hypothermia, the body losing more heat than it creates, can come about rapidly or very gradually.

- Hypothermia can occur quickly due to immersion in cold water on a cold day.

- Gradual onset can take place on a cool day if a person is not wearing adequate clothing.

- Perspiration or rain can dampen clothing, and wind can wick away body heat. A person who has not eaten adequate food will be more susceptible.

Treating Hypothermia

- End exposure. Get the person out of the cold and wet and away from the wind.

- Replace wet clothing with dry or add insulation to clothing—wrap the person in a blanket or sleeping bag.

- Get the person into a warm environment. Offer warm liquids or food if the person is conscious and able to swallow.

- Treat the person gently; hypothermia slows the function of the body and can make it vulnerable to shocks and rapid movement.

getting the person warm and dry. Get out of the wind. Replace wet clothing. Give him warm drinks and food.

Symptoms of moderate to severe hypothermia include: mental confusion, violent shivering, slurred speech, stumbling, unresponsiveness, decreased pulse and breathing, cessation of shivering and physical collapse. This is a very fragile state; treat the person gently. End exposure by covering the person and getting them out of the wind. Remove wet clothing and place victim in a sleeping bag or blanket with another person to re-warm the victim's core temperature. Arrange for medical attention and evacuation immediately.

Untreated hypothermia can progress very rapidly. If someone in your party gets immersed on a cool day respond quickly. Change clothes. Build a fire. Make some hot cocoa. Keep them engaged through conversation and continually monitor their mental and physical status.

It is worth emphasizing that the hypothermic person may not know it! Seriously impaired judgment is a common symptom. If you suspect someone is not doing well, *insist* on a break to get warmed up and rested. It may save a life.

Rewarming the Body

- For moderate hypothermia, the person needs external heat. Get the person near a fire if possible. Insulate from the ground and cover well with sleeping bags and blankets.

- Fill water bottles with hot water and put into a sleeping bag. Put metal water bottles into a sock to prevent burning the victim's skin.

- For severe hypothermia, the person needs external, gentle warmth immediately. Place the person in a sleeping bag with one or two other people to provide skin-to-skin contact.

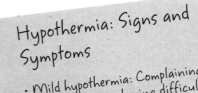

Hypothermia: Signs and Symptoms

- Mild hypothermia: Complaining of cold, shivering, having difficulty using the hands, becoming withdrawn and apathetic

- Moderate hypothermia: Lethargy, confusion, refusal to recognize the condition, uncontrollable shivering, slurred speech, stumbling

- Severe hypothermia: Unresponsiveness, decreased pulse and breathing, cessation of shivering, physical collapse

HEAT EXHAUSTION & LYME DISEASE

Be alert for conditions resulting from exertion or exposure to disease-bearing critters

Heat exhaustion occurs when the body gains heat more quickly than it loses heat. The body overheats. Heat exhaustion usually occurs during warm weather, but it does not have to be hot. Exertion and dehydration are key factors in heat exhaustion. The skin will appear pale and damp with profuse sweating. The pulse rate and oral temperature will be slightly elevated. The patient may experience nausea, weakness, dizziness, thirst, or headache.

Get the patient into a cooler, shady environment. Water should be given in small sips. After the patient has cooled down, replace lost electrolytes by giving bouillon, other salty foods, or an electrolyte replacement drink. Recovery may

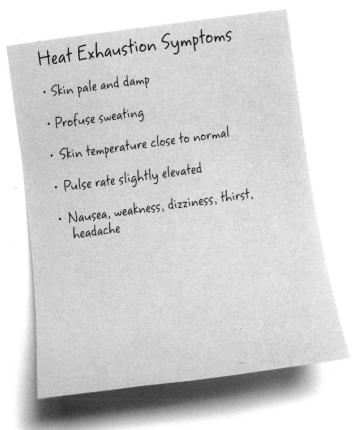

Heat Exhaustion Symptoms

- Skin pale and damp
- Profuse sweating
- Skin temperature close to normal
- Pulse rate slightly elevated
- Nausea, weakness, dizziness, thirst, headache

Heat Exhaustion

- Get the person into a cool, shady environment. If no natural shade is available, rig a tarp or turn a canoe upside down on the shore.

- Give the person sips of water. Have the person lie down and raise his or her feet. After the person cools down, offer salty foods.

- Allow plenty of time for the person to rest and return to normal. Depending on severity, this could take several hours to a whole day.

- Carefully observe the person for recurrence of heat exhaustion.

take up to twenty-four hours.

Ticks are common and can transmit many infectious diseases, including Rocky Mountain Spotted Fever, Q Fever, and Lyme disease. The initial sign of Lyme disease is a distinctive "bull's-eye" rash surrounding the bite that appears within three days to five weeks. Other symptoms include muscular pain, fatigue, and low fever. Lyme disease is often misdiagnosed as the flu. Lyme disease can be successfully treated with antibiotics if it is recognized. Untreated, Lyme disease can lead to serious problems with the nervous system, heart,

and joints. Tick-borne diseases can be prevented by wearing protective clothing and checking the body for attached ticks. Hats, long sleeves, and pants may stop ticks from crawling into hair or onto arms and legs. Spraying clothing with DEET may also dissuade ticks from attaching. Prompt removal of an attached tick lessens the likelihood of infection. Grasp the tick as close as possible to the skin surface using blunt tweezers or fingers. Pull out the tick using steady pressure so that tick body parts are not left in the wound. After removing the tick, wash and disinfect the bitten area.

Ticks

- Ticks are small to very small creatures that feed on the blood of mammals.

- They drop from trees or other foliage onto a person or animal and then crawl into hair, inside clothing, or even under watch bands to find a suitable place to feed.

- It takes some time for a tick to get attached and suck out blood.

- Ticks often carry diseases, including Rocky Mountain Spotted Fever and Lyme disease.

Prevent Tick Bites

- In tick-infested areas, wear a hat and other protective clothing: tight-fitting collars, sleeves, and pants leg cuffs.

- Spray clothing with DEET.

- Carefully inspect the whole body for ticks. Check very closely in hair, groin, and between toes.

- Remove unattached ticks, being careful not to crush or squeeze the tick body. Wash hands afterward.

- If a tick is attached, use tweezers or fingers to pull out using steady pressure. Wash bite and disinfect.

179

CANOE REPAIRS

Canoes and paddles can sustain all sorts of punctures, breakage, or other damage

The nature of a repair depends on the material the canoe is made of and the extent of the damage incurred.

For aluminum, a leaking rivet can often be fixed by placing the outside of the boat at the rivet against a large rock and hitting the inside portion of the rivet with a hammer, the back of a hatchet, or a rock. The holes created by missing rivets can be blocked with duct tape applied on both sides of the canoe. For best adhesion, clean and dry the canoe surfaces before applying tape. Damaged thwarts, gunwales, and seats can be repaired by bending to their original position and lashing them in place with a branch and some wire (or duct tape). Holes and cracks can be repaired by bending

Repair Kit?

- Anything can get broken or damaged. Think of a repair kit as a first aid kit for your boat. You need just enough materials to keep the canoe seaworthy until the end of the trip.

- What are the most likely repairs needed? You must

consider your boat and the type of trip you will be on.

- Be prepared to patch holes and tears in the hull, replace or splint thwarts, reattach seats, and replace bolts or other hardware.

Repair Kit!

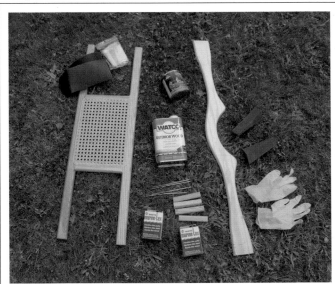

- Commercial repair kits are available for any canoe.

- Fiberglass or Kevlar kits contain various resins, epoxy, or other glues to fill holes, and include sandpaper for smoothing the patched area. Aluminum kits include replacement rivets and a rivet tool.

- Replacement thwarts, seats, and hardware might also be included.

- Devise your own repair kit. Bring the minimum you'll need to get your canoe to the landing site.

the metal back into place and sealing the area with chewing gum, duct tape, or epoxy.

For plastic or Royalex, minor (and often major) dents can be repaired by warming the canoe in the sun and then pressing the hull back into shape. Damaged thwarts, seats, and gunwales can be repaired with wire or duct tape and some kind of "splint." Holes and cracks can be temporarily repaired with duct tape, as with aluminum.

For Kevlar or fiberglass, workable temporary field repairs can be accomplished with duct tape. Commercial repair kits containing resin, a catalyst, fiberglass cloth, and instructions are available.

Depending on the length of your trip and distance from "civilization," you might wish to supplement your roll of duct tape with some of the following materials: an assortment of rustproof nuts and bolts, screwdriver, pliers, flexible steel wire, caulking compound, epoxy, and a commercial repair kit for your type of boat.

Duct Tape

- Bring a roll of duct tape. It can be used to patch holes, splice broken thwarts, and keep split paddles together.

- Duct tape also works for mending clothing and fixing torn or broken shoes.

- To improve adhesion, clean and dry the object that will be taped. Wiping the area with rubbing alcohol and letting it evaporate will give the best surface for tape to stick to.

- Reinforce any patch by taping inside and outside. Replace or supplement tape as needed.

Other Repair Items

- Bring along a multitool or a pair of pliers and a couple of screwdrivers.

- Include a small roll of fine wire, needles and strong thread, and safety pins.

- The back of a hatchet can be used as a hammer. A carefully selected rock will work also.

- Bring a small selection of nuts and bolts. They can hold a thwart or seat or replace missing rivets.

COMFORT & SAFETY
Comfortable kids make happy paddlers

Canoeing with children can be an amazing family experience. It is great fun being on the water together, exploring nature and braving the elements.

However, a successful paddling trip with children requires a little planning and preparation. It is vital that each child have a properly fitted and comfortable PFD. If the child finds the PFD uncomfortable, just keeping it on the child can become an ongoing battle. Resist the urge to emphasize the threat

of drowning just to make the child follow your directions. The goal is a *healthy respect* for the water, not a crippling fear. Make it fun by bringing the kids along to the gear store to help select their own PFD. Before ever getting into the canoe, have children float around in the water in their PFDs. This is fun for them and lets them know that their heads will stay above water.

Dress children as you dress yourself: comfortable clothes in

A Great Family Outing

- Paddling is an awesome family experience. It is a fun way to model respect for the environment and responsible enjoyment of the outdoors.

- Canoeing can include watching animals, swimming, fishing, or just floating around together.

- Children love to be out on the water and will appreciate learning how to be safe while having great adventures.

- Include the kids as much as possible while planning your outings and making preparations.

Child's PFD

- It is vitally important to maintain a high level of safety and alertness.

- Purchase each family member a comfortable PFD that fits well.

- Insist that children wear their PFDs and that the PFDs are fastened.

- Adults must also wear their PFDs! If you don't wear your life jacket, the kids will resist wearing theirs. If you capsize without your PFD on, you will be less able to assist children and more likely to drown yourself. Wear your PFD!

layers that can be easily removed when warm and added to when chilly. An active paddler will stay much warmer than a sitting passenger, so be sure to bring along plenty of clothes, hats, and gloves. Also, have a seat cushion for anyone sitting on the bottom of the canoe. It helps keep the person warm and provides some distance from any water that gets into the canoe.

Bring along lots of healthy food, snacks, and drinks. Kids burn up lots of calories outdoors and need frequent snacks to maintain energy and interest. Pause often to snack and encourage the drinking of water. Make sure that everyone has an individual water bottle.

Scale back your expectations in terms of paddling distance and difficulty. Make the goal being out as a family, not necessarily paddling *x* miles or visiting *x* number of islands.

Plan for Enjoyment

- Carefully consider the needs of children based on their ages and abilities.

- Younger children won't be able to paddle yet, so make sure they are comfortable.

- Each child should have his own seat cushion and perhaps a toy or two that will keep him occupied if he tires of looking at scenery. Bring toys that can get dirty or lost without causing a crisis.

- Each family member should have a water bottle. Encourage frequent drinks of water and tasty snacks.

Sun Protection

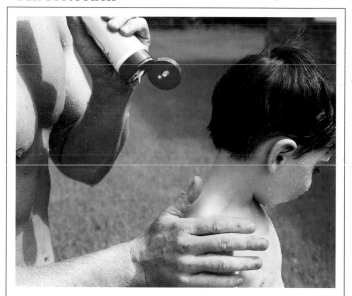

- A sunburned child is a miserable child. Apply sunscreen before getting out in the sun. Bring loose, comfortable clothing to help block UV rays.

- Cover all exposed skin and skin that is likely to be exposed. Hats just don't stay on small heads.

- If swimming is a likelihood, apply sunscreen anywhere not covered by the swimsuit.

- Drinking water helps prevent dehydration and overheating. Invent "drinking games" and toasts to keep everyone well hydrated.

HAVE FUN! SEE NATURE

On the water on a hot day? Be sure to get into the water!

Most kids love swimming. It seems almost like cruel and unusual punishment to take them out paddling but not let them get wet. Of course, all standard precautions should be taken, but if it's warm out make sure to bring along swimsuits. If swimming is a possibility, budget in enough time for a dip. (Swimming is good for grownups, too!)

Assess the water conditions anywhere you let the kids swim. Consider the current and check *under* the water for logs, rocks, and other potentially dangerous objects. Never jump, or let anyone else jump, into water that has not been checked out. Unless you are in a maintained swimming area, everyone should have some kind of shoes on to protect feet. Even if kids are wearing PFDs while they swim, be sure an adult keeps an eye on swimmers at all times.

Paddling takes place outside, so keep an eye open for interesting birds, reptiles, mammals, trees, and cloud formations.

Get into the Water!

- If the weather and the water are warm enough, be sure to bring swimsuits and towels.

- Use all standard precautions when people are swimming. Pay attention to currents and objects in the water.

- When people are swimming nearby, be careful not to hit them with the boat.

- Check with local health officials about the levels of E. coli and other bacteria. Waterways tend to have higher levels of pollutants immediately after heavy rains.

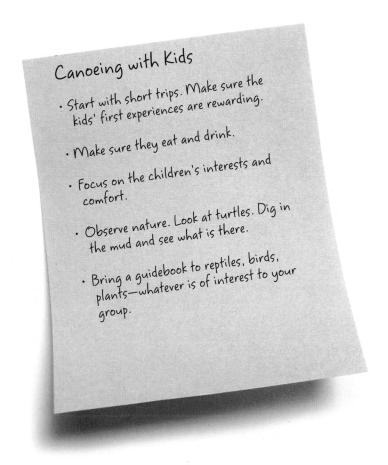

Canoeing with Kids

- Start with short trips. Make sure the kids' first experiences are rewarding.

- Make sure they eat and drink.

- Focus on the children's interests and comfort.

- Observe nature. Look at turtles. Dig in the mud and see what is there.

- Bring a guidebook to reptiles, birds, plants—whatever is of interest to your group.

Become familiar with the common birds in your locale. Then, when you see an unusual bird, it will be easier to identify it. But unless your children are especially interested in names, don't get hung up on identifying.

Watch what the birds are doing. Even "common" birds engage in fascinating behaviors. Small sparrows and blackbirds will gang up and "mob" hawks, owls, and crows. What are the birds eating? Are they eating seeds, insects, fish, other birds? Which ones swoop around, and which ones stay in the shrubs along the shore? Watch for herons lurking in the shadows and ducks dabbling for plants.

Bring along easy-to-use nature guides. Bird and wildflower books organized by color are often a good choice for youngsters. Consider an inexpensive pair of binoculars for anyone old enough to operate them.

Red-tailed Hawk

- The red-tailed hawk is one of the largest and most common of the raptors.

- Hawks can often be seen from the seat of a canoe as they circle over open fields along rivers looking for mice, snakes, birds, or insects to eat.

- Bald eagles and ospreys are often seen while canoeing. Watch carefully, and you may see them dive into the water for fish, their primary food.

- Another common sight is turkey vultures gliding high on the wind currents.

Barn Swallow

- There are frequently several species of swallow performing all kinds of aerodynamic stunts over waterways.

- Swallows swoop and flap constantly so they can feed on airborne insects.

- The barn swallow, startlingly colored blue-black on its back and orange-cinnamon underneath, can be readily identified by its forked tail (remember that pitch*forks* are kept in the *barn*).

- Northern rough-winged, bank, and tree swallows are also common through much of the United States.

WILDLIFE

Watch for mammals, insects, and turtles: They are out there!

There are many species to encounter while you are out paddling. You might ask your children what animals they think they might see. Young children are often a surprising fount of nature lore that they have absorbed while in school, learned from friends, read about in books, or seen on television programs.

The trick to seeing mammals is to remain reasonably quiet and keep scanning the shorelines and open spaces along the banks. Be especially attentive when turning bends in rivers or rounding points of land on lakes. Most mammals will bolt or hide at the first sign of unexpected humans. A canoe allows you to approach quietly and from a direction that most animals aren't expecting humans: the water. You might see deer, foxes, coyotes, raccoons, and porcupines as well as squirrels, rabbits, and chipmunks. In remote areas you may be lucky enough to see moose, bears, or wolves!

Deer

- Although primarily nocturnal, the white-tailed deer may be active at any time.

- Deer eat green plants, including aquatic ones in the summer, acorns, and other nuts, corn, and woody vegetation. White-tailed deer are good swimmers. Their winter coat has hollow hairs that fill with air, making them very buoyant.

- When nervous, the white-tailed deer snorts through its nose and stamps its hooves. This alerts other nearby deer to danger. If alarmed, the deer raises its tail, revealing a flash of white.

Muskrat

- Muskrats are large rodents, up to 24 inches in length from nose to tail. They have dense, glossy fur—dark brown above, lighter on the side, paler on the throat.

- Muskrats eat mostly aquatic vegetation like cattails, rushes, water lilies, and pond weeds.

- Muskrat houses, or lodges, are similar to beaver lodges but much smaller.

- Muskrats can remain submerged for long periods (fifteen minutes or longer) and will travel great distances underwater.

Don't forget to scan the water for swimming mammals. Muskrats, beavers, and river otters can be more prevalent than you imagine.

Although large animals are initially the most intriguing, don't neglect some of the smaller or more secretive inhabitants of the great outdoors. Painted, musk, map, soft-shelled, and snapping turtles are common in many parts of the United States. Turtles can often be seen basking on logs and rocks along the banks. Approach quietly! They will plop off into the water at the slightest noise.

Mosquitoes and black flies can be unbelievably annoying, but some of their insect relatives like damselflies, dragonflies, butterflies, moths, and beetles can be equally beautiful and captivating. Attune yourself to the wide array of insects you might encounter. Try observing insects through binoculars to get a close encounter without disturbing them. What are the insects eating? What is eating the insects?

Damselfly

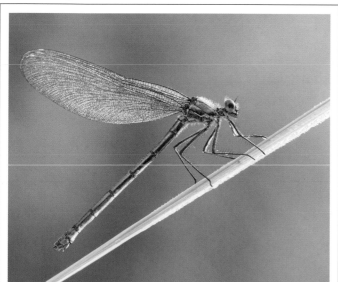

- Dragonflies and damselflies are common insects in the order Odonata. There are over four hundred species.

- Dragonflies are larger and sturdier. They hold their wings horizontally (open) while at rest. The smaller, more delicate damselflies hold their wings vertically,

above their body.

- They have inconspicuous antennae but huge compound eyes that cover almost their whole head.

- Dragonflies are known as *mosquito hawks* because they eat so many of the pesky insects.

Painted Turtle

- The painted turtle is one of the most common turtles. Its upper shell is dark green to almost black with red on the edges.

- The lower shell is yellow, tinged with red. The head, neck, and legs are dark green with bright yellow or red stripes.

- Painted turtles eat aquatic insects, fish, crayfish, snails, tadpoles, and plants. They can live fifteen to twenty-five years or longer.

- These turtles often bask in the sun in large groups.

MACROINVERTEBRATES

Many fascinating creatures can be also discovered living in the bottom sediments

A simple kick net or screen strainer can be used to collect a dozen or more small critters that live among the rocks, stones, and plants of a river bottom. Although at first a little apprehensive, most children become very enthusiastic about collecting and closely studying macroinvertebrates.

A kick net is a piece of cloth netting, about 2½ by 3 feet, connected to two wooden dowels. One person holds the net across the current while facing upstream. A second person, starting 6 or 8 feet upstream of the net, moves toward the net while scuffing up the bottom of the river. This scuffing kicks sediment and critters up into the current, which carries them into the net.

Collect Critters

- Study the small creatures that live on river bottoms.

- Build a kick net from cloth netting and two sturdy sticks. You can also use a wire strainer to gather macroinvertebrates.

- Hold the net or strainer underwater, just at the level of the river bottom. Stir up the sediment just *upstream* from the net.

- The net will catch critters stirred up from the sediment. Lift the net from the water, pick out the critters with your fingers, and place into a basin of water.

Damselfly Nymph

- These are among the most distinctive and common of the critters you will find in our rivers.

- Damselfly nymphs are dull colored and fairly slim. They have three leaf-shaped gills at the tip of the abdomen.

- These three gills look like tails. Many nymphs have lost one or more of these gills.

- Damselfly nymphs are predators and will eat anything they can catch and hold on to, including insects, snails, tadpoles, or small fish.

The net person then lifts the net and lets the water drain off. All eyes are then focused on the net. Look for squirming little critters and then lift them with your fingers into a pan of water. Collect everything you see. In most locales there will not be anything that is poisonous or will bite or sting. The only likely exception is a crayfish. To pick up a crayfish without getting pinched, just push the crayfish into the net with your thumb and forefinger and grab its back behind the front legs and pincers.

After kicking a few times or using a strainer to scrape the river bottom, take your pan of water to shore and investigate what you found. There are hundreds of species of mayfly larvae. You are also likely to see damselfly, caddisfly, stonefly, or dragonfly larvae. Look for water pennies, freshwater leeches, and fingernail clams. To help identify critters, you could bring along a pond life guide or print out a dichotomous key to macroinvertebrates (see "Resources" in Chapter 20). Be sure to return all critters to the river when you are done.

Mayfly Nymph

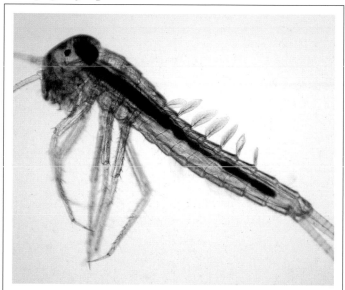

- There are at least 222 species of mayflies in the Great Lakes region and over 600 in North America.

- Mayfly nymphs require relatively clean water to survive. The nymphs feed on algae, diatoms, aquatic plants, and small invertebrate animals.

- As the mayfly nymph grows, it sheds its exoskeleton frequently. Thirty to fifty molts are not uncommon for some species.

- Upon reaching adulthood, mayflies are solely focused on the mating process and die soon afterward.

Adult Damselfly

- Does this adult look like the damselfly nymph? Adult damselflies look like small dragonflies. Their coloring can be varied, including bright blue and emerald green.

- Transformation from nymph to adult takes place on a plant stem, rock, or some other object emerging from the water.

- The nymph's outer skin splits lengthwise along its back, and the adult emerges.

- The new adult must wait for its wings to dry before it can fly.

ADAPTATIONS FOR THE DISABLED

Canoeing is an excellent form of recreation for many people with physical disabilities

Paddling offers many excellent therapeutic benefits for people of all ages and ability levels. Exposure to nature in itself is beneficial, and paddling also provides exercise and opportunities for increased independence, challenges to overcome, and fun with friends and family.

When paddling with people with disabilities, consider what

impairments they are challenged with and how those impairments may impact their experience in a canoe. A person who is usually confined to a wheelchair may need no further assistance than being lifted into the canoe seat. Or he may need a seat back or perhaps a strap to help him maintain balance or position. A visually impaired paddler may be able to

Canoeing Is Easily Adaptable

- Adaptations vary with the type of disability a person has.

- If the paddler has difficulty sitting unsupported, modify the seat with back, side supports. Lowering it a few inches improves balance.

- If there is difficulty enter-

ing or exiting the canoe, mounting grab handles on the boat may help the paddler pull herself into position.

- Pay special attention to fitting PFDs and additional floatation if needed. Make sure that PFDs will keep a person's head above water.

Modified Paddle

- Some people need adapted paddle grips to be able to hold on to the paddle. Velcro strap systems and adapted mitts attach the paddle handle to the person's hands.

- For a paddler with one arm, use a wooden kickboard with a handhold cutout.

- There are also paddle blades combined with a crutchlike upper portion for one-armed paddlers.

- Some companies make attachments for waterproof prostheses that allow the person to hold the paddle.

perform all components of canoeing with verbal guidance. A paddler with arthritis, cerebral palsy, or multiple sclerosis may experience difficulty holding a paddle. An adapted paddle grip can often lead to success.

When paddling with someone with a physical disability, the most important element is a positive attitude. Relax and communicate as you would with someone without a disability. Do not assume that assistance is needed. Ask first and then help as needed.

Plan where you will be paddling and consider accessibility at the site. If people in your party might have trouble lifting things or moving gear or themselves, account for this in your planning. Perhaps a wheeled canoe cart will be useful in moving boats.

Any adaptations needed to ensure a successful paddling experience must be suited to the needs of the paddler. Use as much standard equipment as possible and adapt only as needed. The simpler a system can be, the better.

Pedal Power?

- There are paddle wheel devices available that can be added to canoes.

- This accessory turns your canoe into a paddleboat that can be propelled with either hands or feet.

- According to the manufacturer, the paddle wheel is easy to assemble and adjusts to fit any canoe. It weighs about 7 pounds.

- As with any new equipment, first try it out and see how it works before planning an outing using it.

Why Paddle with the Disabled?

- Paddling emphasizes ability, provides good exercise, and is therapeutic for both mind and body.

- It encourages independence, develops self-confidence, and improves self-esteem.

- The disabled can participate with family and friends.

- Paddling is readily available and requires minimal adaptations.

- It increases upper-body strength and range of motion.

- A wide variety of ages and abilities can enjoy it.

PLANNING THE DAY TRIP
Your first canoe outings should be one day or less

Don't overdo it on the first trip, especially with children. Plan to end while everyone is still having fun or at least before youngsters are exhausted, crabby, and miserable.

Most people don't have to travel too far to get a paddle into the water, so you will likely have multiple options for one-day and partial-day excursions. Choose a spot that matches your experience level. Do not pick a swift, rock-filled river for your first outing.

If you have a canoe or are borrowing one, where will you launch and take out? Is there a dock, a sandy beach, or other designated launch site? Don't forget parking for your car. Many state and county parks have ideal spots on small lakes and reservoirs for an afternoon's paddle. If you haven't visited the park before, call ahead or check its website so you will know what to expect.

If you don't have your own boat, going through a canoe

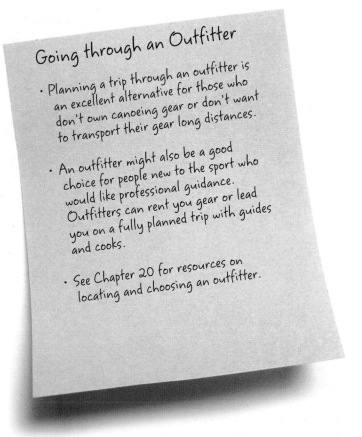

Going through an Outfitter

- Planning a trip through an outfitter is an excellent alternative for those who don't own canoeing gear or don't want to transport their gear long distances.

- An outfitter might also be a good choice for people new to the sport who would like professional guidance. Outfitters can rent you gear or lead you on a fully planned trip with guides and cooks.

- See Chapter 20 for resources on locating and choosing an outfitter.

Canoe Livery

- The livery will provide canoes, paddles, PFDs, and usually transportation to the launch site or from the take-out spot.

- Livery staff members will provide information about what to expect on the part of the river you will be paddling. Let them know

- your level of experience or inexperience.

- Because liveries often operate on popular rivers, you are likely to encounter lots of other paddlers. Some rivers, especially on weekends, offer more of a party atmosphere than a tranquil retreat.

livery is a great way to get onto the water. Liveries often operate on accessible, scenic rivers that are relatively easy to paddle.

If you are able to transport a canoe, renting from a paddle shop is a great option.

Even though it may be a short trip, there are a few basics to take care of to make the trip a success. Bring water and food. Be prepared for changes in the weather. Have enough clothing to stay warm and enough rain gear to stay dry. Consider the sun; apply sunscreen, wear a brimmed hat, bring sun-

glasses. Have a basic first aid kit: Band-Aids, aspirin, tweezers. Anything that must stay dry must be in a sealed dry bag and attached to a thwart.

Leave behind anything you don't need: jewelry, money, wallet. If you must wear a watch, make sure it is waterproof.

Shuttle Options

- Arrange for a pickup at take-out or a dropoff at launch. Liveries sometimes offer shuttle services.

- Leave one car at the take-out and pile people, gear, and boats into other car(s) for the trip to the launch site.

- It is hard to eliminate all waiting. Plan a task or activity for the people who have to wait for the drivers to shuttle vehicles.

Bicycle Shuttle

- Some energetic and ingenious paddlers can tow their boat behind their bike to the launch site. They then load the cart and bike into the canoe for the paddle downstream.

- Pick a bicycle and canoe cart that will break down, or fold, to fit into the canoe.

- Paddlers with one car can leave a locked bike at the take-out site.

- At the end of their paddle, one person pedals back to get the car and then drives to pick up the boat.

193

GEAR YOU'LL NEED
Bring what you will need but not too much

To point out the obvious, you will need a canoe. Perhaps you own a canoe or can borrow one. That is great, but make sure the canoe will meet your needs. It should be in good working order. An old aluminum tanker, dug out from under years of leaves, might float, but it might not be worth the time and trouble. If the bottom is crushed in, or some ribs are broken, the canoe may hardly move in the water or might be difficult to steer. Avoid any canoe with missing or broken thwarts.

Watch for splintery wooden components or for sharp or jagged edges.

Know what style of boat you are using. It can be difficult to cover much distance on a lake if you are paddling a whitewater river canoe. A river canoe is designed to turn quickly and easily. If you are on flatwater, you probably want a canoe that tracks well (moves in a straight line easily).

Select paddles that are the right size. A paddle that is too

Clothes and Gear for a Day Trip

- Comfortable clothes, layered for the weather, and shoes that will stay on

- Extra clothes in a dry bag

- Water and food

- First aid kit, sunscreen

- Canoe, paddles, PFDs, painters and cord for tying gear into canoe, seat cushion for a duffer (passenger sitting on floor of canoe), sponge to use as a bailer

- Hat, eyeglasses strap

- Camera, cell phone, wallet in a small dry bag

- Optional: binoculars, nature guidebooks, swimsuit, towel

Change of Clothes

- One key to an enjoyable day trip is having everything you'll need without toting along stuff you won't need.

- A dry change of clothes on a cool day or at the end of the trip will feel great. Keep them dry inside a waterproof bag.

- Pack wisely and keep all items tied down or inside a bag that is tied or clipped to a thwart.

- In the event of a capsize, the river will claim *anything* not secured. This includes shoes, glasses, and hats.

short will be tiring because it is less efficient. A paddle that is too long will be cumbersome and unwieldy. Wooden paddles should be smooth and free of splinters.

By now you know the importance of a well-fitting PFD.

Bring plenty of drinking water and snacks or lunch. Unless you enjoy soggy bread, pack food in plastic bags inside a dry bag. Bring sunscreen and a broad-brimmed hat to protect from the sun. Bring rain gear, even if the day starts out sunny. You don't want to end up cold and wet halfway through the trip. Keep extra clothes in a dry bag. Bring a first aid kit in a waterproof container.

If you are new to this location, bring a map. If the map isn't laminated, keep it in a plastic zip bag or map case.

The Weather Can Change

- A lot of factors impact feeling hot, cold, or comfortable. These factors include air temperature, rain, wind, sun, clouds, exertion, clothing, and getting wet.

- All of these factors can change in a brief period of time, and the only ones totally within your control are your level of activity (exertion) and what you are wearing (clothing).

- Make sure you have the clothing to handle the other factors. Have a jacket for the cold, a hat and sunglasses for the sun.

Rain Gear

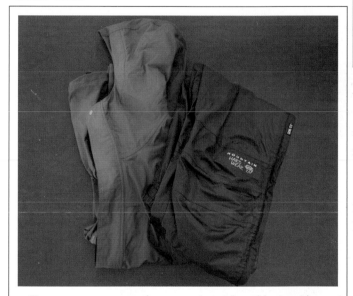

- No one can guarantee that it will stay sunny all day. Get into the habit of always bringing rain gear.

- A good nylon rain jacket and rain pants, in their own nylon storage bag compress quite small and are not heavy.

- A steady, cold rain without protection is miserable. In rain gear you will be warm and dry and can enjoy the phenomenon of a rain-pelted river.

- A rain jacket serves double duty as a windbreaker on breezy or gusty days.

BEING PREPARED

It is wise to be ready for any foreseeable mishaps and inconveniences

At the risk of sounding repetitive, there are preparations you should make for any trip to keep it safe, fun, and comfortable. After a couple of outings, it will become second nature to include a small first aid kit, tuck a second car key into a secure pocket, and bring along some extra candy bars or trail mix. It will also become second nature to rehearse some "what if?" scenarios in your head and contemplate how you would respond.

What if you lose a paddle? What if the weather forecast is wrong, and a storm develops? What if it takes longer to get to the take-out point than you estimate? What if your companion cuts his hand while fixing lunch? What if your canoe hits

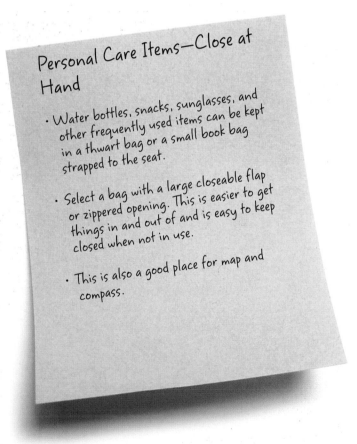

Personal Care Items—Close at Hand

- Water bottles, snacks, sunglasses, and other frequently used items can be kept in a thwart bag or a small book bag strapped to the seat.

- Select a bag with a large closeable flap or zippered opening. This is easier to get things in and out of and is easy to keep closed when not in use.

- This is also a good place for map and compass.

Water, Snacks, and Food

- Bring lots of clean drinking water. Each person should have an accessible individual water bottle.

- For an all-day trip, bring extra water. An empty milk jug works fine, although a rigid camping jug is more durable.

- Keep some trail mix, cookies, or energy bars near at hand to maintain energy.

- Have lunch well protected so that it doesn't get soggy. Sandwiches and fruit work well. A Thermos of hot soup tastes great on a cool day.

a rock, and you flip over? What if you see an unusual bird and would like to get a photo of it? What if the water is shallow in spots, and you need to walk the canoe?

If you can answer these and other similar "what if?" questions, you are in a good position to embark on an enjoyable and successful outing.

A canoe trip involves more than canoeing, so it pays to be ready for other potential mishaps. Does the car have a spare tire and a jack? Don't wait until you are out on a remote gravel road to ask that question. Make sure you have gas in the tank and booster cables in the trunk.

Write down and bring with you any emergency phone numbers you might need. Your cell phone may not get reception, the battery could die, or the phone might get wet. Then you have no phone numbers!

Be prepared for unexpected wait time. Have a couple of kids games up your sleeve, concoct a scavenger hunt on the spot, or keep a book of short stories handy to read aloud.

Map and Compass

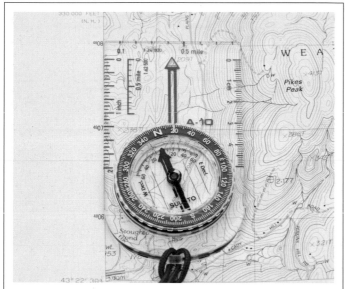

- Taking a map for any location you haven't paddled before is highly recommended.

- If the map is not waterproof, keep it in a sealable plastic map case or in a plastic zip bag.

- Keep the map accessible and refer to it often. It is much easier to stay oriented to where you are on the map than try to figure out where you are without definite landmarks.

- Fasten the compass to a thwart, keep it on a lanyard around your neck, or stow it with the map.

Camera and Dry Bag

- Some people are satisfied with a waterproof disposable camera. Others require elaborate gear: multiple lenses, spare camera bodies, tripod, lighting. Most bring along a small digital camera.

- Keep your camera safe, dry, and functional. Store it in a dry bag or keep it in a plastic, crushproof, watertight gear box.

- Use a container that is easy to use and keeps the camera protected except when you are snapping a photo.

GETTING ONTO THE WATER
Most of the work is getting to the water and getting launched

Lining up the gear, getting the vehicle loaded, securing the canoe, and driving to the launch site can seem to take longer and use more energy than actually canoeing. But don't get discouraged and don't take shortcuts. After you are on the water, the details and stresses fade into the background.

Be sure to secure the canoe carefully to the vehicle. Use appropriate straps, ropes, and knots (see Chapter 14). If driving more than a few miles or on the freeway, stop to check for loosening. Don't wait for the canoe to slide off the roof to find out that the ropes need to be adjusted.

To the degree possible, pack dry bags and food bags at home. Then, when you arrive at the put-in site you can get launched more quickly. Launch sites can be crowded and busy places, and the more organized you are, the less time you will have to spend there.

When getting ready to launch, have a job for everyone.

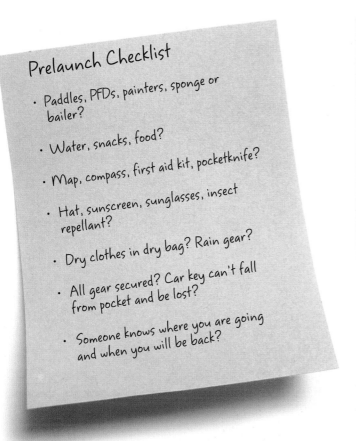

Prelaunch Checklist

- Paddles, PFDs, painters, sponge or bailer?

- Water, snacks, food?

- Map, compass, first aid kit, pocketknife?

- Hat, sunscreen, sunglasses, insect repellant?

- Dry clothes in dry bag? Rain gear?

- All gear secured? Car key can't fall from pocket and be lost?

- Someone knows where you are going and when you will be back?

Load the Canoe

- Strap down the canoe so that it will not slide sideways. Run straps or ropes under the rack right next the gunwale.

- If the bow painter does not provide tension that will keep the boat from sliding forward when the car brakes, secure a line around a bar on the canoe rack and a thwart in front of the bar.

- Review how to tie two half hitches and the trucker's hitch (pages 156–57).

- Ropes can loosen during transit! Frequently check tightness of ropes and knots.

While two adults are unloading the canoe(s), other members of the group can move paddles and gear to shore. Stack gear neatly out of the way of people moving the canoe and with an awareness of other groups using the launch site. If a car(s) needs to be shuttled or just moved to a parking place, have the drivers move vehicles while others are getting the canoes and gear ready. This will minimize waiting time.

With all this emphasis on saving time, don't rush when it is time to launch. That is the most common time for someone to fall into the water or to capsize a canoe. Have a plan for who gets into the canoe first. Only one person should move at a time; communicate whose turn it is to do what.

The Launch Site

- Organize your gear at home so that you will be able to just unload the canoe, stow the packs, and get under way.

- Be considerate of other paddlers and set your canoe and equipment off to the side until you are ready to launch.

- Be sure that all packs and gear are secured! Clip or tie dry bags to thwarts. Tie painters out of the way or tuck under bungee cords.

- Before shoving off, scan the launch area for any belongings.

Don't Forget!

- Spare paddle
- Painters (ropes on bow and stern of canoe)
- Everyone wearing a fastened PFD
- Toilet paper in a zip bag inside a dry bag
- Spare car key
- To tell someone where you are going and when you expect to return
- Drinking water and snacks

LOADING THE CANOE

Careful placement of equipment and people enhances the performance of the canoe

A canoe is not a yacht. How gear is loaded, where you step, and how you shift your weight have an immense and immediate impact on the canoe. In most cases, a canoe should be flat on the water with bow and stern level. The canoe should also be level from side to side.

Distribute people and gear so as to keep the canoe as flat and level as possible.

If one paddler is heavier than the other, shift any gear toward the lighter paddler to help balance the load. If one paddler is significantly heavier than the other, it is usually preferable to have more weight toward the stern of the canoe. However, this imbalance can be corrected by placing the heavier stern

Paddler's "Garage Sale"

- A capsize can occur in any water and to paddlers of all experience levels.

- Items that don't float will sink, and items that do float can get swept away.

- Be prepared for the unexpected capsize by keeping all gear, equipment, and clothing stowed in bags or tied to thwarts.

- Knowing that your gear won't sink or float away allows you to focus on responding to the capsize.

Tie Down Gear

- Consolidate individual items and smaller gear bags into a few larger bags.

- Attach bags to thwarts with rope or clips. A single attachment point will keep the bag connected to the canoe, but if the canoe flips, the bag can flop about and become unwieldy.

- Lash bags in place so that they won't roll around or flop out during a mishap.

- Plan ahead and store lunch and frequently needed items where you can get at them easily.

paddler closer to the middle of the canoe. He could kneel in front of the stern thwart or rig a temporary seat. Don't sit on a thwart! This raises the center of gravity and makes the canoe quite unstable. Another option is to add extra weight to the bow of the canoe. A bag of sand or a heavy concrete block under the bow seat can help trim the canoe.

When selecting gear bags, consider size and shape. Overly large gear bags can become too heavy to easily move around, and they can be difficult to effectively stow in the space available between thwarts or under seats. However, it is easier to portage a few large, well-loaded packs than a bunch of smaller bags. Over time you will develop your own system, but look for bags that will hold your gear, keep it dry, fit into your canoe, and be easy to carry. Be sure that handles and shoulder straps are durable and comfortable to use.

Comfortable Seat for the Duffer

- When you have a third paddler or passenger sitting in the middle of the canoe, bring along a seat cushion.

- A seat cushion makes the bottom of the canoe more comfortable and warmer.

- The passenger is known as the *duffer* because he sits on his *duff*.

- The duffer can also sit on a Crazy Creek-type chair or sit so that she can use a thwart for a backrest.

Remember to Take It Easy on Your First Trips

- This advice is especially important with children and youth or others you haven't paddled with before.

- The goal is an enjoyable experience.

- Plan to stop while everyone is still having a good time.

- First trips are to learn skills; later trips can emphasize distance or adventure.

201

KEEPING CANOE TRIM

A canoe flat on the water steers better and goes faster than an uneven canoe

Draft is how deep in the water a canoe is. *Trim* is the difference between the draft at the bow and the draft at the stern. A properly trimmed canoe will sit perfectly level in the water. Trim is impacted by how people and gear are loaded into the canoe (see pages 200–201).

A well-trimmed canoe will steer more easily, travel more quickly over the water, and be less susceptible to being blown around by the wind.

A canoe with its bow sticking up in the air is like a weather vane. The wind will push on the bow, and the canoe will pivot around the stern instead of pivoting from the middle of the canoe. A poorly trimmed canoe will move more slowly

Distribute Weight Evenly

- Arrange gear and people to keep the canoe trim from bow to stern and balanced from side to side.

- Minor shifts of weight can greatly affect how the canoe sits in the water. Secure bags so that they won't shift as the canoe moves.

- Remember to stow gear so that whatever is needed while paddling is within reach.

- If you do need to move about the canoe, keep your weight low and centered over the keel line.

Arrange People and Gear Evenly

- Consider the relative weights of paddlers when loading the canoe.

- Shift a particularly heavy paddler toward the middle or arrange gear and other paddler to compensate.

- A sand bag, a couple of large rocks, or some other ballast can be used to supplement a very light paddler.

- Adjust people, gear, and ballast so that the canoe is level from side to side and trim from stern to bow.

through the water because the weight of the canoe is concentrated toward one spot rather than being spread out along the keel.

A poorly trimmed canoe is less stable and harder to control than a flat and level canoe. Keeping the canoe level from side to side is common sense. Pay attention to how gear is stowed and how children and duffers are moving around in the boat. Sometimes a minor shifting of weight can make a noticeable difference in how well the canoe responds.

A canoe with a single paddler in the back, bow jutting up into the air, is an unmistakable sign of an amateur. Kneel in the middle of the boat or add some ballast to the bow. The canoe will handle much better, and you will command a little more respect from any onlookers.

A well-loaded canoe is trim, handles well, and has needed gear close at hand but still secured against loss. Keep map, water bottle, and snacks in a small dry bag or pack clipped to the nearest thwart.

Wrong!

- This seating arrangement makes for inefficient, difficult, and awkward-looking paddling.

- With the bow sticking up out of the water, the canoe will behave like a weather vane and spin around.

- The less surface area of the hull that is touching the water, the harder the boat is to steer, and the more waves bounce the canoe about.

- The raised bow also significantly blocks the eyesight of the paddler.

Right!

- A solo paddler should be positioned very near the middle of the canoe.

- Kneel or devise a comfortable seat that puts you at the right height for efficient paddling.

- A properly trimmed craft will handle more easily, track better, and go faster than a canoe that is not level on the water.

- A trim canoe is also far less likely to get hung up on a rock or log or to capsize.

PLANNING AN OVERNIGHT TRIP

An overnight trip requires more gear and more planning

After developing basic paddling skills and experiencing a degree of relaxed ability on short day trips, you may want to extend your adventures to canoe camping. It is a great feeling of independence to load up the canoe with gear for a few days, paddling by day and camping near the water by night.

The same spirit of being well prepared that allows for successful brief canoe trips applies to longer paddles. There are just a few additional commonsense considerations to factor in to assure a safe, enjoyable trip. These include shelter, adequate clothing, food, and the equipment to prepare it. In addition, you will need to have adequate maps, a plan for where you will camp, and information regarding your route.

Information on where to take longer canoe trips is readily available. Numerous local paddling guidebook s are available in most areas. Check the library and the local/regional shelves of bookstores. Paddling clubs exist in many areas;

The Weekend Trip: Reservations Required?

- Don't assume that there will be available camping. Most waterways are lined with private property. State and federal lands have varying regulations regarding camping. Inquire beforehand.

- Some rivers have large and plentiful sandbars, which make for great camp spots. No reservations required.

- State parks and private campgrounds often take reservations for campsites months in advance. Call the park or campground for information or check its website.

- Some sites are available only on a first-come, first-served basis.

Canoe Camping

- There is a great sense of freedom, adventure, and remoteness to be gained from camping by canoe.

- To find remote canoeing destinations, know what kind of trip you want to take, do lots of research, and ask lots of questions.

- For your first overnight canoe trips, start small: just one or two nights. You will learn a lot that will prepare you for longer journeys.

- Select a medium-sized lake with established campsites or broad, predictable rivers with large sandbars.

their members are happy to share information. The Internet can provide loads of information regarding possible trips and paddling groups.

The gear needed for canoe camping can be adapted from what you would use for car camping or backpacking. Questions regarding weight are usually less critical than when backpacking unless you will be doing numerous long portages. The gamut of suitable gear runs from economical discount store gear and garage sale finds to highly engineered equipment sold through specialty outlets. The gear you se-lect will depend on your needs and budget. Unless you anticipate camping very often or in extreme conditions, moderately priced tents, sleeping bags, and stoves should be just fine. As with most outdoor endeavors, you will discover your own preferences and make adaptations over time.

Approaches to Gear

- Canoeing permits you to bring more equipment than if you were backpacking.

- Although you *can* bring more gear, you will still have to carry it at some point. Make an effort to select items you will use and need.

- Most people will bring a full tent, although some opt to travel light and bring just a tarp to keep the rain off while they sleep.

- For your initial trips, bring the gear you are accustomed to camping with.

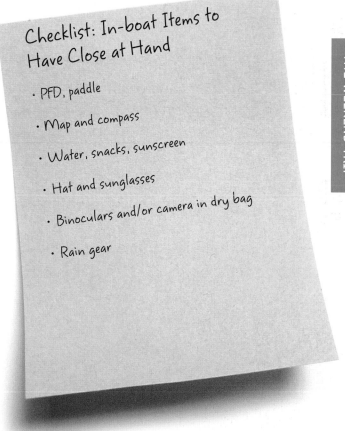

Checklist: In-boat Items to Have Close at Hand

- PFD, paddle

- Map and compass

- Water, snacks, sunscreen

- Hat and sunglasses

- Binoculars and/or camera in dry bag

- Rain gear

TENTS & SHELTER

When traveling outdoors, you'll need to bring adequate shelter with you

Temporary shelters should protect you from rain, wind, and insects, be easy to set up and take down, and be reasonably lightweight. The array of tents available can be mind boggling. Generally, any sturdy three-season backpacking-type tent will meet your needs while canoeing.

Avoid large "family tents." They tend to be heavy and cum-

bersome when rolled up and require a lot of space to set up. Many canoeing campsites have limited tent space.

Select a tent with sturdy zippers and durable mosquito netting. The netting keeps out insects while allowing ventilation and a cooling breeze. Most tents come with a rain fly that covers the tent by resting on the pole structure. It is the dis-

Three-season Tent

- A sturdy three-season tent is suitable for most canoe camping.

- A dome tent will allow you to set up the tent on any surface without stakes.

- Set up the tent at home before your trip. This will

assure that you know how to set up the tent in camp and that you have all needed parts.

- Make sure the tent is the right size for you. A "two-person" tent may be big enough for two, but it might be very cramped.

Rain Fly

- The rain fly keeps the tent dry by creating a gap between the fly and the tent fabric. The fly keeps the rain out but allows for ventilation and air circulation.

- If the fly and the tent touch, water can soak through at that point and drip all over you and your sleeping bag.

- Some tent flies attach to the poles, and some require stakes to stay stretched out far enough.

- Make sure the fly covers all parts of the tent fabric that aren't waterproofed.

tance between the fly and the tent that keeps the rain out. If the fly and tent are touching, water will seep right through.

A dome-type tent can be freestanding. It doesn't require stakes or rope to maintain its structure. This can be especially helpful in places where stakes are hard to use: big, flat rock, hard ground, or sand. But if not using stakes, be sure to weight down the tent with gear or rocks so that it doesn't blow away.

Become familiar with your tent in a controlled environment. Practice setting up at home any tent that is new to you. Make sure it has all the poles, stakes, and cord it needs to be set up properly. You do not want to set up a tent for the first time in the dark, in the rain, or without all the parts you need.

Some people forgo a tent and take along just a tarp for sleeping under. This can work just fine for rain but does not keep out the mosquitoes. Tarps are also a great idea for sheltering cooking and dining areas.

Ground Cloth

- The ground cloth is placed between the ground and the floor of the tent.

- It keeps moisture from seeping up from the earth and protects the tent floor from being punctured by rocks, sticks, or roots.

- Some tents have a "foot-print," a factory-made ground cloth designed for those tents. A plastic utility tarp cut to the size of the tent floor also works quite well.

- If the ground cloth sticks out from under the tent, it can funnel water right underneath the tent.

Vestibule

- Some tents come with a vestibule that attaches around the door to create a porchlike area.

- The vestibule provides a place to keep gear out of the elements while preserving space inside the tent.

- The vestibule is a good place to keep wet shoes, packs, or other gear you want within reach.

- If you don't have a dining tarp, the vestibule can be a place to cook during inclement weather. But avoid cooking near your tent in bear territory.

SLEEPING BAGS & PADS
A good night's sleep makes the next day more enjoyable

Available sleeping bags range from cheap and flimsy slumber party bags to highly engineered and very expensive Arctic expedition bags. The sleeping bag needed for a decent night's sleep on a typical canoe trip is somewhere in the middle.

Most suitable bags are made of nylon and filled with a number of different synthetic fibers or with goose down. Different filling materials have different advantages and disadvantages.

Down bags are incredibly warm. They are lightweight and compress very tightly for easy packing. However, down is expensive and if it gets wet provides zero insulation. If you use a down bag, be sure to keep it in a waterproof stuff sack or a sturdy plastic bag packed inside of a dry bag.

Synthetic sleeping bags will retain their loft and ability to insulate even if they get wet. However, synthetic fill does not compress as well as down and takes up more space in your

Clothes and Equipment for a Weekend Trip

- Tent with ground cloth, sleeping bag, and pad

- Large dry bag or Duluth-style pack and plastic liner

- Nylon cooking tarp, stove, fuel, cooking and eating gear, food

- Clothes: T-shirt, lightweight, long-sleeved shirt, sweater, or fleece, long pants, shorts, wool socks, nylon rain jacket and pants, wide-brimmed hat for sun, wool stocking cap, shoes for canoeing, shoes for camp

- Flashlight, toiletries, towel

Mummy Bag

- The mummy bag is contoured to fit closely to your body, maximizing the insulation potential of the filling. Mummy bags have close-fitting hoods to keep cold air out and warm air in.

- Some people find the mummy bag constricting and difficult for movement.

- Quality usually increases with price. Pick a bag with a durable, easy-to-operate zipper.

- Select a bag in which the sewn seams are offset between the interior and exterior layers. Seams that go through both layers don't insulate well.

pack. But research and innovation are occurring constantly, so the available equipment and its attributes are always changing.

In addition to a choice of fill, sleeping bags come in different styles. Rectangular bags are the same width at the top and bottom and have a full-length zipper that runs down the side and along the bottom. Two rectangular bags, with similar zippers, can be zipped together to form a large double bag.

Mummy bags are wide at the shoulder and narrow at the bottom. This shape keeps the sleeping bag contoured to the sleeper and eliminates "dead" air spaces that waste heat. Most mummy bags also have hoods that can be tightened down to keep cold air out.

Even the very best bag won't keep you very warm on cold ground without some kind of sleeping pad. Bring along a closed-cell foam pad or a self-inflating Therm-A-Rest pad.

Rectangular Bags

- Rectangular bags are fine for mild weather. They tend to be less warm than mummy bags.

- A rectangular bag is roomier and sometimes the preference for sleepers who move around or don't like a snug sleeping bag.

- Couples can zip two rectangular bags together to make one bag large enough for two people.

- A mild weather bag can be supplemented with a flannel or fleece liner for colder nights.

Sleeping Pads

- A closed-cell foam pad or a self-inflating open-cell pad insulates the sleeper from the cold ground and provides some cushion.

- The best sleeping bag without a pad will not be as warm or comfortable as it should be.

- Closed-cell pads provide less cushion than inflatable pads but are much less expensive.

- Self-inflating Therm-a-Rest pads are comfortable and roll up fairly small. However, they can be punctured. Consider having a patch kit.

STOVES

A good camping stove is lightweight and provides clean, efficient, and reliable heat

Although campfires add a delightful ambience to many trips, you will probably want to do most of your cooking on a stove. A camp stove allows you to cook dinner quickly and easily without the hassle of collecting wood, maintaining a fire, or getting smoke in your eyes. Stoves can be started easily in the rain and can also be hauled out at lunch or rest stops to heat water for tea or cocoa. Also, some canoeing areas have permanent or temporary fire bans, depending on the weather or threat of wildfires.

There are numerous types of stoves to choose from. Outdoor stoves can be fueled by gasoline, white gas, propane, butane, alcohol, or kerosene. Most stoves burn liquid white

Whisper Lite

- This is a powerful, lightweight stove that packs up fairly small. The Whisper Lite runs on white gas.

- The refillable fuel bottle is attached to the burner by a flexible metal hose. The hose attachment includes a pump to pressurize the fuel,

although the stove also needs to be "primed."

- Priming is done by releasing some liquid gas into a small trough at the base of the burner and then lighting it. The flaming gas warms up the burner and helps pressurize the stove.

Coleman Peak 1

- This stove is sturdy and reliable. It is heavier than some other stoves but light and small enough for canoeing.

- The Coleman runs on liquid fuel, which must be poured into the fuel tank. This process can lead to spills.

- This stove is pressurized with a pump. There is no need to prime, but the stove sometimes has to burn for a minute or two to get to the right pressure.

- Both the Coleman and Whisper Lite can have occasional "flame-ups."

gas or canisters of butane or propane.

Butane or propane canister stoves are convenient and easy to use. However, the canisters tend to be expensive and aren't always widely available. It is also hard to tell how full or empty a canister is. Butane burns less efficiently at low temperatures and is hard to light at 32 degrees or colder. (Butane can be kept warm overnight inside your sleeping bag.) Empty canisters need to be packed out.

White gas stoves require a little more attention to operate. They require pumping or priming to attain adequate pressure, and it's easy to spill fuel. White gas is cheaper than canister fuels and widely available. It can often be found at hardware stores, big box stores, and bait shops. Some stoves are multifuel and can be run on white gas, unleaded gasoline, or kerosene. Multifuel stoves are preferred for international or very remote trips because gasoline or kerosene are almost always available. Read stove instructions carefully before using any new stove. Follow any advice given regarding maintenance and stove repairs.

Fuel Canister Stove

- This stove burns prepressurized butane. Attach the canister and light the stove.

- Butane burns evenly with no flame-ups unless the temperature is low. Butane can be hard to light at 32 degrees or less.

- Butane canisters (or cartridges) are more expensive than white gas. It's hard to tell how much fuel is left in them, and they seem to run out quickly.

- Each stove has its own type of canister. Replacements can be difficult to locate in remote areas.

Jet Boil

- A specialized canister stove, the Jet Boil has a customized pot that attaches directly to the burner.

- It is an efficient way to heat water very quickly. This is handy if most of your meals are freeze dried or prepared by just adding hot water.

- The insulated pot is a little bulky, although it also can be used as a cup or bowl.

- Fuel for the Jet Boil shares the advantages and disadvantages of all canister fuels.

211

COOKING GEAR
Select cooking and eating utensils according to your menu

The camping kitchen can range from extremely simple to very elaborate, depending on your approach to food and cooking. For some people, the entire emphasis of a trip is on paddling, and they want to spend as little time cooking and cleaning up as possible. Other people revel in gourmet-style meals cooked and eaten outside and plan their time accordingly. Your cook kit will reflect your approach.

Depending on the size of your party, two or three nested pots with covers, a coffee pot or tea kettle, and a skillet will suffice for most cooking needs. Add a large spoon, spatula, ladle, and kitchen knife, and you have the basics covered. Some people include a wire strainer for draining pasta. A plastic roll-up cutting board is a handy addition, although a metal dinner plate or flat lid will suffice.

Individual utensils include a cup, bowl, and spoon for each person. Forks and plates can be added but aren't necessary.

Eating Utensils

- Minimalists will need only a spoon and a cup to meet their dining needs. Add a bowl, and you can drink coffee while eating your oatmeal.

- Most canoeists accept the increased weight of forks and plates to accommodate a variety of foods.

- Cups, bowls, and plates can be made from plastic, aluminum, titanium, or ceramic-coated steel.

- Select durable items that nest easily for packing. Keep eating utensils together in a nylon mesh bag.

Cooking Pans

- Camping cookware should be durable, versatile, and lightweight. It can be made of aluminum, stainless steel, or titanium.

- In general, a cook set composed of two pots with lids, a kettle or coffee pot, and a skillet will be adequate.

- A Teflon-coated skillet works great for eggs, pancakes, and fish. Select one with a folding or removable handle.

- If the handles of your gear get hot as the food cooks, bring some pliers or a pair of leather work gloves to use as hot pads.

Bowls and plates can be metal or plastic. Get those that stack or nest easily to save space. An insulated cup keeps beverages hot. Bring a pair of leather gloves for handling hot pans.

Develop a system for packing cooking gear. Have a designated pack for kitchen equipment. Keep pans in a cloth bag. Utensils can be kept in a lidded plastic box or wrapped in a cloth roll. Keep the stove packed in its bag or other container. This keeps all parts together and prevents soot from getting on other gear. Load the kitchen pack so that the stove, kettle, and cups are accessible for lunch or rest stops.

For clean-up bring Camp Suds or another biodegradable, concentrated soap and scrub pad. Scrub food scraps off with sudsy water and rinse well with hot water. Let dishes air dry.

Cooking Utensils

- Bring a large cooking spoon, a spatula, and a kitchen knife. Use a cup as a ladle. Plastic utensils can melt and are more likely to break than metal.

- Make sure all knives have a sturdy sheath.

- Don't forget a can opener. Bring a basic kitchen model, buy a small camping-style can opener at any outdoor store, or use the can opener feature on your pocketknife or multitool.

- Optional: a wire strainer for draining pasta.

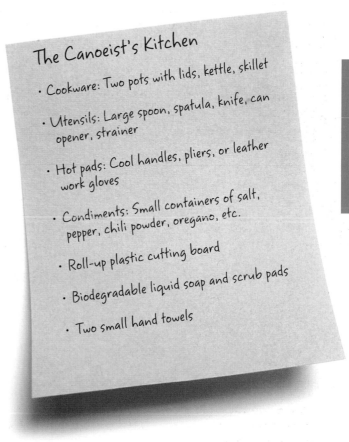

The Canoeist's Kitchen

- Cookware: Two pots with lids, kettle, skillet

- Utensils: Large spoon, spatula, knife, can opener, strainer

- Hot pads: Cool handles, pliers, or leather work gloves

- Condiments: Small containers of salt, pepper, chili powder, oregano, etc.

- Roll-up plastic cutting board

- Biodegradable liquid soap and scrub pads

- Two small hand towels

FOOD

Simple menus or gourmet meals, select nourishing foods that fit your style

For your first trip, go with a fairly simple menu. Canoeing allows a little more extravagance than backpacking. You can bring fresh fruit and vegetables for the early part of the trip. A cooler or ice chest can be very manageable on short canoe trips. Prefreeze any items you can; they will keep longer and provide coolness for other items. Canned goods are also easier to take canoeing than backpacking. Avoid glass containers because of the risk of breakage.

Easy, tasty meals include soups, pasta, and rice dishes. Burritos are great favorite early in the trip with beans, green peppers, and onions. If you include ground beef, precook it at home, store in a zip bag, and freeze. Another creative op-

Perishable Foods

- On short trips lacking long portages, you can bring an ice chest to preserve perishables like milk, meat, fruit, vegetables, and eggs.

- Ice will last only a day or two, so plan your meals to use fresh items first.

- Prefreeze meats and any other foods that you can so they will last longer and help keep the ice chest cold.

- Use a strap or bungee cord to ensure that the cooler will stay closed if there is a capsize or other mishap.

Durable Foods

- Canned, dried, and boxed foods make good options for canoe camping. Pack rice, pasta, flour mixes, and other dry foods inside sealed plastic bags.

- Repack boxed items in plastic bags to save space and to keep food dry until you need it.

- Carefully read directions so that you will have all the ingredients. Bring powdered milk in a plastic bag or plastic container.

- Bring margarine or vegetable oil in a small plastic container. Store this container inside of a plastic bag.

tion is pita bread pizzas. Bring a can of tomato sauce, mix in some oregano or Italian spice, spoon onto a pita, add grated cheese and your other favorite toppings (olives, onions, pepperoni—whatever you want), and then heat on the stove in a covered skillet. Include fresh fixings for salads; greens, carrots, peppers, nuts, and a plastic bottle of salad dressing.

Breakfasts can include pancakes, eggs, and hot cereals. For an easy, hot breakfast, put about a half cup of couscous into your cup with raisins or apricots and a handful of walnuts and pecans. Cover with hot water and let sit for a minute. For a quick start, have granola bars and fruit with your hot beverage of choice.

Keep lunches simple but varied. Crackers, cheese, and summer sausage are a traditional favorite. Add an apple or carrot and a chunk of chocolate, and you'll have plenty of energy to paddle for a few more hours. Foil envelopes of tuna can be mixed with restaurant-size packets of mayonnaise and mustard and spread onto bread or crackers. Other options include bagels and cream cheese and tortilla wraps.

Outdoor Cooking

- Camp food does not have to be bland or boring.

- Burritos are surprisingly easy. Saute onions and peppers. Add prebrowned ground beef and stir in a packet of Mexican spices.

- Instead of ground beef you can use wheat bulgur or TVP (textured vegetable protein). These are vegetarian and do not need to be refrigerated.

- Cheeses like cheddar, Colby, and provolone will keep for several days if they are covered in wax or sealed in plastic.

Foil Dinners

- If there will be a campfire, you can have foil dinners. Also known as *silver dollars, hobo dinners,* and *silver turtles,* these can be constructed in camp or premade at home.

- Place sliced potatoes, onions, carrots, and ground beef in the middle of a large square of aluminum foil.

- Carefully fold and seal the foil. Then wrap in a second layer of foil, crimping the edges to keep moisture inside.

- Place onto hot coals for about twenty to thirty minutes. Turn halfway through.

PLANNING A LONGER TRIP

For many people, the wilderness canoe trip is the essence of canoeing

With solid intermediate paddling skills and several overnight and weekend canoe camping trips under your belt, it is very feasible to successfully lengthen your canoeing adventures to four or five days, then to a week, and then maybe longer. The key to doing this safely is preparing, planning, and staying within your abilities while remaining aware of the power of nature. It is best to increase the length and intensity of trips gradually. The more isolated your paddling destination, the more preparation and experience you will need.

However, the steps that ensure a successful longer trip are the same as those for a shorter trip: take appropriate equipment, be prepared for the weather, and know how to re-

Touring

- Imagine a week-long trip in the Great North Woods or an exploration trip down that big river you have driven over hundreds of times.

- There is nothing quite like a touring canoe trip to get a break from the daily grind.

- The sense of independence and the ability to visit remote or unusual places are a compelling lure for many people.

- After developing your skills over several canoe camping trips and doing detailed planning, you will be ready for a longer adventure.

Considerations for the Week-long Trip

- Location: Cool North Woods lakes, large, winding rivers, or remote wilderness regions? Make sure your paddling destination is at your paddling skill level.

- Who will be on the trip? What size group is best for you? Some wilderness areas limit group size; plan accordingly.

- Food: Are you ready for several days without fresh food or cold soda?

- Transportation: Will you bring your own canoe or rent from an outfitter?

spond when things don't go according to plan.

Learn as much as you can about your destination. Managed wilderness areas often require permits and registration. Permitting helps protect wilderness areas from the damages of overuse. Registration can also help authorities provide assistance in emergency situations. Inquire early about permits. Popular destinations during busy times of the year can fill quickly. Paddling in the off-season, late spring, and early autumn makes it easier to obtain permits and avoid crowds.

Talk to area rangers and outfitters about what to expect. Do online research; lots of people post trip reports and can provide helpful information. Gather all the information you can but take everything with a grain of salt; remember that you are ultimately responsible for your trip. Buy the most detailed maps available and become familiar with them.

Know the average temperatures and weather patterns for the time of year you will be paddling but don't assume that those conditions are what you will encounter! Check weather predictions but remember that they are called *predictions* for a reason.

Permits

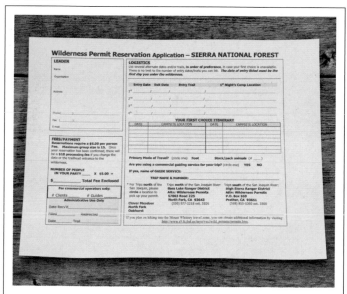

- Permitting helps prevent overuse of, and damage to, wilderness areas.

- During the busy season, permits must be secured in advance. During the off-season, when use is low, permits can be purchased at park headquarters the day you launch. But don't count on this! Call ahead.

- Call or write the park or wilderness headquarters for information.

- Often visiting its website is the most efficient way to get answers to your questions.

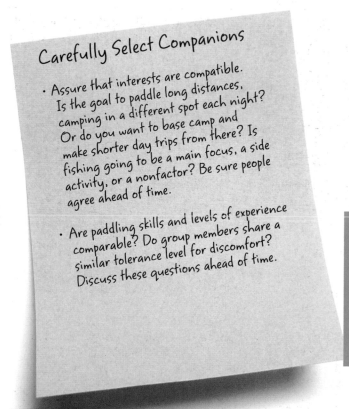

Carefully Select Companions

- Assure that interests are compatible. Is the goal to paddle long distances, camping in a different spot each night? Or do you want to base camp and make shorter day trips from there? Is fishing going to be a main focus, a side activity, or a nonfactor? Be sure people agree ahead of time.

- Are paddling skills and levels of experience comparable? Do group members share a similar tolerance level for discomfort? Discuss these questions ahead of time.

TREAT DRINKING WATER
On a longer trip, you can't take all your water with you

Safe drinking water is key to a healthy trip. It is no longer wise to assume that clean-looking water is safe to drink. Perhaps that was never a safe assumption. Water can contain bacteria or viral pathogens that can cause serious diarrhea or other intestinal discomfort.

It is important to treat any water that is of suspect quality. There are different technologies and processes available to treat water.

A water filter pump forces water through a charcoal or ceramic filter that removes many impurities and pathogens. Filters can be quick and efficient, treating water without adding any unpleasant taste, but they have potential drawbacks. Any filter will eventually get blocked up due to use and needs to be cleaned or replaced. Pumps can break and then be useless. The quality of filters and the amount of water they can treat vary with price.

Water Filter Pump

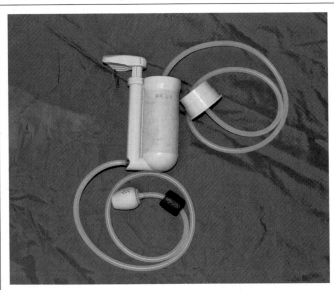

- Filter pumps are a good "first line of defense" against waterborne pathogens.

- A preference of many paddlers, pumps can treat water instantly without any chemical aftertaste.

- However, filters can get clogged, and pumps can break. Always have at least one backup method for water treatment.

- Heating water to 160 degrees will kill all pathogens. You must wait for it to cool, and it may taste "flat."

Gravity Filter Bag

- This is a filtering system that doesn't require a pump. Fill the bag in the lake, seal the top, and hang from a tree or pole.

- Gravity pulls the water through the filter as you fill pans or water bottles.

- This is great for groups because it treats a large amount of water fairly quickly.

- However, it can be hard to fill in shallow areas. Be sure to bring a spare filter in case the first one gets clogged.

Water can be treated chemically. Iodine water purification tablets are readily available at outdoor stores. They are easy to use: Put one or two tablets into a liter of water and wait thirty minutes. This will kill most common bacteria and viral pathogens in the water.

Household bleach is even more accessible, economical, and easy to use. Add two drops of standard bleach, containing 6 percent sodium hypochlorite with no other additives, per liter and let sit for ten minutes. The swimming pool taste can be reduced by leaving the lid off of your water bottle, al-lowing the chlorine to dissipate. Powdered drink mix can also mask chemical flavors.

Heating water to 160 degrees will kill off pathogens. So there is no need to pump or chemically treat water heated for cooking or hot drinks. However, select water carefully. Avoid sticks, leaves, and other sediment. Collect water from a moving source if possible, well away from campsites, beaver dams, and other animals.

Chemical Treatment

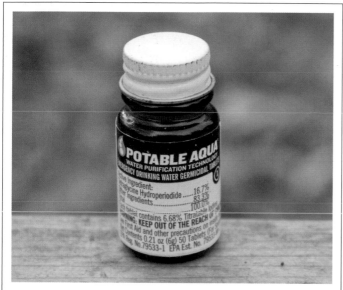

- Iodine tablets are available at outdoor stores, drug stores, and big box stores.

- They are easy to use. Put one or two tablets into a liter of water and wait thirty minutes. Has a chemical taste and can stain water containers.

- Plain household bleach is equally effective and quite inexpensive. Use two drops per liter of water and wait at least ten minutes.

- The chlorine taste can be reduced by letting the water stand with the lid off.

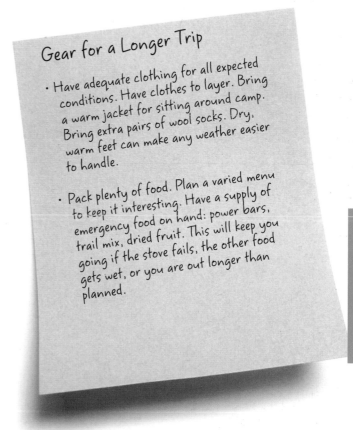

Gear for a Longer Trip

- Have adequate clothing for all expected conditions. Have clothes to layer. Bring a warm jacket for sitting around camp. Bring extra pairs of wool socks. Dry, warm feet can make any weather easier to handle.

- Pack plenty of food. Plan a varied menu to keep it interesting. Have a supply of emergency food on hand: power bars, trail mix, dried fruit. This will keep you going if the stove fails, the other food gets wet, or you are out longer than planned.

FOOD

Longer trips require durable, nonperishable foods, but they can still be tasty

For longer canoe trips, build on your menu experiences from overnight and weekend trips. The concepts are similar, although you will be cooking and eating for longer without fresh groceries.

Many paddlers plan a basic, quick breakfast of granola bars, coffee, and maybe instant oatmeal so that they can get on the water more quickly. Lunch will be crackers, cheese, summer sausage or some variation, including bagels, tuna, trail mix, and dried fruit. But then dinner will be more of an affair: spaghetti, garlic bread, and a cup of wine followed by cobbler or cake.

Freeze-dried foods are convenient and have become much

Menu Planning

• Plan out each meal. Develop a shopping list of the items you'll need. Some things can be bought in bulk: granola, trail mix, powdered milk, dried fruit, nuts.

• Repack groceries into single meal packets. Then have separate bags for all the breakfasts, all the lunches, and all the dinners.

• Remember that you will be packing out all trash, so the less packaging you take in, the less you will have to bring out.

Storing Food Items

• Keep dry foods dry. Double-bag powdered items, grains, and pastas. If the Bisquick gets wet, you will have to use it right away or throw it into the garbage bag to be hauled out.

• Nonzipping plastic freezer bags can be tied off with an overhand knot or closed with twist ties.

• High-quality resealing plastic boxes work well for food storage. The lids can accidentally come off of lower-quality plastic containers during travel.

more tasty over time. Freeze-dried meals tend to be a little expensive for the budget-minded. Many of the freeze-dried offerings can be approximated from the aisles of a large grocery store or supermarket. There are lots of tasty rice, pasta, and soup packets on the shelves. Instant mashed potatoes, with margarine and garlic, taste pretty good with a bowl of minestrone or mushroom soup after a long day of paddling. Pan breads and coffee cakes can be baked in a skillet with a lid.

Plan your menu carefully and repack the items you will need for each meal in their own zip bag. Include recipes or directions with each meal. Then pack dinners, lunches, and breakfasts in their own bag. Have a nylon bag or plastic box for salt, pepper, and sugar and small containers of other spices. Bring vegetable oil in a small plastic bottle stored in its own zip bag. Powdered milk, instant coffee, and powdered drink mixes can be stored in zip bags or recloseable plastic bottles. If you plan to eat fish, bring cornmeal or other mix for frying. One key to more enjoyable meal preparation is organization. Plan ahead, know what you brought, and know where to find it in your gear.

Creative Meals

- Soups can be varied by adding marble-sized dumplings made from Bisquick.

- Bring corn tortillas and cheese to make quesadillas in the skillet. Pita bread tuna melts can be made the same way. Put a lid on the skillet to keep heat in.

- Make mini-pita pizzas. Spoon tomato sauce onto a pita and add cheese, olives, and pepperoni slices. Heat in a lidded skillet.

- Instant mashed potatoes with gravy make a nice side dish for soups or fish. Have pancakes, syrup, and canned bacon for dinner.

Fish Fry

- If you plan to catch fish for eating, bring along some cornmeal or a breading mix and some vegetable oil for frying.

- After cleaning the fish, gently shake the fillet in a plastic bag with some cornmeal in it to evenly coat the fillet.

- Heat the skillet and oil before adding the fish to prevent the breading from becoming mushy.

- Don't *count* on catching fish for meals. Sometimes they just aren't biting, so bring enough food with you.

HANGING A BEAR BAG

The best way to keep animals away is to keep a clean camp

Bears, raccoons, chipmunks, squirrels, and numerous other critters have been known to eat, steal, or otherwise destroy a week's worth of food in very little time. The best way to avoid this inconvenience (or catastrophe, depending on your situation) is to keep a clean camp and do little to attract animals. Set up your kitchen area a little distance from the tents. Wash all dishes and pans right after dinner and stow them away. Do not throw garbage or leftover food onto the ground or into the woods near your camp!

All food items should be kept wrapped in plastic and stored in the food pack. Don't bring any food into your tent! Any food packaging and garbage should also be wrapped in plastic and stowed in the food bag.

Hang food bags from tall, sturdy trees. Hanging a food bag will protect it from mice and other gnawing critters as well as from bears. (Probably hundreds more dry bags have been

Prepare to Throw

- A bear bag can be hung a number of ways, depending on the available trees.

- The most effective way is to find two sturdy trees 20 feet or farther apart. Look for trees where you can throw the rope with minimal interference from branches.

- A very large single tree with a stout branch 15 to 20 feet up will also work.

- Loosely coil the rope so it will unwind after going over the target branch. If you weight the rope with a rock, tie it securely.

Perfect Toss

- An underhand toss is most likely to place the rope where you want it to go.

- If you use a rock or other weight, take heed what the rock can hit if it comes loose.

- Don't rush. This usually takes a few tries. A "hole-in-one" is as rare as in golf.

- Aim to get the rope over a sturdy branch or close to the trunk of the tree.

chewed through by mice than have been ripped open by bears.)

Dispose of fish entrails by burying them some distance from your camp. Leaving them on the rocks for the gulls may attract bears as well. If there are not suitable trees for hanging a food pack, improvise with what is available. Try to get the pack off the ground to dissuade mice. You can place the pack on a rock and then put empty pans on it to act as a burglar alarm. Raccoons and black bears can usually be driven off with lots of noise and commotion.

But it is best to keep a clean camp and feel confident that your food is well packed and out of the way.

Hoist the Food Bag

- One-tree method: After the rope is tossed over a sturdy branch, tie it to the food bag. Hoist the food bag at least 10 feet above the ground and tie off the rope to the tree trunk.

- Two-tree method: Tie off the rope to the trunk of the first tree. Attach the food bag to a middle point on the rope.

- Toss the other end of the rope through a crotch of the second tree.

- Hoist the food bag and tie off the rope.

Use a Pulley

- Food bags are heavy, especially at the start of the trip. Use a small pulley to make hoisting the bag easier.

- One tree: Toss a rope over a branch. Tie a pulley to the end of the rope. Then run the food bag rope through the pulley.

- Raise the first rope until the pulley is at the branch, then tie off the first rope.

- Tie the food bag rope to the food bag and then pull on the other end of the rope to hoist the bag.

223

PORTAGE

Moving your canoe and gear between lakes or around rapids and dams

The experienced paddler plans for the portage and considers it part of the canoeing trip. Gear is loaded in easy-to-carry packs, and forethought has been given to how to secure paddles and fishing poles to the thwarts. There is no miscellaneous, loose gear rolling around in the bottom of the canoe. Upon arriving at the portage, one paddler carries the gear packs, the other hefts the canoe, and off they go down the trail. That is the ideal, anyway.

Novice paddlers tend to have loose gear strewn around the landing site and make numerous trips over the trail. Sometimes multiple trips are unavoidable, but watch the experts and learn to minimize unnecessary work.

Simplify the Portage

- Anticipate the portage. Pack your gear so that it is easily carried. Use large dry bags, Duluth packs, or duffel bags that have shoulder straps.

- Ideally, you will be able to make a portage in one trip.

- Be able to stow all items in as few bags as possible. Don't have any loose items; water bottles, map, compass, and binoculars all go into a day pack.

- Tie paddles and fishing poles to the thwarts. Secure painters.

One-person Canoe Carry

- Keep your PFD on. It's easier to carry that way than wasting space in your hand.

- The paddler portaging the canoe also wears the day pack holding small items.

- The yoke of the canoe should ride just fine over the straps of your PFD and the day pack.

- The other paddler can assist with getting the canoe up onto your shoulders by holding the bow end high while you get under the canoe and get the yoke situated.

Portages range from only a few yards around some rough rapids to several miles between lakes. On some maps, portages are measured in *rods*. A rod is 16.5 feet or roughly one canoe length. Sometimes the hardest part of a portage is finding it. Portages can be marked with signs, but signs can fall down, and trails can become overgrown. Some trails are wide, well maintained, and smooth. Others are narrow, rocky, and hilly. When paddling on rivers, there will be portages for rapids, falls, and dams. Be sure to pull to the bank as soon as you realize you are approaching one of these features.

MAKE IT EASY

Keep your gear to a minimum. Load equipment in packs that have comfortable shoulder and waist straps. Tie paddles and fishing poles to thwarts: Have pieces of cord or small bungees in place to simplify this. Have painters tightly secured. If a painter is loose, it will get underfoot or tangled in the underbrush.

Yoke Made from Paddles

- A straight thwart makes an uncomfortable portage yoke.

- You can lash two paddles to the thwarts so that the blades will serve as yoke cushions for your shoulders.

- It takes some work to tie the paddles so that they will be secure and not slide around.

- With a little practice, you will be able to do this in just a few minutes.

How to Carry Packs

- The paddler portaging the packs can wear one pack on her back and then push her arms through the straps so that she can wear the second pack in front.

- This can be a little awkward and limit vision.

- The second bag can be cradled in the arms or thrown over one shoulder and partially resting on the first pack.

- Depending on the length of the portage, two trips may be preferable to struggling the whole way with multiple bags.

LINING & TRACKING

Lining is guiding a canoe downstream with ropes; tracking is hauling a canoe upstream

There may be occasions when you encounter some rapids that are too challenging to paddle through, but you would rather not portage. One option is to lead the canoe from the shore using ropes tied to the bow and stern. This can be a difficult and tricky procedure, hopping from boulder to boulder. The water is powerful and the rocks frustrating.

You want the lining ropes to be fastened as low and close to the keel as possible. If your painters are attached to rings that are halfway down from the tip of the bow or stern, you can leave them there. If not, tie a lining bridle underneath the end of canoe, having attached the line to the seat or thwart. If the lining ropes are attached too high, it is easier for the

Canoe Bridle: Part 1

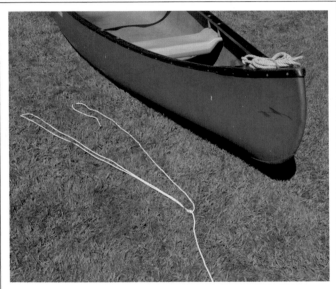

Canoe Bridle: Part 2

- To maximize control, you want the lining rope to be attached close to the water line.

- Fashion a lining bridle by looping the rope around one end of the seat. Both pieces of the rope then pass underneath the canoe.

- The two ends are tied together so that the long leading end will run out under the bow or stern at the keel line.

- The short piece is tied to the other end of the seat.

- Attach a lining bridle to both ends of the canoe.

- The low placement of the line will help keep the canoe from being tipped over by the current.

- Don't tie knots or loops in the lining rope. If it does get pulled from your hands,

a knot can get wedged between two rocks, allowing the current to flip the canoe.

- Never tie yourself to a lining rope or painter. The canoe could yank you into the river and cause serious injury or drowning.

canoe to get pulled under the water.

Usually lining requires two people, although it is sometimes possible to lower the canoe through rapids using only a stern rope. The procedure is to maneuver the canoe along the edge of the rapids, keeping the stern end from being swept out into the current. If the back end gets pulled out, the canoe turns sideways in the current and is likely to be swamped and may be pinned against rocks.

Tracking is like lining, but it is pulling a canoe upstream. To get the canoe around obstacles near shore, pull on the back rope. This turns the upstream end of the canoe outward. Then walk upstream, letting the current push the canoe around the obstacle. Don't let the bow get too far out in the current, or else it can pull the canoe all the way around. If the bow does get too far out, let up on the stern line so that the canoe stays parallel to the current.

Lining Downstream

- Holding on to the lines, walk the canoe downstream through the rapids.

- The key is to keep the stern from getting swept out away from the shore.

- If the stern starts to get pulled into the current, ease up on the bow line so that the canoe can stay parallel to the shore. It is sometimes possible to line using only a stern line.

- Try to keep the canoe near the shore, out of the main force of the current.

Tracking Upstream

- Tracking is using ropes to move the canoe upstream.

- Ferry around an obstacle by letting out a little on the upstream line. This will angle the canoe outward.

- The current pushes the canoe sideways; you can then pull it past the obstacle.

- Do not let the upstream end get pulled around by the current. If it starts to get pulled, let loose with the downstream line. This allows the boat to become parallel to the current.

RESOURCES

The world of canoeing and gear is immense and constantly changing. The following list of resources will provide you with a good start for finding further information. While on-line information is almost limitless, be sure to check out the library and local bookstores for paddling titles.

Books

Gullion, Laurie. *Canoeing: A Woman's Guide*. McGraw-Hill Professional, 1999.

Kesselheim, Alan S. *Wilderness Paddlers Handbook* Camden, ME. Ragged Mountain Press, 2001.

Kraiker, Rolf and Debra. *Cradle to Canoe: Camping and Canoeing with Children*. Boston Mills Press, 1999.

Jacobson, Cliff. *Canoeing and Camping: Beyond the Basics*. Globe Pequot, 2007.

Organizations

American Canoe Association
www.americancanoe.org

American Whitewater
www.americanwhitewater.org

National Organization for Rivers
www.nationalrivers.org

Paddle Canada
www.paddlingcanada.com

United States Canoe Association
www.uscanoe.com

River Conservation and Protection

American Rivers
www.americanrivers.org

Waterkeeper Alliance
www.waterkeeper.org

Information about outfitters

America Outdoors
PO Box 10847
Knoxville, TN 37939
800-524-4814
www.americaoutdoors.org

Paddlesports Industry Association
   PO Box 7189
   Silver Spring, MD 20907
   703-451-3864
   800-789-2202
   www.paddlesportsindustry.org

Paddling with the Disabled

Zeller, Janet and Anne Wortham Webre, *Canoeing & Kayaking for Persons with Physical Disabilities* American Canoe Association, 1990.
   Disabled Sports USA
   451 Hungerford Drive, Suite 100
   Rockville, MD 20850
   www.dsusa.org

Wilderness Inquiry
   808 14th Ave SE
   Minneapolis, MN 55414-1516
   612-676-9400
   800-728-0719
   www.wildernessinquiry.org

Periodicals

The Boundary Waters Journal
www.boundarywatersjournal.com

Canoe & Kayak Magazine
www.canoekayak.com

Canoe Sailing Magazine
www.canoesailingmagazine.com

Paddler Magazine
www.paddlermagazine.com

Building Your Own Canoe

Here are plans for a simple canoe you can build in one weekend. There are also more elaborate plans and kits available.
www.wikihow.com/build-a-plywood-canoe

General Canoeing Web sites

Canoeing and Kayaking Information
www.paddling.net

Information about planning a paddle trip in the United States
www.canoeingUSA.com

JoJaffa Goes Canoeing
www.jojaffa.com/guides/canoe.htm

Paddling Tales and Trip Reports from the Boundary Waters
www.canoestories.com

Solo Tripping: The Solo Tripper's Online Community
www.solotripping.com

Canoe Sailing

Conversion kits
www.lostinthewoods.ca/conversion

Tides

www.saltwatertides.com

Paddling Clubs

These are examples of club web pages. There are hundreds of paddling clubs. Explore your area for a local club. If you can't find anything online, inquire at a paddle shop.

Crystal Coast Canoe and Kayak Club
www.ccckc.org

A Directory of Canoeing and Kayaking Clubs
http://peteandedbooks.com/cclubs.htm

Prairie State Canoeists
www.prairiestatecanoeists.org

Southern Wisconsin Paddlers
www.wi-paddlers.net

Regulations and Laws

Boat registration: Check with your state. Some states require all boats, including canoes and kayaks, to be registered. Some states do not require non-motorized craft to be registered.

Lights: All states require some sort of illumination at night so that other boaters can see you. The Coast Guard requires all boats on the seas at night to have some sort of emergency signal: strobe lights, flares, etc. as well as a flashlight for identifying yourself and avoiding collisions.

Games

The following games can be used with multiple canoes. They work well with groups for teaching steering, partner cooperation, increasing a sense of comfort, and building confidence.

Dead Fish Polo: Throw a number of dish sponges into the water (they will float for quite a while before sinking). The goal is to pick up dead fish (the sponges) with the paddle blade and toss the dead fish into someone else's canoe.

   Rules: You can't touch the fish with your hands. Once the sponge is inside of a canoe, it must stay there until the end of the round. Blocking and splashing is allowed, but paddles must not hit or touch opponents. At the end of the round the canoe with the least sponges in it wins.

Duct Tape Tag: Each canoe has a duct tape "tail" attached to the bow and stern. The goal is to paddle around collecting other canoe's tails, while not losing your own tails. Your canoe is "out" after losing both of your tails. The last canoe with a tail wins.

Follow the Leader: The first canoe leads other canoes through an obstacle course of floats or other objects that can be canoed around. Include left and right turns, pivots, and parallel moves.

GEAR LISTS

Day Trip

- ❑ Canoe
- ❑ Paddle
- ❑ Spare Paddle
- ❑ PFD
- ❑ Painters
- ❑ Bailer and sponge
- ❑ Small dry bag or thwart bag for accessible items
- ❑ Large dry bag for extra clothes, other items
- ❑ Water bottle
- ❑ Lunch, snacks, emergency food
- ❑ Layering clothes appropriate for the weather
- ❑ Fleece, sweater or light jacket
- ❑ Protective foot wear
- ❑ Rain gear
- ❑ Hat, sunglasses
- ❑ Sunscreen
- ❑ Insect repellant
- ❑ First aid kit
- ❑ Map and compass
- ❑ Flashlight or headlamp

- ❑ Knife
- ❑ Matches
- ❑ Duct tape
- ❑ Binoculars
- ❑ Camera

Weekend Trip (add to Day Trip list)

- ❑ Tent
- ❑ Sleeping bag
- ❑ Sleeping pad
- ❑ Toiletries
- ❑ Hand towel
- ❑ Extra clothing
- ❑ Additional water containers
- ❑ Food
- ❑ Condiments and Spices
- ❑ Cooking gear
- ❑ Stove
- ❑ Fuel
- ❑ Eating utensils

❑ Dish scrubber and soap

❑ Tarp and tie lines

❑ Lantern

❑ Hatchet or saw, if you will have a fire

Extended Trip
Repair kit:

❑ Fiberglass: resin and catalyst, fiberglass cloth, disposable rubber gloves, plastic wrap

❑ Inflatable: patching adhesive and patches, spare valve and pump parts

❑ Duct tape

❑ Spare fasteners (nuts, bolts, screws)

❑ Wire

For coastal paddling:

❑ Strobe light or flares

❑ VHF radio

❑ GPS (optional)

❑ Coastal charts

❑ Current tables

❑ EPIRB

GLOSSARY

Bow: The front of the canoe.

Beam: The widest part of the canoe.

Blade: Part of the canoe paddle that is put in the water.

Bridging: When a canoe rests partially on water and partially on land. Makes canoe very unstable and tippy.

Deck plate: Flat portion at the bow and stern, level with the gunwale.

Dry bag: A water tight plastic, rubber, or nylon bag that varies in size from big enough for a camera, to full backpack or duffel bag size (It must be sealed properly to remain waterproof).

Duffer: The middle paddler or passenger in a tandem canoe; name is derived from the opinion that this person just sits on his or her "duff" while the bow and stern paddler do all the work.

Flatwater: Calm water without rapids; may be a lake or slowly moving river. Also call quietwater.

Floatation: Material that is built into the canoe to make it more buoyant like Styrofoam or air pockets; or inflatable plastic bladders, bags, or inner tubes that are tied into the canoe to displace water and make the canoe more buoyant.

Grip: The handle of the canoe paddle that is held by the upper hand.

Gunwale: The upper edge, or rail of the canoe (pronounced "gunnel").

Hole: Spot beneath a ledge, dam, waterfall or other obstacle, where water collects. Holes can be difficult to maneuver through or get out of.

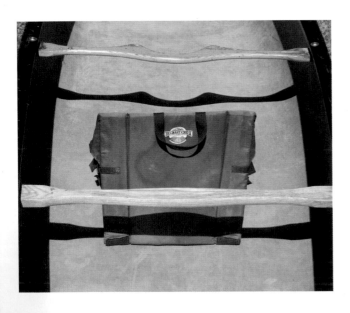

Keel: A strip of wood or metal, or a plastic ridge, that runs from the bow to the stern along the keel line. The keel is intended to help the canoe move in a straight line on windy lakes. Many canoes do not have keels.

Keel line: The imaginary line that runs along the middle of the bottom of the canoe from bow to stern. This is the line around which weight is balanced to keep the canoe from leaning to one side.

Painter: A length of cord or rope tied to the bow or stern of the canoe.

PFD: Personal Floatation Device. Lifejacket.

Portage: To carry canoes and gear over land.

Powerface: The side of the power blade that pushes against the water.

Solo: Either to paddle by oneself, or a canoe designed for one paddler.

Stern: The back end of the canoe.

Tandem: A canoe designed for two paddlers.

Throat: The part of the canoe paddle above the blade that is gripped by the paddler's lower hand.

Thwart: Cross brace in the canoe that goes from side to side.

Whitewater: Fast moving turbulent water. Rapids.

Yoke: A specially shaped crossbar for carrying the canoe overhead on one's shoulders. Is often the middle thwart.

INDEX

INDEX